Book of Worship
United Church of Christ

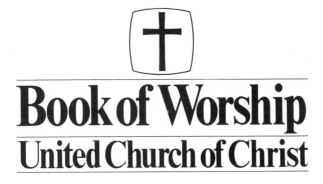

Book of Worship
United Church of Christ

United Church of Christ
Office for Church Life and Leadership
New York

Printed in the United States of America.
International Standard Book Number: 0-940615-00-2
Library of Congress Catalog Card Number: 86-051338

Table of Contents

Services of a Church's Life 167

Seasonal Services

Occasional Services

Services of Reconciliation and Healing

Services of Marriage 321

Services of Memorial
and Thanksgiving 357

Preface

It is with great delight and enthusiasm that the Office for Church Life and Leadership offers this *Book of Worship* to the United Church of Christ. Because the church is formed and reformed by its worship life, we trust that this resource will be a means of and a contributor toward renewal and enrichment for the church.

In July 1977 the General Synod adopted a resolution which directed the Executive Council "to request the Office for Church Life and Leadership to develop, if feasible, a book of worship for the United Church of Christ using inclusive language." A sampling of the United Church of Christ in early 1978 affirmed the importance of a book of worship. This book is the result of the work which began with that vote of the General Synod and the urging of people within the United Church of Christ.

From 1979 through 1981 a group created a draft of a book of worship. Staff members Ralph C. Quellhorst, Dorothy L. Robinson, and Robert D. Witham worked with Thomas E. Dipko, Lynne S. Fitch, Jerry P. Hankins, Peter V. Hayn, R. Howard Paine, William C. Royster, Catherine E. Thiedt, Frederick S. West, Bertrice Y. Wood, and Barbara Brown Zikmund. Their tireless and insightful endeavors provided the foundation for ensuing work. We are indebted to them for sharing their gifts with the church, and we thank them for their work. Their gifts were many and diverse, yet flowed from one spirit as they worked individually and together.

We acknowledge and thank the numerous people who responded willingly to our requests. A special word of thanks goes to Sarah R. Bentley, Ruth C. Duck, Louis H. Gunnemann, Lyman G. Potter, Virtie Stroup, Mark H. Wayne, Frederick S. West, and Paul H. Westermeyer.

A book of worship needs the scholarship of those who know the history and tradition of the church and its worship life and the language of the poet and pastor. The United Church of Christ has been blessed by the rare combination of these gifts in the person of Thomas E. Dipko, who invested himself in both the design and the language of the liturgies. These services, while built on the rich traditions of the church and the work of the draft group, are fresh and original. Their beauty and majesty owe much to Thomas Dipko and his loving commitment to the centrality of worship in the church. We are deeply in his debt.

Since 1982, when a series of booklets of the proposed services was printed, ecumenical partners and innumerable pastors and lay leaders of the United Church of Christ have provided guidance to the Office for Church Life and Leadership. Their comment and critique substantially influenced this final version. Many people submitted material for consideration for inclusion in the book as the resource section reflects. We thank those who shared their labors in all ways, including ecumenical friends who were generous and helpful as we prepared a book rooted in historic documents.

While many persons participated in the development of this *Book of Worship*, the assignment was given to the Office for Church Life and Leadership. We have directed its development and are responsible for its contents. A word of thanks goes to the directorate and staff of the Office for Church Life and Leadership for their participation in this labor of faith. We are affectionately indebted to two staff colleagues in the Office for Church Life and Leadership, Dorothy Robinson and Robert Witham, for managing and coordinating this project with care and sensitivity.

We offer the book in the hope that those who call on it as a resource for worship and those who lead worship from it may discover that it is instrumental in bringing them closer to the Holy One in whom we live and move and have our being.

Blessing and honor, glory and power be to God.

Reuben A. Sheares, II
Executive Director
Office for Church Life and Leadership

Use of This Book

This *Book of Worship* is intended to be a resource for the public worship of God in local churches of the United Church of Christ. It is offered to all who plan and lead that worship to the end that the spirit and form of worship in the church may be enhanced and the potential for the local church as the center for the Spirit's life may be realized.

Words, signs, and movement have been carefully molded to help create worship that has integrity and power. The introductions and instructions are integral parts of the book which seek to inform and instruct for the most effective use of the resource. In using the book, you will need to choose among the options offered those most appropriate for the worship life in your local church. You may want to adjust and adapt the material to fit the tradition and experience of your church.

This *Book of Worship* attempts to express the diversity of the United Church of Christ while at the same time lifting up the common liturgical threads which flow through the church, linking the tapestry of the past and weaving the fabric of the future. Informed and imaginative use of this resource can open the rich liturgical history of the church and enhance the particular traditions of the local church. In doing this, it is hoped that the *Book of Worship* will be a means of praise and thanksgiving of the living God by God's people in this time.

The format is designed to help make the book's use easier. Note that:

✸ Introductions preceding the orders provide a context and rationale for the liturgical text.

✸ Outlines preceding each order list parts of the service that are headlined in the text.

✸ When appropriate, instructions are given for incorporating other orders into the orders for the Service of Word and

Sacrament or the Service of the Word from this *Book of Worship*.

- ✠ Except where clearly marked *pastor*, a lay or a clergy representative of the congregation may be the leader.
- ✠ Instructions for leaders are printed in red italic type.
- ✠ Words to be read by a leader, including those read in unison with the congregation, are in bold type.
- ✠ Options are clearly indicated by letters in boxes. It is not necessary to follow one option throughout a service; new choices may be made for each part of the service.
- ✠ In addition to the options marked by letters, the option always exists that the leader may choose other words.
- ✠ Guidance is given for offering prayers in the words of the worship leader.
- ✠ Musical settings for service music are included in the Resource Section, beginning on page 449. Two composers have prepared new music for which both accompaniment and melody lines are provided. Page references in the services are to the accompaniment.
- ✠ Footnote numbers in the services generally denote material of other copyright holders. Information about sources and copyrights is provided in Notes, beginning on page 555.

Introduction

What is Christian worship? The answers to that question reflect the rich diversity of Christ's church and account for more than a few of its divisions. There is no definition that exhausts the scope of the question. Every answer raises more questions and cautions humility in the presence of all that is holy. Where definitions are elusive, descriptions become an alternative.

Christian worship cannot be understood apart from the Jewish worship that first cradled and nurtured it. Like worship in Judaism, Christian worship is the glad response of total individuals—through "heart, soul, strength, and mind"—to the saving acts of God in history.[1] It is the communal and personal celebration in the universal church of God's love for creation and for every human being. This divine love is revealed in God's gracious covenant with the people of Israel and in God's coming into the world in Jesus Christ.

Christian worship is more than a passive response to God's revelation. It is in itself a Pentecostal proclamation. It both announces the good news of God's love for all the world and invites all people to share God's saving embrace. This active response would not be possible without the presence of the Holy Spirit. It is the Holy Spirit who endows the community of faith and individual Christians with the gifts that are necessary for God's service. All that Christians are and do, corporately and individually, is worship, liturgy, the work of praise and thanksgiving.[2] The words and acts commonly called *worship* cannot rightly be separated from Christians' faithful response to God in words and acts of love and justice for all people.[3] That is the transparent meaning of Jesus' liberating command: "You shall love your neighbor as yourself."[4]

BIBLICAL HERITAGE

Christian worship, because it is the active response to God's loving initiative, is rooted in the biblical witness to God's saving deeds in history.[5] From the saga of Adam and Eve to John's mystical vision of a new heaven and a new earth, the Bible tells the story of God's redeeming love. Holy scripture provides the trustworthy and normative record of the history of salvation. Its luminous pages inspire, inform, and instruct the church's worship through all the centuries.

It is clear in the New Testament that Jesus Christ cherished and shared in the three fountains of Jewish spiritual nurture that flowed from the Old Testament and shaped the worship of the early church: the temple, the synagogue, and the Jewish home. Each provided distinctive but complementary contributions to the full worship life of faithful Jews.[6] Although Jesus occasionally criticized the abuse of customs and ceremonies practiced in these places, Jesus honored them with his presence, prayer, and preaching.[7] At the Last Supper, Jesus' very choice of words indicated that he knew and willingly used the prayers and blessings familiar to the people of his time.[8]

After the resurrection, Christians, at first, continued to participate in the worship at the temple and the synagogue and to observe the set hours of daily prayer, certain fasts, and other acts of domestic Jewish piety. When resistance to the Christian movement made association with the temple and the synagogue untenable, Christians opened their own homes as places for the church to gather.

Within the New Testament itself, there is evidence of the gradual coming together of customs and ceremonies formerly celebrated separately in the temple, synagogue, and Jewish home. Christians assembled in homes on Sunday, the weekly commemoration of the resurrection of Jesus Christ. There they participated in worship, incorporating both a scripture service and a meal that included bread and wine.

Worship in word and sacrament, celebrated weekly on the little Easter that Sunday quickly became, emerged in a primitive pattern that has shaped Christian liturgy to the present day.[9] This *Book of Worship* seeks to be faithful to this heritage and crowns every service of the church with the abundant witness of scripture.

ECUMENICAL HISTORY

Ecumenism is the vocation of separated Christians to celebrate their unity in Jesus Christ and to make that unity more visible as the Holy Spirit guides the church into all truth. It is a vocation as old as the church itself. Within the New Testament, Christians of differing points of view struggled to live in harmony in the one Body of Christ. The Council of Jerusalem is evidence enough that Jewish Christians and Gentile Christians labored patiently to affirm diversity that did not compromise the identity and unity of the church as one people of God.[10]

Current understanding of the worship of the New Testament church is assisted by insights made available from the literature of the church of the first four centuries. The discovery in modern times of much of this literature, particularly the *Didache*, the Apostolic Tradition of Hippolytus, and the journal of Egeria, provides texts more ancient than those available to the Protestant reformers of the sixteenth century.[11] This informative literature, when studied in relation to the New Testament, leads to fuller appreciation of the trials and treasures of Christian worship in the formative centuries of the church, better understanding of the liturgical development of the medieval period, and the discernment of the broad shape that gives Christian worship its enduring identity.[12]

Ironically, many insights into the worship that united the early church have developed as a consequence of disputes that threatened Christian unity. Were it not for the impassioned concern of Hippolytus to interpret his beliefs to those who disagreed with him, there would be no detailed description of Christian worship in A.D. 215.[13]

In a similar way, modern Christians are the beneficiaries of other information because one part of the church tried on occasion to force its form of worship on some minority, only to discover that uninvited ecumenical contact of this kind rarely left the majority unchanged![14] The sixteenth century Reformation provides a wealth of evidence that the various Protestant reformers and their Roman Catholic colleagues did not permit fragmentation of the church to isolate them from one another. The extent to which they maintained ecumenical dialogue as they led their respective movements puts their zealous followers of later generations to shame. Nowhere does their devotion to ecumenical faithfulness show itself more profoundly than in their common concern for the right worship of God.[15] The confessional liturgies developed during this time are full of ecumenical affinities.

More recently, a liturgical renewal movement has arisen that is so thoroughly ecumenical that the strands of its history are difficult to trace.[16] Protestants rejoice to find in Roman Catholicism a renewed emphasis on the place of preaching and full congregational participation in worship. Roman Catholics celebrate the renewed interest of Protestants in the sacrament of Holy Communion and in the power of liturgical symbols.

This renewed appreciation for the unitive wholeness of word and sacrament promises to correct what Karl Barth defined as *torso* worship. After criticizing Roman Catholics for sacramental worship that lacks responsible preaching and Protestants for sermon services that lack the sacraments, he remarked, "Both types of service are impossible."[17] He cautioned that in Sunday worship the preaching and hearing of the sermon are compromised when the opportunity to participate in Holy Communion is denied. In a similar way, faithful sharing in the sacrament is compromised when the preaching of the word is omitted or diminished in its importance.

Although John Calvin spoke eloquently of the place of the sermon, as did Luther and other reformers of the sixteenth century, he resisted every attempt to drive a wedge between word and sacrament. He boldly asserted that the sermon is itself sacramental in the sense that it is the verbal articulation of the same Word met in the sacrament of Holy Communion. Nonetheless, one does not displace the other. An order for word *and* sacrament remains normative for Sunday worship.

This conviction has been reaffirmed recently by Christians of diverse traditions who see word and sacrament as a unitive whole. *Baptism, Eucharist and Ministry* states: "Since the *anamnesis* [recalling, remembering] of Christ is the very content of the preached word as it is of the eucharistic meal, each reinforces the other. The celebration of the eucharist properly includes the proclamation of the word."[18]

In addition to this convergence, from the rich worship life of the Eastern Orthodox churches, Protestants and Roman Catholics are learning how to stand in awe of the mystery of God and how to resist the scholasticism that reduces an individual to intellect alone. Everywhere, Christians moved by the Holy Spirit remind the churches of the charismatic treasury of gifts among the people of God.

In 1963 the Faith and Order Commission of the World Council of Churches reported that "there is in the New Testament a greater variety of forms and expressions of worship than in the majority of divided churches and traditions today."[19] Since that time, the churches, often acting ecumenically, have experienced growth in their liturgical life that reflects the closeness of their ecumenical relationships. They have discovered the richness of an enlarged diversity within themselves that makes each of them more truly universal and sets aside many of the confining stereotypes of the past. There are responsible voices currently saying for the first time that "the liturgies now in use in the separated churches are no longer a cause of division. Such causes lie elsewhere."[20]

THE UNITED CHURCH OF CHRIST

The youthfulness of a church born in 1957 might suggest to some that it has not yet had adequate opportunity to accumulate what purists call *history*. It has! Behind its recent past stand the distinguished histories of the Evangelical and Reformed Church and the Congregational Christian Churches. Through these churches, roots are deep in the reform movements of the American frontier and the Swiss, German, and English Reformations and also penetrate beyond the sixteenth century to the Latin church of the West and to the early church that once knew a remarkable degree of unity throughout the Roman Empire. In matters of worship, and all other matters, the United Church of Christ is the inheritor of this history with all its splendor and shame and is responsible for appropriating now the great lessons this history is able to teach.

Religious history in the United States of America affirms that the United Church of Christ is a church of European origins. It is also a church of Black, American Indian, Hispanic, Oriental, and other people who share one diverse household of faith that makes the United Church of Christ a humble microcosm of the church throughout the world. It is also a church of women and men, ordained people and lay people, single people and married people, children and youth and adults, rich and poor, people with few disabling conditions and those with more. The United Church of Christ is local churches, associations, conferences, instrumentalities, and the General Synod.

At the same time, the United Church of Christ claims its place in the one, holy, catholic, and apostolic church of

Jesus Christ which is the home of all Christians. It strives to participate responsibly in the ecumenical movement.

The United Church of Christ is not only these things. It is also becoming. The clock and the calendar announce that the United Church of Christ is making history. Part of that unfolding history is represented in this *Book of Worship*, requested by the Eleventh General Synod in 1977 for use in the United Church of Christ. This endeavor has looked thankfully to the traditions of the churches that presently constitute the United Church of Christ. In the preparation of the *Book of Worship*, earlier service books of these churches, along with documents that represent the Puritan and free church traditions, were carefully studied.

Like the venerable publications used in its preparation and in words borrowed from three of them, this *Book of Worship* seeks to "conserve the best in the tradition of worship" found in the denomination's past and to "draw upon the treasures of the historic and universal church."[21] It is "offered as a guide and help in public worship"[22] in order "to preserve unity of spirit within diversity of forms"[23] in the proclamation of the word of God and the celebration of the sacraments. Its only authority is its intrinsic worth as an imperfect human resource for those who seek to worship God in the beauty and duty of holiness.

THE CONTEMPORARY CONTEXT OF WORSHIP

The church is called in every generation to celebrate the full message of salvation in the context of the particular time and place given it by God. Jesus Christ is "the same yesterday, today, and for ever,"[24] but the language, customs, and historical situation of the people of God are continually changing. The *Book of Worship* reflects the intention of the United Church of Christ to respond faithfully to God's saving initiative in ways that speak to the spiritual hunger of all people in this time and place. Several contemporary emphases that stem from this intention inform the services contained in the *Book of Worship* and deserve brief attention.

The Eleventh General Synod explicitly instructed that a *Book of Worship* be characterized by language that is truly inclusive with respect to God and to human beings. Although the generic use of masculine terms may have been acceptable in the past, it excludes and offends many sensitive people of faith today. Further, the use of only masculine nouns and pronouns for God and of masculine generic terms for humankind has hidden the rich feminine imagery for God and God's people in scripture. The rediscovery of the complementarity of female and male metaphors in the Bible and the literature of the early church forbids Christians to settle for literary poverty in the midst of literary riches.[25]

In response to this rediscovery, care has been taken to avoid exclusively male terms for God. For example, the word *God* is frequently used where the masculine word *Lord* predominated in the past. *Lord* is retained as an important title to identify Jesus Christ, but not the only title. In general, masculine language is not used in reference to Jesus Christ except where there is some necessity to identify Jesus by gender. In a similar way, diverse masculine and feminine images are used for the people of God. The witness of women of faith in the biblical story is treated with the same dignity accorded the witness of men of faith.

Inclusive language is far more than a matter of male and female imagery. Behind the aesthetic dimension of human words towers the prophetic issue of social justice. It is obvious to people of goodwill that words have the power to exploit and disfranchise as well as to affirm and liberate those to whom they refer.[26] Language that is truly inclusive affirms not only human sexuality but also racial and ethnic background and diverse stages of maturity from infancy to old age. It shows respect for people with handicapping conditions, people who do not live in the traditional nuclear family, people who suffer addictions, and others who intentionally identify themselves by some particular need or characteristic. If people do not find themselves in the language of worship or find themselves there in derogatory images, it should not be surprising if they absent themselves from the worshiping community.[27]

This *Book of Worship* seeks to underscore the inseparable connection between liturgy and ethics not only by means of inclusive language but also by maintaining a biblical tension between Christian nurture and Christian witness. The services show that liturgy is a recalling of God's acts in history for the world and its salvation and at the same time a communal and personal answering of God's call to service in the world.

The issue of inclusive language and other concerns for social justice point toward even larger areas of wholeness. In practically all churches that are experiencing liturgical renewal, there is a deep regard for denominational traditions that have been cherished, as well as an ecumenical longing to explore parts of the gospel that have received inadequate attention within a particular denomination.[28] This *Book of Worship*, for example, reflects with a new clarity not only the cross of Jesus Christ that dominates much of Reformation theology but also the fullness of Christ's life, death, and resurrection. The services, especially the services of word and sacrament, invite participants to remember the whole story of the history of salvation and to celebrate that story as the church that stands on the Easter side of the cross and tomb.

Out of respect for the total person, the services address human senses as well as rational minds. They offer opportunities for music and other arts, various postures and movements, silence, and the full active participation of the congregation in acts and words that are readily shared. The services also recognize that people have differing abilities to use these senses and acknowledge that physical limitations are to be considered as worship is planned. There is a reverence before God's mystery and majesty and a reticence to use power language, military imagery, or the jargon of triumphalism either for God or the church.

This reverence for God calls forth reverence for the image of God in all human beings including children. Today the question of how children relate to worship is being pursued with renewed interest. The central place given to children in the preaching of Jesus and the caution that unless people become like little children they cannot enter the realm of God call into question some prohibitions concerning children at worship.[29]

The role of children in Holy Communion is especially debated. Until recently the principal objection to their participation in the sacrament was their inability to "discern the body of Christ" in the meal (1 Corinthians 11:29). Recent biblical scholarship challenges this interpretation of scripture. It recognizes in Paul's words not a concern for a cognitive understanding of *sacramental* presence but a concern for an *experience* of the body of Christ present in the *community* of faith that Christ gathers as the church.[30]

With this communal understanding, in which discernment is primarily a recognition of *belonging* and not merely a matter of intellectual comprehension, adult Christians are urged to ask "whether, by excluding children from the Lord's Supper, we are not equally guilty [with the offending Corinthians] of failing to 'discern the body' and, therefore, of endangering the reality of the supper."[31]

In *Baptism, Eucharist and Ministry*, the churches are asked to study the place of children in worship with specific reference to Holy Communion.[32] Churches are urged by Christian educators and others to include children in all aspects of church life as fully as possible. How churches respond to children "is of importance, not simply as a liturgical concern but as an ethical concern," because God calls the church to "receive them as gifts."[33]

There is a renewed awareness in the *Book of Worship* of the church as the church of Pentecost, the church of the Holy Spirit, living between the time of Christ's coming at Bethlehem and Christ's coming again at the close of history. The full texts of the prayers for Holy Communion and baptism include reminders that the great cloud of witnesses and the church of today form the one, holy, catholic, and apostolic church. At the center of all the human words stands the Word made flesh, Jesus Christ, the firstborn of all creation, who says to the servant church anew, "If I be lifted up, I will draw all unto me."[34]

THE LEADERSHIP OF WORSHIP

The line between leading the people of God in worship and displacing them in worship is a precariously thin one. It is significant that in the New Testament, as in Judaism, the leadership of worship was a shared responsibility. In the church of the first four centuries, this collegial model of leadership prevailed. It was common for several people to concelebrate word and sacrament in services full of congregational participation.

Then leadership fell into the hands of an officiant acting alone. "Services came to be celebrated for the people rather than by them," and the worship of God "became a spectator sport."[35] In churches in the East and West alike, liturgical action became remote from the laity, who often paid for rites they did not bother to attend.

The Reformation of the sixteenth century only partially restored the active role of the congregation. In the twentieth century there has been a remarkable resurgence of congregational involvement in the planning and leading of worship. There are hopeful signs that Christian worship today is approaching the level of participation evident in the early church.

This *Book of Worship* is offered to all who plan, lead, and participate in the worship of God. It is especially important in the United Church of Christ, where the freedom of local churches to order their own worship life is steadfastly maintained, that great care be taken to exercise that freedom with the commensurate responsibility that it requires. It is also a matter of honesty to recognize that the distinction between *liturgical* worship and *free* worship is often more imagined than real. It has rightly been observed that fixed orders can breathe with variety, that informal ones are characterized by discernible patterns, and that both "are equally ritual because it is impossible to vary them every time they are used."[36] John Calvin, a pioneer in liturgical reform, cautioned even as he reshaped the worship of his time that "we ought not to resort to innovation rashly or frequently, or for trivial causes."[37] His counsel is of special relevance during the liturgical revolution of this generation.

What is the relationship between a service book of any kind and freedom, spontaneity, and informality in the worship life of the church? In the United Church of Christ the relationship is determined by each local church. Even local churches of the United Church of Christ that share the heritage of using a book of worship covet nonetheless the right to do so in ways appropriate to their local customs and felt needs.

Contrary to popular stereotypes, those local churches that trace their roots to the Puritan and free church traditions have consistently reserved the right not only to refrain from using prayer books but also to *use* them. Henry Martyn Dexter, writing about Congregational worship from the colonial days to 1880, made this assessment of how *free* the free church tradition can be:

> Any Congregational church, whose taste and sense of expediency may so incline it, is at perfect liberty to order its worship by the liturgy of the Church of England, or the Protestant or Reformed Episcopal Church of the United States, or by a liturgy of its own. So long as it does nothing which shall give reasonable ground of offense to the other churches with which it is in fellowship, it may order its prayers, its praise, and all the methods of its worship, to its own entire content; and its pastor, remaining true to our fundamentals of doctrine and polity, though enrobed and endowed . . . with "chasuble, albe, amice, stole, maniple and zone, with two blessed towels, and all their appendages," would remain, in good faith and entirely, a Congregational minister still.[38]

Clearly, free church does not translate simplistically into a church free *from* all forms. Rather, it denotes a church that includes within the parameters of its freedom the uninhibited liberty to use whatever forms prove to be consistent with its understanding and practice of the gospel.

Where the *Book of Worship* is received in this spirit, it will not compromise the freedom, spontaneity, or informality of the worship life of any local church. It may, in fact, broaden the diversity and deepen the experience of those very characteristics. One thing that it will not do, when used properly, is relieve the local church of the responsibility of providing careful planning and prepared leadership for its worship life. History is replete with examples of empty and corrupt worship that afflicted the people of God precisely because a responsibility that belonged to the whole people of God was abandoned into the hands of the few who eagerly assumed it. The *Book of Worship* is an invitation to every local church to commit itself anew to the hard work of the people of God—the *lietourgia* (worship)—that is the vocation of every Christian and of every local church.

PASTORAL LEADERSHIP

Ordained ministers of the United Church of Christ, by virtue of their ordination vows, the traditions of the church, and the constitutions and bylaws of local churches, are entrusted with primary responsibility for preaching and teaching the gospel, administering the sacraments and rites of the church, and exercising pastoral care and leadership. Their role in leading worship has been compared with that of a first chair musician or a concertmaster rather than with that of a conductor. It is clearly the function of ordained ministers to work in close collaboration with lay people in planning and leading worship. This role presumes that adequate preparation is provided and that ordained ministers seek constantly to grow in their understanding of the theology and practice of worship.

As ordained ministers seek to fulfill their partnership with lay people in worship, it is imperative that adequate time be allowed for study, creative planning, and the rehearsal of services that may require it. Attention will be given not only to the words of worship but also to symbolism, choreography, and dramatic integrity. Shared leadership in the conduct of services will permit different people to fulfill specific roles without leaving the assembly confused about who is presiding.

Ordained ministers and lay people who share the leadership of worship have a particular responsibility to consult and cooperate with church musicians. If the ecumenical lectionary or another schedule of readings, the church year, and special emphases of any other kind are to inform worship in an integrated manner, church musicians will need opportunity for the selection and rehearsal of appropriate music.

LAY LEADERSHIP AND PARTICIPATION

Lay leaders of worship, in the exercise of the priesthood of all believers, bear a responsibility to prepare for their ministry. They need to be people of prayer, informed concerning the worship heritage of the church, and willing to participate in available training for the roles they assume. Their ministry may include roles of leadership—leading various parts of the service, reading scripture, preaching the sermon. Their roles may be supportive—ushers, acolytes, servers of Holy Communion, choir members, greeters, floral artists, or other roles approved by the local church.

The entire worshiping congregation is called to exercise its priesthood through dynamic participation in all aspects of the church's liturgical life. Christians do not go to church; they gather as the church. There is mutual responsibility of chancel and pew for the proclamation of the word and the celebration of the sacraments.

This full involvement of the whole people of God in worship is affirmed not only by churches of the Protestant Reformation but also by the Eastern Orthodox and Roman Catholic churches as well. In answer to those who say, "I don't get anything out of going to church," an Orthodox theologian replies, "If you really expect to 'get something' out of church attendance, you must give. It is not enough just to sit in church. You must take an active part in its worship."[39] The Second Vatican Council of the Roman Catholic Church urged that all the faithful "be led to that full, conscious, and active participation in liturgical celebrations which is demanded by the very nature of the liturgy."[40] Concerning the focus of the current liturgical renewal taking place in that church, the Council added, "This full and active participation by all the people is the aim to be considered above all else, for it is the primary and indispensable source from which the faithful are to derive the true Christian spirit."[41]

What does this active participation require? Clearly it involves more than being present at a place of worship at a stated hour. That approach to worship presumes that worshipers are the audience and that God, or God's servants in the chancel, are the performers. The action, in fact, is the other way around. The worshiping congregation, including those who lead it, are the ones who offer worship, and God is the one to whom it is offered. This awareness places significant responsibility upon all the people of God to live daily lives rooted and grounded in the gospel of Jesus Christ and to seek the presence of the Holy Spirit in prayer, study, planning, and preparation, culminating in acts of worship filled with the grace and power of Pentecost. When reflection and action are joined in this way, Luther's emphasis on the *consolations* of grace and Calvin's emphasis on the *demands* of grace find mutual correction and wholeness.[42] Responsibility is also placed on churches to break down barriers that prevent all people from worshiping together.

No other obstacle to congregational participation in worship looms larger than human resistance to change. It is instructive that even churches accustomed to authorized prayer books affirm "the liberty wherewith Christ has made us free" and admonish succeeding generations to change the forms of worship "according to the various exigencies of times and occasions."[43]

No book of worship or mimeographed service or spontaneously announced order of worship can assure that people will worship God in spirit and truth. In order for any of these forms to become more than disconnected dry bones of devotion, it is necessary that every Christian, inspired by

the Holy Spirit, actively take his or her place in the body of
Christ, the living and breathing community of faith that is
"a chosen race, a royal priesthood, a holy nation, God's
own people."[44]

MUSIC AND OTHER ARTS

"The Christian liturgy was born singing and has never
ceased to sing."[45] Music is a treasure of the people of God
that has held a place of singular honor from Old Testament
times to the present as a principal means by which praise
and adoration are offered to God in communal worship.
The psalter and other hymns of Israel testify to the power of
vocal and instrumental music as artistic forms nobly suited
to the celebration of God's saving deeds. In the New Testament, from the song of Mary to the hymn of the angels at
Jesus' birth to Paul's great hymns about Christ to the
trumpets and victorious doxology of the heavenly host in
the book of Revelation, God's love for humanity is proclaimed in music that continues to fill the spheres.

The literature of the church of the first four centuries echoes
the Bible's "joyful noise" and provides magnificent hymns.
Augustine, a champion of sacred music, believed that those
who sing pray twice. The Protestant reformers of the sixteenth century, although they held different views on the use
of organs and other musical instruments, affirmed the singing of psalms as one means by which the priesthood of all
believers may be expressed.[46] The Roman Catholic Church
shares this view and has declared boldly that "the music tradition of the universal church is a treasure of immeasurable
value, greater even than that of any other art."[47]

This *Book of Worship* honors the place of music in the continuing pilgrimage of the people of God and invites musicians to employ their art fully in the worship life of the
church. Opportunity is given for the singing of hymns,
psalms, anthems, or other parts of the liturgy. Provision is
made for instrumental music, including the sounds of
instruments other than the organ. Choirs, whether large or

small in number, have a special responsibility to enrich the services with anthems and to lead the people in congregational singing. Musicians who are diligent stewards of their art are knowledgeable concerning diverse ways of presenting hymns and psalms. They are able to open to the worshiping community the vast treasury of the church's sacred music.

It is the "task of the musician to bear the word faithfully," through music; it is the task of the worshiping congregation to offer musicians cooperation and support.[48] This requires an openness to learn new hymns and a willingness to grow in the breadth of understanding and appreciation of diverse styles of music. It calls for patience with congregational rehearsals and the commitment to serve on music committees, sing in choirs, and provide for the cost of the ministry of music.

Through full partnership in this ministry, the worshiping congregation is able to become an anthem of praise to God in words, acts, and sounds that unite the church in heaven and on earth.

Other forms of art also have their rightful place in the worship of God. The Old Testament honors silversmiths, cabinetmakers, architects, and other artisans who offered their skills to the glory of God. The New Testament affirms the diversity of human gifts and calls upon all Christians to use their talents for the common good in service rendered to God. The early church, worshiping in homes and later in simple buildings called the "Lord's" house, created symbols to announce the Christian message visually. Some frescoes and other works of art that were ancient symbols have survived to the present day.

Another element common to early Christian worship was the use of gesture and movement. Their Jewish heritage had steeped the first Christians in an appreciation of the body as an instrument of praise and supplication. Prayers were fulsome gestures, with participants' arms lifted high in outreach to God. Celebrations of salvific events were seldom complete without a processional dance, whether solemn or exuberant in spirit. Prophets and rulers sought inspiration and expressed faithful dependence on God in movement and dance.[49] Psalms, and later Christian hymns, were often accompanied by the movement of the entire congregation in simple line or circle formations.[50]

As such expressions were lost or overtly secularized, liturgical use of movement was minimized, especially after the Reformation. The twentieth century church, particularly in the United States, has seen a renewal of interest in sacred dance.[51] Dancers and those who do not dance alike are engaged in this recovery of the biblical and early Christian sense of worship through movement, a type of discourse especially appropriate to express the rich diversity of spirit of the church year.[52]

A confession, an offertory, or a blessing in dance will be a new experience for some, so judicious planning and thoughtful preparation are needed when introducing movement into worship. When movement, such as a procession, is planned for the whole congregation, consideration must be given to the physical abilities of the people.

In creative partnership with the best of music and other arts, this form of praise is well adapted to both small and large churches. Through movement, many may come to appreciate the symbolic nature of truly embodied faith, fitting testimony to the presence of the Incarnate One.

The arts are not immune to abuse. Frequently the church has had to deal with the issue of artistic forms that obscure the gospel rather than proclaim it. This sometimes occurs with the space used for worship. Forms of worship change, but buildings yield to change reluctantly and usually only at considerable expense. Church architecture is a sermon in walls, floors, and ceilings. If its form no longer relevantly announces the good news of God's love that is celebrated in Christian worship, it is the responsibility of the people of God, with the assistance of able architects, to reform the space and rearrange or replace the furniture. Where this is not done, buildings erected to be servants of right worship become rulers that prohibit liturgical renewal or barriers to worshipers because of inaccessibility.

The proper use of the arts is one way the church celebrates creation as God's gift and echoes God's pronouncement that all that has been made is "good." To hearts of faith, the entire creation points to God. The arts are called to do the same. The signs through which the liturgical arts are expressed, including the literary signs of words printed in worship books, "are not there to reflect our own light. Neither are they themselves a source of light. They refract into our bodily and worldly existence a light that comes from elsewhere. They are not there to be seen but to see by. They are to open our eyes to other things."[53] The test of the liturgical arts is whether they merely point to themselves or whether they point to God and thereby summon worshipers to unite with their neighbors on the pilgrimage toward the holy city, the New Jerusalem not made by human hands, eternal in the heavens, whose builder and maker is God.

RELATIONSHIP OF THE
CHURCH YEAR AND THE LECTIONARY

Christians, from the New Testament age to the present, regard time not only as a product of nature but also as a parable of God's saving action in human history. The people of Israel, in an earlier age, transformed the festivals of Canaan's agricultural cycle into a sermon-in-time that proclaimed the Exodus and other saving events. In a similar way, the church transformed Jewish festivals and secular holidays into a calendar of salvation history.

The expectation of the early return of Jesus Christ conditioned the New Testament church on the side of restraint and simplicity in the development of its worship life.[54] Nevertheless, the New Testament itself contains the first evidence of the evolution of a calendar of holy days and of a schedule of readings for special occasions. Easter and Sunday, respectively, became the annual and weekly signposts in time of the resurrection of the crucified Christ. There is reason to believe that the Gospel of Mark is organized for the purpose of relating its contents to a pattern of readings for a primitive version of the church year.[55] The very concept of such a schedule of readings, or a lectionary, was already an intrinsic part of the synagogue worship of Jesus' day.[56]

The relationship between the church year and the lectionary is more than coincidental.[57] When either is neglected, the other suffers as well.[58] The two are bound closely in their historical development. Although there was great diversity among the churches during the formative period of this development, there were also common factors. Consequently, by the end of the fourth century A.D., it is clear that various primitive lectionaries were in use, and that "before the Roman Empire had passed away, the majestic structure of the church year was established, representing the conquest for Christ of the invisible world of time."[59]

THE CHURCH YEAR

The brief descriptions of the seasons and days of the church year are ordered here by current use rather than by their historical development.

Advent is the season of anticipation and preparation that precedes Christmas in the churches in the West. It was first identified in the fourth century by Hilary of Poitiers who indicated that it was observed for a three-week period in Gaul.[60] In some instances the season was related not to Christmas but to the older Eastern feast of Christ's birth, Epiphany.[61] In the Middle Ages, the Western church gradually reduced the period from an eighth-century pattern of six weeks to four weeks.

Now the first Sunday in Advent is the fourth Sunday before December 25. The focus of the season includes not only preparation for the anniversary of Christ's birth but also the anticipation of Christ's return at the close of history. The early festal nature of the season has been rediscovered in this generation.[62] Consequently, the penitential emphasis no longer dominates. The seasonal color, purple, announces Christ's royalty. In some traditions blue is used, jointly symbolizing royalty and hope.

Christmas, the festival day of the birth of Jesus Christ, falls on December 25 in the church in the West. This date in the ancient Roman calendar was observed as a winter solstice holiday associated with non-Christian rituals of light. By the year A.D. 354, the church in the West had transformed the day into the annual festival of the one born to be the Light of the World.[63] White, the color of the season, is appropriately used from Christmas Eve through at least the first Sunday in Epiphany. The season is one of joyful celebration.

Epiphany, which means manifestation or disclosure, is observed on January 6. Its origins are rooted in the winter solstice holiday of the eastern regions of the Roman Empire. In Jerusalem, the day was transformed by the church into a festival of the incarnation.[64] Egeria, a Spanish woman of the fourth century, provided an eyewitness account of the celebration of Epiphany in Bethlehem.[65] Although other Christians in the eastern provinces celebrated both Jesus' birth and baptism on this day, in the region of Jerusalem only the incarnation was observed.

At a very early time in the East, the visit of Jesus to the marriage feast of Cana became part of the Epiphany celebration.[66] In later developments in the West, the visit of the Magi became the predominant theme of the day. Today, these several strands continue to influence Epiphany, with the baptism of Jesus being observed on the first Sunday of the Epiphany season. Although the color of the day of Epiphany and the first Sunday of the season of Epiphany is white, different practices exist for the remainder of the season. Some churches, emphasizing the person of Christ, continue with white. Others, emphasizing the manifestation of Christ to the whole world, change to green from the second Sunday until the close of the season. Green is the color of the church in mission and symbolizes its life and growth. In some traditions, the last Sunday of the season is observed as the Festival of the Transfiguration, with white as the liturgical color.

Lent is a penitential season of self-examination, prayer, and fasting that precedes the observance of the Triduum (Maundy Thursday evening, Good Friday, and the Vigil of Easter which begins on Saturday night). In Western churches, the season opens on Ash Wednesday and consists of forty days excluding Sundays. The term *Lent* is derived from roots that mean *to lengthen.* The Lenten season points to the spring of the year and to the increasing daylight hours which spring brings.

Lent is first clearly documented in Canon Five of the Council of Nicaea (A.D. 325).[67] However, the practice of a pre-Easter period of discipline is much older. A century earlier, Hippolytus of Rome mentioned a two-and-one-half-week fast prior to Easter. In some places this season was the intensified period of preparation for those who were to be baptized on the eve of Easter.

The color for the season of Lent, beginning with Ash Wednesday and including Sundays, is purple. Some traditions, however, recommend black for Ash Wednesday.

The earliest extant reference to Ash Wednesday is in the Gelasian Sacramentary of the seventh century. It is customary in some traditions to mark the forehead of Christians with ashes on this day. The use of ashes is based on several scriptural texts, including Genesis 3:19 and 18:27, Jeremiah 6:26, and Jonah 3:6.

Holy Week, beginning with Palm/Passion Sunday, marks the final week of Lent. Egeria described a procession to Bethany "six days before the Passover," on which occasion the story of the raising of Lazarus was read in anticipation of Christ's passion.[68] She placed the event on the Saturday before Palm Sunday. In the medieval period, churches in the West began to observe Passion Sunday on the Sunday before Palm Sunday.[69] In recent calendar revisions, most churches have combined the Passion and Palm Sunday themes. They have reduced the Palm Sunday observance of Christ's triumphant entry into Jerusalem to an opening or entrance rite and have made the sixth Sunday in Lent predominantly an anticipation of Christ's passion. In some traditions the color recommended for Palm/Passion Sunday and the weekdays before Maundy Thursday is red. The color is reminiscent of martyrdom.

Maundy Thursday commemorates the institution of Holy Communion and the giving of the new commandment (*mandatum*) that people should love one another even as Christ loves them (John 13:34-35). It also is an appropriate occasion for the rite of washing the feet. In most traditions the color for the day is white in keeping with the glad receiving of the gift of Holy Communion. In those churches where red is introduced on Palm/Passion Sunday, it may remain in use on Maundy Thursday. It is the custom of many churches at the conclusion of the last service on Maundy Thursday to strip the chancel of all paraments and altar hangings in preparation for Good Friday.

Good Friday and Easter, in the earliest celebrations of the church, were combined in a unified rite. Peter Cobb has stated: "Originally, when the Feast of Feasts emerges into the light of history in the second century, it is a unitive commemoration of the death and resurrection of the Lord, a nocturnal celebration of a single night, constituting the Christian Passover."[70] However, very early, as Egeria attested, special services were held on Good Friday. She described a fourth century vigil at the site of the cross that began at noon and ended at 3:00 P.M.[71] This separation of the events of Good Friday from those of Easter Sunday, especially in the West, contributed to an emphasis on the death of Christ in the celebration of Holy Communion "to the exclusion of the resurrection and ascension."[72]

Easter, in the most ancient celebrations of the church, was a vigil service that began on Saturday night of Holy Week and extended into the dawn of Easter day. The Eastern church has preserved this order without interruption to the present time. In the West, the Easter Vigil is now being reintroduced in many churches. This noctural service announces with great power that "certainly the cross and resurrection, seen as a unity, did constitute the new Exodus."[73] White is the color for all the services of Easter Day and the Easter season, including the vigil. The services are the most joyful of all the celebrations of the church year. In many churches this Resurrection Day remains the principal festival on which Christian baptism is celebrated.

Pentecost, the fiftieth day after Easter, closes the Easter season. During this entire period of fifty days, the oldest of the seasons in the church, Egeria reported that "not a single person fasts."[74] Pentecost, borrowed from the Jewish calendar of feasts but transformed by the experience of the church described in Acts 2, originally combined the themes of Christ's ascension and the descent of the Holy Spirit. In the fourth century the two events were separated, and the ascension was placed on the fortieth day after Easter, a Thursday ten days before Pentecost.[75] The color for the day of Pentecost is red in vivid commemoration of the tongues of fire described in Acts 2.

In some churches the Sunday following Pentecost is observed as Trinity Sunday. However, this festival in observance of a doctrine about God rather than of an event in history lacks ancient precedent. Where it is celebrated, white is the usual color.

The Sundays following the day of Pentecost are usually identified by their numerical sequence: the first Sunday after Pentecost, etc. The seasonal color is green. This is the long season of the church in mission.[76] In some traditions the last Sunday in the season, the Sunday before Advent begins, is observed as the Festival of Christ the Sovereign. The color, white, associated with all the festivals of Christ's life, is used when this occurs.

THE LECTIONARY

The use of lectionaries or schedules of readings for particular days is one way the church has labored to guarantee that the story of the Christian faith is grounded in divine revelation and in history. Egeria wrote that on the weekly commemoration of Easter, "the bishop reads the Gospel of the Lord's resurrection at first cockcrow, as he does on every Sunday throughout the year."[77] It is not surprising, especially in the land of Christ's ministry, that special readings became attached to particular days, events, and places that eventually shaped the core of the church year.

The oldest extant manuscript of a lectionary currently available is one developed in Edessa in A.D. 475.[78] Considerable freedom was left to church leaders to choose readings spontaneously. However, as early as Augustine's time, there is evidence that the people frowned upon any departure from the scheduled readings for major holy days.[79] The earliest fully developed lectionary now known is that of Alcuin of York. It dates to A.D. 790 and includes readings for the major festival days, the Sundays within the seasons, and for twenty-four Sundays after Pentecost.[80]

In the sixteenth century, most Protestant reformers at first retained the old Roman lectionary. However, a preference soon developed for the continuous reading of the Bible in sequence, leading to the widespread custom in reformed churches of leaving the choice of readings to the clergy. By 1758, a lay person in the Church of Scotland criticized the clergy for choosing the readings arbitrarily, so as to "mangle them" and "make them say" what the preacher desired.[81] In the past two hundred years, diverse lectionaries have been developed by the churches of the Reformation. In some instances the old Roman lectionary was revived and revised.

In the twentieth century, a resurgence of biblical scholarship moved the churches to reexamine the question of a lectionary. The Roman Catholic Church, in response to the reforms mandated by the Second Vatican Council, published a new three-year lectionary in 1969. This lectionary contained three readings and a psalm for each major Christian festival and for all Sundays of the year. The reintroduction of an Old Testament reading, along with the Epistle and Gospel selections, corrected a deficiency that dates to the fifth century.

This contemporary lectionary, acclaimed and significantly revised by representatives of the churches participating in the Consultation on Common Texts, holds great promise for gaining widespread acceptance in North America and throughout the English-speaking world. This *Common Lectionary* contains a valuable introduction in which its history, structure, and function are carefully explained.[82]

The *Common Lectionary* is commended to all local churches of the United Church of Christ for study and use. Its schedule of readings is published annually in the *United Church of Christ Desk Calendar and Plan Book*.

Why use a lectionary in a denomination that cherishes the freedom of its local churches to order their worship according to their own norms? One reason is that given by the Second Vatican Council and affirmed by uncounted voices throughout the ecumenical church: "The treasures of the Bible are to be opened up more lavishly so that richer fare may be provided for the faithful at the table of God's Word. In this way a more representative portion of the holy scriptures will be read to the people over a set cycle of years."[83] In local churches in which the *Common Lectionary* is used, worshipers are assured of hearing in the period of three years most of the Old Testament and practically all the New Testament.

The readings are ordered, in part, by the selection of Old Testament readings that are thematically related to the Gospel for the day, with a semicontinuous reading of the assigned Epistle. In some seasons a more continuous reading of the Old Testament is provided. The Psalms, once the honored hymn book of Reformation churches, are reintroduced and coordinated thematically with the Old Testament reading. Where non-canonical readings are indicated, alternate selections from the canonical scriptures are included.

Among the benefits of the *Common Lectionary*, few are more coveted than the sharing of the same Bible readings on any given occasion by Christians who worship in different communions but are called to live their faith in a common world. The use of the lectionary makes it possible for laity as well as clergy, ecumenically if they wish, to study the readings with others prior to hearing them offered in worship. It holds the promise of allowing the full message of the Bible to address the attentive heart that is open not only to favored texts but also to the entire word of God.

The church year and the lectionary deserve thoughtful use, not because they are law. They witness to the Word made flesh and enable the church to proclaim faithfully the story it has been told, the story that it lives, and the story that it is privileged to tell to the end of time.

LINKING THE CHURCH

Faithfulness to God's call in Jesus Christ requires that Christians respond in timely ways to the One who is the same yesterday, today, and for ever. This *Book of Worship*, like all books of worship, is transitional literature. It seeks to provide a small span in the bridge that will traverse and link the worshiping church of the twentieth century with the church of the past and the church of the twenty-first century. To the extent that it serves faithfully in this endeavor, it deserves careful study, prayerful reflection, and imaginative use.

Services of Word and Sacrament

Order for the Service of Word and Sacrament I

INTRODUCTION

This order is shaped by traditional forms characteristic of orders of worship found in the Western church. It reflects the unitive structure of the primitive Services of Word and Sacrament known to us by the witness of Justin Martyr, Hippolytus, Egeria, and others. It is also informed by insights of the Protestant Reformation and the most recent ecumenical consensus concerning worship, including the recommendations of *Baptism, Eucharist and Ministry* from the Faith and Order Commission of the World Council of Churches.

This order reflects the human response found in the sixth chapter of Isaiah. Here the prophet first answers God's mysterious presence with adoration and then experiences contrition, confession, and absolution. Instruction from God and a call to God's service follow. Isaiah's "yes" to God is celebrated in a divine commissioning. This order is informed by Isaiah's experience and conveys a sense of the majesty of God. Its central focus is God's victory over sin and death in the resurrection of Jesus Christ.

In this order, as in the second order, the confession of sin is integrally related to the passing of the peace as a reminder that Christians ask God to forgive them "as we forgive those who trespass against us." Peace with God is inseparable from peace with neighbors. In ancient times those not yet baptized were dismissed following the Service of the Word prior to the prayers and the offertory that introduced the Service of the Sacrament. For this reason, the confession of sin occurred midway in the total service and was often integrated within the general prayers of intercession. In later times when the worship of the church was open to the public, the confession of sin was moved to a much earlier place in the opening acts of the Service of the Word. The use of the prayer for mercy in this part of the order and the use of other traditional forms elsewhere provide an opportunity to express the universal heritage of the Christian faith. Through the use of words and acts common to the church across the centuries and around the world, participants show that they are equally "citizens with the saints and members of the household of God."[1]

The sermon, in the early church and the churches of the Reformation, is essential to worship rightly ordered. The proclamation of the Christian message by this means was so treasured among early Christians that more than one sermon in a given service was not unusual. Christ's presence in the act of preaching is a real presence of the one who promised, "where two or three are gathered in my name, there am I in the midst of them."[2] The sermon, though not sacramental in the tangible sense made possible by material signs, is a witness endowed with grace through which human words attest to the Word that became flesh and dwelt among us.

The prayers of the people and the concerns of the church are closely related to the offertory. This placement is a sign that they are part of the worship offered to God with monetary gifts and the bread and wine, all of which represent the life and labor of the community of faith.

The invitation and the call to the supper emphasize that all people of faith are welcome at Christ's table. The invitation and call celebrate not only the memory of a meal that is past, but an actual meal with the risen Christ that is a foretaste of the heavenly banquet at which Christ will preside at the end of history. The texts and outlines for the communion prayer seek to summarize God's words and deeds in history for the world and for its salvation. Provision is made for the entire congregation to say or sing parts of this central prayer that stands at the heart of the order, and comes to its climax in the Prayer of Our Savior.

The visible breaking of the bread and pouring of the wine are symbolic actions with double significance. The wheat that is gathered to make one loaf and the grapes that are pressed to make one cup remind participants that they are one in the body of Christ, the church. But the breaking and the pouring also announce the costliness of Christ's sacrificial life and of the discipleship to which all are called. The use of the traditional "Lamb of God," whether said or sung, reintroduces the theme of penitence just before Holy Communion is received.

The manner of distributing Holy Communion is not prescribed in the United Church of Christ. The practice of using individual cubes of bread and individual cups was introduced in the nineteenth century. Prior to that time, the usual mode of distribution was a common loaf and a common cup. Where the congregation received the bread and wine in their pews, it was sometimes necessary for those charged with serving the people to use a portion of the loaf and a separate cup adequate to serve one section of the room. The mode of intinction—dipping the bread in the wine and receiving both simultaneously—is an ancient custom still practiced as the norm in Eastern Orthodox churches. Also in the nineteenth century, grape juice became available and replaced wine in some churches. The biblical record supports most clearly the custom of one loaf and one cup shared in sequence.

The post-communion prayer is both a prayer of thanksgiving and an affirmation of the willingness of those who received communion to serve God.

The service concludes with the Song of Simeon, followed by a commissioning and a blessing. The movement is from meal to mission.

In this order, as in others, the prelude and postlude are an intrinsic part of the worship and stand within the total order of the service.

OUTLINE

Prelude
Greeting
Sentences of Adoration
Hymn of Adoration
Confession of Sin
Silence
Prayer for Mercy
Assurance of Pardon
Passing the Peace
Act of Praise
Reading of Scripture
Sermon
Affirmation of Faith
Hymn, Anthem, or Other Music
Prayers of the People
Concerns of the Church
Offertory
Invitation
Communion Prayer
Prayer of Our Savior
Breaking Bread and Pouring Wine
Lamb of God
Call to the Supper
Sharing the Elements
Prayer of Thanksgiving
Hymn of Parting
Song of Simeon
Commissioning
Benediction
Postlude

PRELUDE

The service may begin with music as the congregation gathers. The greeting and sentences of adoration or the hymn may follow, according to local custom.

GREETING

All who are able may stand for one of these or another greeting informed by scripture.

A
LEADER
**In the name
of the triune God:
the Creator,
the Christ, and
the Holy Spirit.**

ALL
Amen.

B
LEADER
**The grace
of our Lord
Jesus Christ
and the love
of God and
the communion
of the Holy
Spirit be
with you all.**[3]

PEOPLE
And also
with you.

C *for use except during Lent*
LEADER
**Alleluia!
Christ is risen.**

PEOPLE
Christ is risen
indeed.
Alleluia!

SENTENCES OF ADORATION

All who are able may stand as one or more of the following sentences or others appropriate for the day or season are said.

A
LEADER
**Our help is in the name of the Holy One,
who made heaven and earth.**[4]

B
LEADER
**Christ, our paschal lamb, has been offered for us.
Let us, therefore, celebrate the festival.**[5]

C

LEADER

**In the beginning was the Word,
and the Word was with God,
and the Word was God.**[6]

D

LEADER

**God's love has been poured
into our hearts
through the Holy Spirit
which has been given to us.**[7]

E

LEADER

**God has brought the people of the covenant
from the land of bondage
into freedom.**

F

LEADER

**Jesus came to preach good news to the poor,
to proclaim release to the captives
and recovery of sight to the blind,
to liberate those who are oppressed,
and to proclaim the year
of God's favor.**[8]

HYMN OF ADORATION

*All who are able may stand. This may be a processional
hymn.*

CONFESSION OF SIN

*The people may be seated. A leader may offer one of these
prayers or one in his or her own words.*

A

LEADER

**We are called to examine
our faithfulness to God's
covenant with us.**

B

LEADER

**If we say we have no sin,
we deceive ourselves,
and the truth is not in us.**

God, in whose presence
we gather,
promises us grace
and pardon when we
acknowledge our
weakness and shame.
Let us confess our sin
to almighty God.

ALL
Eternal God,
whose Word is a lamp
for our feet
and a light for our path,
we recognize and confess
that we have failed
to respond fully
to your gracious presence
in our lives.
Through Jesus Christ you
have offered us new life,
fulfillment,
and the freedom
to serve you.
We confess
that we are captive to sin,
that our sin binds us
with false pride,
and that the wrong we do is
made worse by the good
we leave undone.
Reconcile us to you
and to all people.
God of mercy,
forgive all our sin and
strengthen us anew for life
as you intend it;
through Jesus Christ
our Savior.
Amen.

PEOPLE
But if we confess our sins,
God, who is faithful and just,
will forgive our sins
and cleanse us from all
unrighteousness.[9]

LEADER
Let us confess our sins
before God
and one another.

ALL
Most merciful God,
we confess that we are
in bondage to sin
and cannot free ourselves.
We have sinned against you
in thought, word, and deed,
by what we have done
and by what we have
left undone.
We have not loved you
with our whole heart.
We have not loved our
neighbors as ourselves.
For the sake
of Jesus Christ,
have mercy on us.
Forgive us, renew us,
and lead us,
so that we may delight
in your will
and follow in your ways,
to the glory
of your name.
Amen.[10]

SILENCE

Silence may be observed for reflection and prayer.

PRAYER FOR MERCY

The Kyrie, Trisagion, *or other words may be said or sung. Musical settings are on pages 449, 450, and 459.*

A

LEADER
Lord, have mercy.

PEOPLE
Christ, have mercy.

LEADER
Lord, have mercy.

B

LEADER
Holy God,
Holy and mighty,
Holy Immortal One,

ALL
Have mercy upon us.

ASSURANCE OF PARDON

A leader may speak of God's pardon and mercy, using one of the following or her or his own words.

A

LEADER
God hears the confession of our hearts and lips. Through Jesus Christ we are forgiven all our sins, and by the Holy Spirit we are empowered for new life.

ALL
We believe the good news of Jesus Christ. Amen.

B

LEADER
Anyone in Christ becomes a new person altogether; the past is finished and gone, everything has become fresh and new.

Friends, believe the good news of the gospel:

ALL
In Jesus Christ, we are forgiven.[11]

PASSING THE PEACE

As a sign of their reconciliation with God and each other, all may greet those around them with an embrace or a handshake, accompanied by such words as: "The peace of

God be with you," and the response: "And also with you."
All who are able may rise for the passing of the peace.
Leaders of the service may move among the congregation
to share the signs of peace.

ACT OF PRAISE

All who are able may stand for a call to praise and a
hymn, psalm, or gloria.

LEADER
Let us sing praise to God.

ALL
We will continually praise God's holy name.

A

A hymn, psalm, or gloria
such as the following may
be read or sung.

ALL
Glory to God
in the highest,
and peace
to God's people on earth.

Holy One, heavenly God,
sovereign God and Creator,
we worship you,
we give you thanks,
we praise you
for your glory.

Lord Jesus Christ,
God's only begotten one,
Lord God, Lamb of God,
you take away the sin
of the world:
have mercy on us;
you are seated
at the right hand

B

This gloria may be said or
sung. Musical settings are
on pages 451 and 460.

ALL
Glory to God the Creator,
and to the Christ,
and to the Holy Spirit:
as it was in the beginning,
is now,
and will be for ever.
Amen.

of Majesty:
receive our prayer.

For you alone are the Messiah,
you alone are the Lord,
you alone are the
Most High, Jesus Christ,
with the Holy Spirit,
in the glory
of the triune God.
Amen.

READING OF SCRIPTURE

The people may be seated as the scripture lessons are intro-
duced. It is recommended that the schedule of readings
found in the ecumenical lectionary be used. If it is not,
care should be taken to maintain a balance in readings
from the Old Testament, the Epistles, and the Gospels.

A collect for illumination, a seasonal collect, or an extem-
poraneous prayer asking for attentive hearts may precede
the first reading. A brief introduction to the theme of each
lesson may be offered. In order to distinguish the lesson
from the commentary, the reader may announce the lesson
as indicated.

OLD TESTAMENT LESSON
READER
before the lesson
Listen for the word of God in _____.

After the lesson, a psalm may be said or sung, followed by
a gloria, unless one has been said or sung earlier, or the
following or a similar announcement may be made.

READER
Here ends the Old Testament lesson.

EPISTLE LESSON
READER
before the lesson
Listen for the word of God in _____.

READER
following the lesson
Here ends the Epistle lesson.

GOSPEL LESSON
*In some local churches, standing, by those who are able,
for the reading of the Gospel is customary as it is a sign of
respect for Jesus Christ, who addresses the congregation.
Responses before and after this lesson may be said or sung.*

READER
before the lesson
Listen to the Gospel of Jesus Christ according to _____ .

PEOPLE
Glory to you, O Christ.

READER
following the lesson
This is the good news.

PEOPLE
Praise to you, O Christ.

SERMON

AFFIRMATION OF FAITH

*All who are able may stand for a form of the Statement of
Faith of the United Church of Christ, a creed, or a church
covenant. Forms of the statement of faith, historic creeds,
and other affirmations are in the Resource Section, beginning on page 509.*

HYMN, ANTHEM, OR OTHER MUSIC

PRAYERS OF THE PEOPLE

*The people may be seated for the prayers. Leaders may
announce special concerns for prayers and invite the people to indicate needs or to name causes for thanksgiving.
Intercessions may include prayers for:*

- *The church universal, including ecumenical councils, specific churches in other places, the United Church of Christ and its leaders, and this local church.*
- *The nations and all in authority.*
- *Justice and peace in all the world.*
- *The health of those who suffer in body, mind, or spirit.*
- *The needs of families, single people, and the lonely.*
- *Reconciliation with adversaries.*
- *The local community and all other communities.*
- *All who are oppressed or in prison.*

A litany of prayers and responses, with silences, may be used; a pastoral prayer may be offered; petitions may be offered by anyone present, ending with a phrase to which all may respond, such as those below. A longer period of silence may precede or follow the prayers.

🅰
LEADER
Christ, in your mercy,

PEOPLE
Hear our prayer.

🅱
LEADER
Holy Spirit, our Comforter,

PEOPLE
Receive our prayer.

CONCERNS OF THE CHURCH

Leaders and people may announce information concerning the program, ministry, and people of the church.

OFFERTORY

A leader may introduce the offertory and give an invitation to Holy Communion, using his or her own words or one of the following.

🅰
LEADER
Through Christ let us continually praise God and share what we have, for such sacrifices are pleasing to God.

🅱
LEADER
Let us present with joy our offerings of commitment and support for the work of Christ's church.

PEOPLE
**Let us prepare Christ's table
with the offerings
of our life and labor.**

*Music may be offered to God's glory while the tithes and
offerings are being received. Silence is also appropriate.
The people may express their dedication and thanksgiving
to God through music, prayers, dance, and other acts.*

*The people who are able may stand as representatives
bring the gifts to the table. The communion elements may
be brought to the table with the other gifts.*

A

*A doxology, such as the
following to the tune "Old
Hundredth," may be sung.*

ALL
**Praise God from whom
all blessings flow;
Praise Christ the Word
in flesh born low;
Praise Holy Spirit evermore;
One God, Triune,
whom we adore.
Amen.**

B

*This doxology may be
sung. Musical settings are
on pages 452 and 461.*

ALL
**Praise God from whom
all blessings flow;
Praise Christ,
all creatures here below;
Praise Holy Spirit,
the Comforter;
One God, Triune,
whom we adore.
Amen.**

AND

A prayer of dedication may be said.

**If there is to be no celebration of Holy Communion, the
service may be concluded with the Prayer of Our Savior,
a hymn, a benediction, and a postlude.**

INVITATION

*While all who are able stand, a leader may use these or
other words informed by scripture. The people respond.*

LEADER
Beloved in Christ,
the Gospel tells us that on the first day of the week
Jesus Christ was raised from death,
appeared to Mary Magdalene,
on that same day sat at the table with two disciples,
and was made known to them in the breaking of the bread.

The people may sing or say the following. Musical settings
are on pages 453 and 462.

ALL
This is the joyful feast
of the people of God.
Men and women,
youth and children,
come from the east and the west,
from the north and the south,
and gather about Christ's table.[12]

LEADER
This table is for all Christians
who wish to know the presence of Christ
and to share in the community of God's people.

COMMUNION PRAYER

All who are able may stand.

PASTOR
God be with you.

PEOPLE
And also with you.

PASTOR
Lift up your hearts.

PEOPLE
We lift them to God.

PASTOR
Let us give thanks to God Most High.

PEOPLE
It is right to give God thanks and praise.

The pastor leads in thankfully recalling God's great acts of salvation, using the outline on page 49 or one of these.

A

PASTOR

**We give you thanks,
God of majesty and mercy,
for calling forth the creation
and raising us from dust
by the breath of your being.**

**We bless you for the beauty
and bounty of the earth
and for the vision
of the day
when sharing by all will
mean scarcity for none.**

**We remember the
covenant you made
with your people Israel,
and we give you thanks for
all our ancestors in faith.
We rejoice that you call us
to reconciliation with you
and all people everywhere
and that you remain faithful
to your covenant
even when we are faithless.**

**We rejoice that you call
the entire human family
to this table
of sacrifice and victory.
We come in remembrance
and celebration of the gift
of Jesus Christ,
whom you sent,
in the fullness of time,
to be the good news.
Born of Mary,**

B

PASTOR

**We give you thanks,
Holy One,
almighty and eternal God,
always and everywhere,
through Jesus Christ,
the only one begotten by you
before all time,
by whom you made
the world and all things.**

**We bless you for your
continual love and care
for every creature.
We praise you
for forming us in your image
and for calling us
to be your people.**

**Although we rebelled
against your love,
you did not abandon us
in our sin,
but sent to us prophets
and teachers to lead us
into the way of salvation.**

**Above all, we give you
thanks for the gift of Jesus,
our only Savior,
who is the way, the truth,
and the life.**

**In the fullness of time
you came to us
and received our nature
in the person of Jesus,**

our sister in faith,
Christ lived among us
to reveal the mystery
of your Word,
to suffer and die
on the cross for us,
to be raised from death
on the third day,
and then to live in glory.

*A seasonal preface from
Resources for the Church
Year, beginning on page
476, may be said here.*

We bless you, gracious God,
for the presence
of your Holy Spirit
in the church
you have gathered.
With your sons and
daughters of faith
in all places and times,
we praise you with joy.

who, in obedience to you,
by suffering on the cross,
and being raised
from the dead,
delivered us from the way
of sin and death.

We praise you that Jesus
now reigns with you in glory
and ever lives to pray for us.

We thank you
for the Holy Spirit
who leads us into truth,
defends us in adversity,
and gathers us from every
people to unite us
in one holy church.

Therefore, with the entire
company of saints
in heaven and on earth,
we worship and glorify you,
God Most Holy.

*All may sing or say the following. Musical settings are on
pages 454 and 463.*

ALL
Holy, holy, holy God
of love and majesty,
the whole universe speaks of your glory,
O God Most High.

Blessed is the one
who comes in the name of our God!
Hosanna in the highest!

*The people may be seated as option A or B of the prayer
continues. As the following words are spoken, the pastor
may indicate the communion elements.*

PASTOR
**We remember
that on the night
of betrayal and desertion,
and on the eve of death,
Jesus gathered the disciples
for the feast of Passover.**

**Jesus took bread,
and after giving thanks to you,
broke it, and gave it
to the disciples, saying:
"This is my body
which is for you.
Do this
in remembrance of me."**

**In the same way also the cup,
after supper, saying:
"This cup is the new
covenant in my blood.
Do this,
as often as you drink it,
in remembrance of me."**[13]

**Therefore we proclaim
the mystery of our faith.**

PASTOR
**For in the night of betrayal
Jesus took bread, and
after giving thanks to you,
broke the bread,
and gave it to the disciples,
and said: "Take, eat:
This is my body
which is given for you.
Do this
in remembrance of me."**

**In the same way
also after supper,
Jesus took the cup,
and after giving you thanks,
gave it to them and said:
"Drink this, all of you:
This is my blood
of the new covenant,
which is poured out
for you and many,
for the forgiveness of sins.
Do this,
as often as you drink it,
in remembrance of me."**[14]

*Either of these may be said or sung with option A or
option B of the prayer.*

A

*Musical settings are on
pages 455, 456, and 464.*

ALL
**Christ's death, O God,
we proclaim.
Christ's resurrection
we declare.
Christ's coming we await.
Glory be to you, O God.**

B

ALL
**Christ has died.
Christ is risen.
Christ will come again.**

Option A or B of the prayer continues.

PASTOR
**Eternal God, we unite
in this covenant of faith,
recalling Christ's suffering
and death, rejoicing
in Christ's resurrection,
and awaiting Christ's return
in victory.**

**We spread your table
with these gifts of the earth
and of our labor.
We present to you
our very lives,
committed to your service
in behalf of all people.**

**We ask you
to send your Holy Spirit
on this bread and wine,
on our gifts, and on us.
Strengthen your universal
church that it may be the
champion of peace and
justice in all the world.
Restore the earth with your
grace that is able to make
all things new.**

ALL
**Be present with us
as we share this meal,
and throughout all
our lives,
that we may know you
as the Holy One,
who with Christ
and the Holy Spirit,
lives for ever.
Amen.**

PASTOR
**Holy One,
show forth among us the
presence of your life-giving
Word and Holy Spirit,
to sanctify us and your
entire church through these
holy mysteries.
Grant that all who share
the communion
of the body and blood
of our risen Savior
may be one in Jesus Christ.**

**May we remain faithful
in love and hope,
until the perfect feast
with our exalted Savior
in the eternal joy
of your heavenly realm.**

ALL
**Gracious God,
accept with favor
this our sacrifice of praise,
which we now present
with these holy gifts.
We offer to you ourselves,
giving you thanks for the
perfect offering of the only
one begotten by you,
Jesus Christ our Savior:**

**By whom and with whom
and in whom, in the unity
of the Holy Spirit,
all honor and glory be
to you, eternal God,
now and for ever.
Amen.**

*If option A or B of the communion prayer has been used,
the service continues with the Prayer of Our Savior.*

C

*The pastor, following this or a similar outline, may offer
the prayer of great thanksgiving in her or his own words.*

- *Give thanks for God's goodness to us shown in the
  creation of the world and in the events of history.*
- *Remember people of faith through whom God has
  spoken to the human family as witnessed in scripture.*
- *Give thanks for the birth, life, death, and resurrection of
  Jesus Christ.*
- *Recall Jesus' words at the institution of the supper in
  the upper room.*
- *Remind us that our participation in Holy Communion
  is a sacrifice of praise which includes the offering of our
  lives to God.*
- *Briefly proclaim faith in Christ who has died, is raised,
  and will return at the close of history.*
- *Give thanks for the gift of the Holy Spirit whose
  presence is invoked.*

PRAYER OF OUR SAVIOR

*Standing, sitting, or kneeling, all may sing or say the
prayer received from Jesus Christ.*

LEADER
Let us pray as Christ our Savior has taught us.

A	B	C
ALL	ALL	ALL
Our Father in heaven, hallowed be your name, your kingdom come, your will be done, on earth as in heaven.	**Our Father, who art in heaven, hallowed be thy name. Thy kingdom come. Thy will be done on earth as it is in heaven.**	**Our Father, who art in heaven, hallowed be thy name. Thy kingdom come. Thy will be done on earth as it is in heaven.**

Give us today
our daily bread.
Forgive us our sins
as we forgive those
who sin against us.
Save us from the
time of trial
and deliver us
from evil.
For the kingdom,
the power,
and the glory
are yours now
and for ever.
Amen.[15]

Give us this day
our daily bread.
And forgive us
our trespasses,
as we forgive those
who trespass
against us.
And lead us not
into temptation,
but deliver us
from evil.
For thine
is the kingdom,
and the power,
and the glory,
for ever and ever.
Amen.

Give us this day
our daily bread.
And forgive us
our debts,
as we forgive
our debtors.
And lead us not
into temptation,
but deliver us
from evil.
For thine
is the kingdom,
and the power,
and the glory,
for ever.
Amen.

BREAKING BREAD AND POURING WINE

The bread is broken and the wine is poured as visible and audible reminders of the sacrificial self-giving of Jesus Christ. These actions call to mind the cost as well as the joy of Christian discipleship.

PASTOR
while taking the bread and breaking it
**The bread which we break
is the communion of the body of Christ.**

PASTOR
while pouring the wine and raising the cup
**The cup of blessing which we bless
is the communion of the blood of Christ.**

LAMB OF GOD

Either version of the ancient Agnus Dei[16] *may be said or sung by all.*

A

ALL
**Lamb of God,
you take away the sins
of the world:
have mercy on us.**

**Lamb of God,
you take away the sins
of the world:
have mercy on us.**

**Lamb of God,
you take away the sins
of the world:
grant us peace.**

B

*Musical settings are on
pages 457 and 465.*

ALL
**Jesus, Lamb of God:
have mercy on us.
Jesus, bearer of our sins:
have mercy on us.
Jesus, redeemer of the world:
give us your peace.**

CALL TO THE SUPPER

A

PASTOR
**The gifts of God
for the people of God.
Come,
for all things are ready.**

B

PASTOR
**The gifts of God
for the people of God.
Take them in remembrance
that Christ died
and was raised for you.**

SHARING THE ELEMENTS

*In giving the bread and cup, the pastor and those assisting
may use their own words or one of the following, and the
people respond.*

A

while giving the bread

PASTOR
**Take and eat,
this is the body of Christ,
broken for you.**

PEOPLE
Amen!

B

while giving the bread

PASTOR
**The body of Christ,
the bread of heaven.**

PEOPLE
Amen!

while giving the cup

PASTOR
**Take and drink,
this is the cup
of the new covenant,
poured out for you.**

PEOPLE
Amen!

while giving the cup

PASTOR
**The blood of Christ,
the cup of salvation.**

PEOPLE
Amen!

After the distribution of the bread and cup, the elements may be covered, according to local custom.

Words of dismissal may precede the prayer of thanksgiving if people have moved from their seats to receive communion.

PRAYER OF THANKSGIVING

All who are able may stand. A leader may give thanks in her or his own words or may use one of the following.

LEADER
Let us pray.

A

ALL
**Almighty God,
we give you thanks for the
gift of our Savior's presence
in the simplicity and
splendor of this holy meal.
Unite us with all who are fed
by Christ's body and blood
that we may faithfully
proclaim the good news
of your love and that your
universal church may be
a rainbow of hope
in an uncertain world;
through Jesus Christ
our Redeemer.
Amen.**

B

ALL
**Bountiful God,
we give you thanks
that you have refreshed us
at your table
by granting us
the presence of Christ.
Strengthen our faith,
increase our love
for one another,
and send us forth
into the world
in courage and peace,
rejoicing in the power
of the Holy Spirit.
Amen.**[17]

HYMN OF PARTING

All who are able may stand. Depending on local custom, the commissioning and benediction, with or without the Song of Simeon, may precede the hymn.

SONG OF SIMEON

All may sing or say the ancient Nunc Dimittis. *Musical settings are on pages 458 and 466.*

ALL
**Holy One,
now let your servant go in peace;
your word has been fulfilled:
my own eyes have seen the salvation
which you have prepared
in the sight of every people:
a light to reveal you to the nations
and the glory of your people Israel.**[18]

COMMISSIONING

All who are able may stand as a leader says these or other words of commissioning.

LEADER
**Go forth into the world
to serve God with gladness;
be of good courage;
hold fast to that which is good;
render to no one evil for evil;
strengthen the fainthearted;
support the weak;
help the afflicted;
honor all people;
love and serve God,
rejoicing in the power of the Holy Spirit.**[19]

BENEDICTION

A leader may offer one of the following or another blessing.

A

LEADER
**The blessing of God Almighty:
the Creator,
the Redeemer,
and the Sanctifier,
be with you all.**

PEOPLE
Amen.

B

LEADER
**Now may the God of peace
who brought again
from the dead
our Savior Jesus,
the great shepherd
of the sheep,
by the blood
of the eternal covenant,
equip you
with everything good
that you may do God's will,
working in you that which
is pleasing in God's sight;
through Jesus Christ,
to whom be glory
for ever and ever.**

PEOPLE
Amen.[20]

POSTLUDE

*The congregation may be seated and remain until the
postlude is concluded.*

Order for the Service of Word and Sacrament II

INTRODUCTION

This order, like the first one, is shaped by the customs and practices of the church in every century and is faithful to the ecumenical convergence published in *Baptism, Eucharist and Ministry*.[21] It includes all aspects of our human response to God found in Isaiah's vision but for particular reasons places them in a different sequence. The flow is from adoration to instruction and only then to contrition, confession, and absolution. This flow is explained in part by the awareness that contrition and confession of sin are sometimes a response to the word of God proclaimed in the reading of scripture and the preaching of the sermon, more than an immediate response to the presence of God announced at the beginning of worship. This order concludes with a call to God's service and a commissioning in a manner that reflects Isaiah 6 and the Order for the Service of Word and Sacrament I.

In this order an effort is made to remind each worshiper not only of God's presence, but also of the presence of all other worshipers who constitute the community of faith. Without diminishing the immediate relationship of each person directly with God, all are called to recognize God's presence in the lives of those for whom Christ died. For this reason, a responsive greeting that points to human relationships is placed early in the order, and the same theme is repeated in the invocation.

Although the confession of sin, silence, assurance of pardon, and passing of the peace come later in this order than the first, they are kept as an integral unit in both orders. This is done to indicate that the passing of the peace is more than a social courtesy. It presumes that people have first asked for God's forgiveness and sought reconciliation with their neighbors. In this order, because of the Matthean influence, the passing of the peace is placed immediately prior to the offertory.

Following the offertory, the principal prayer used at the table to mark the beginning of the eucharistic meal is the one given by Jesus. Through the centuries, this prayer has appeared at various places in orders for worship. In the earliest orders it is not mentioned. Consequently, there is uncertainty about its placement in antiquity. However, there is evidence that this great prayer of Jesus was reserved for the use of the baptized community. It likely came at some point after the offertory which marked the time when those who were not baptized were dismissed. Later it was placed in close proximity to the breaking of the bread or just before the reception of Holy Communion. John Calvin and John Knox placed it after the offertory and prior to the words of institution in a position similar to the one in this order.

At various points, two full texts are provided. The option is offered for the leader to speak extemporaneously or to prepare a text for the occasion. When a printed option is not chosen, adequate preparation will be necessary to assure that the biblical integrity of the order is maintained.

In both orders, the risen Christ is the central focus. However, this order is more explicit in its attempt to call forth the joy of Christ's victory over death. This is expressed, for example, by the placement of the resurrection acclamation in the position where the first order calls for the "Lamb of God." The prayer of thanksgiving and the dismissal accent the call of the people of God to be the church dispersed. As in the first order, the movement is from meal to mission.

OUTLINE

Concerns of the Church
Prelude
Hymn of Adoration
Greeting
Invocation
Act of Praise
Reading of Scripture
Sermon
Affirmation of Faith
Hymn, Anthem, or Other Music
Prayers of the People
Confession of Sin
Silence
Assurance of Pardon
Passing the Peace
Offertory
Lord's Prayer
Invitation
Communion Prayer
Breaking Bread and Pouring Wine
Resurrection Acclamation
Sharing the Elements
Prayer of Thanksgiving
Benediction
Hymn of Parting
Postlude

CONCERNS OF THE CHURCH

Leaders and people may announce information concerning the program, ministries, and people of the church here or at the offertory.

PRELUDE

Music may be played as the congregation gathers.

HYMN OF ADORATION

All who are able may stand. According to local custom, the hymn may follow the prelude or the greeting.

GREETING

All who are able may stand as a leader offers one of these or another greeting informed by scripture.

A

LEADER
The grace of our Lord Jesus Christ and the love of God and the communion of the Holy Spirit be with you all.[22]

PEOPLE
And also with you.

B

LEADER
Dear friends, let us love one another, because love comes from God. Whoever loves is a child of God and knows God.

PEOPLE
Whoever does not love does not know God, for God is love.[23]

C

LEADER
With what shall we come before the Holy One, and bow ourselves before God on high?

PEOPLE
Shall we come before God with burnt offerings, with calves a year old?

LEADER
God has showed you, O people, what is good; and what does the Holy One require of you?

PEOPLE
To do justice,
and to love
kindness,
and to walk
humbly with
our God.[24]

INVOCATION

All who are able may stand.

A

LEADER
Christ is with us.

PEOPLE
Christ is in our midst.

LEADER
Let us pray.

B

LEADER
God be with you.

PEOPLE
And also with you.

LEADER
Let us pray.

One of these prayers or one in a leader's own words may be offered, asking for the congregation to be made responsive to the presence of God.

A

ALL
**Eternal God,
companion of all
who seek you,
and seeker of all
who turn away from you,
draw near to us that
we may draw near to you,
and grant us the grace
to love and to serve you that
we may find in your will
our true freedom;
through Jesus Christ,
the way, the truth,
and the life.
Amen.**

B

ALL
**Gracious God,
gentle in your power and
strong in your tenderness,
you have brought us forth
from the womb
of your being
and breathed into us
the breath of life.
We know that we do not
live by bread alone
but by every word
that comes from you.
Feed our deep hungers
with the living bread
that you give us**

in Jesus Christ.
May Jesus' promise,
"Where two or three are
gathered in my name,
there am I
in the midst of them,"[25]
be fulfilled in us.
Make us a joyful company
of your people
so that with the faithful
in every place and time
we may praise and honor
you, God Most High.
Amen.

ACT OF PRAISE

All who are able stand as a hymn, psalm, or gloria is read
or sung. During Lent, it is appropriate to omit hymns that
contain the alleluia.

A

*This hymn (tune: "*Lasst Uns Erfreuen*") or another hymn*
of praise may be sung.

ALL
From all that dwell below the skies
Let the Creator's praise arise;
Alleluia! Alleluia!
Let the Redeemer's name be sung.
Let God the spirit free each tongue!
Alleluia! Alleluia!
Alleluia! Alleluia! Alleluia!

Eternal is your glory, God.
Eternal Word we give you laud;
Alleluia! Alleluia!
Eternal Spirit we adore,
Your praise shall sound from shore to shore!
Alleluia! Alleluia!
Alleluia! Alleluia! Alleluia!

B

A gloria such as the following may be said or sung. Musical settings are on pages 451 and 460.

ALL
**Glory to God the Creator,
and to the Christ,
and to the Holy Spirit:
as it was in the beginning,
is now,
and will be for ever.
Amen.**

C

A psalm may be read or sung. This may be a responsive reading.

READING OF SCRIPTURE

The people may be seated as the scripture lessons are introduced. It is recommended that the schedule of readings found in the ecumenical lectionary be used. If it is not, care should be taken to maintain a balance in readings from the Old Testament, the Epistles, and the Gospels.

A collect for illumination, a seasonal collect, or an extemporaneous prayer asking for attentive hearts may precede the first reading. A brief introduction to the theme of each lesson may be offered. In order to distinguish the lesson from the commentary, the reader may announce: "A reading from _____" and may conclude: "Here ends the lesson."

OLD TESTAMENT LESSON
After the Old Testament lesson, a psalm may be said or sung, followed by a gloria.

EPISTLE LESSON

GOSPEL LESSON
In some local churches, standing, by those who are able, for the reading of the Gospel is customary as it is a sign of respect for Jesus Christ, who addresses the congregation in words remembered by the early church.

SERMON

AFFIRMATION OF FAITH

All who are able may stand for a form of the Statement of Faith of the United Church of Christ, a creed, or a church covenant. Forms of the statement of faith, historic creeds, and other affirmations are in the Resource Section, beginning on page 509.

HYMN, ANTHEM, OR OTHER MUSIC

PRAYERS OF THE PEOPLE

The people may be seated. Leaders may announce special concerns for prayers and invite the people to indicate needs or to name causes for thanksgiving. Intercessions may include prayers for:

- *The church universal, including ecumenical councils, specific churches in other places, the United Church of Christ and its leaders, and this local church.*
- *The nations and all in authority.*
- *Justice and peace in all the world.*
- *The health of those who suffer in body, mind, or spirit.*
- *The needs of families, single people, and the lonely.*
- *Reconciliation with adversaries.*
- *The local community and all other communities.*
- *All who are oppressed or in prison.*

A litany of prayers and responses, with silences, may be used; a pastoral prayer may be offered; petitions may be offered by anyone present, ending with a phrase to which all may respond, such as those below. A longer period of silence may precede or follow the prayers.

A

LEADER
God, in your mercy,

PEOPLE
Hear our prayer.

B

LEADER
O God, hear our prayer.

PEOPLE
Let our cry come unto you.

CONFESSION OF SIN

A

LEADER
**Let us confess our sin
against God and each other.**

ALL
**Merciful God,
we know that you love us
and that you call us
to fullness of life,
but around us and within us
we see the brokenness
of the world
and of our ways.
Our successes leave us empty;
our progress does not satisfy.
Our prosperous land
is not the promised land
of our longing.
Forgive our willful neglect
of your word,
our insensitivity to the
needs of others,
and our failure to feed
the spirit that is within us;
through Jesus Christ
our Redeemer.
Amen.**

B

*An introduction and
prayer from scripture may
be used, such as the following paraphrased verses
from 1 John and Psalm 51.*

LEADER
**If we say
we have no sin,
we deceive ourselves,
and the truth is not in us.**

PEOPLE
If we confess our sins,
God is faithful and just
and will forgive our sins
and cleanse us
from all unrighteousness.[26]

LEADER
**Sisters and brothers,
in the words of the psalmist,
let us ask for the forgiveness
we need.**

ALL
**Have mercy on us, O God,
according to your
steadfast love;
according to your
abundant mercy
blot out our transgressions.
Wash us thoroughly
from our iniquity,
and cleanse us from our sin.
Create in us a clean heart,
O God, and put a new and
right spirit within us.
Cast us not away
from your presence,**

**and take not your Holy
Spirit from us.
Restore to us the joy
of your salvation,
and uphold us
with a willing spirit.**[27]
Amen.

SILENCE

Silence may be observed for reflection and prayer.

ASSURANCE OF PARDON

*A leader may speak of God's pardon and mercy in his or her
own words or may use one of these, and the people respond.*

Ⓐ

LEADER
**Almighty God has forgiven
you all your sins
and has promised to bring
you to everlasting life.**

PEOPLE
Amen.

Almighty God has forgiven
you all your sins
and has promised to bring
you to everlasting life.

LEADER
Amen.

Ⓑ

LEADER
**Since we are
justified by faith,
we have peace with God
through our Lord
Jesus Christ.**

PEOPLE
Through Jesus Christ
we have obtained access
to this grace
in which we stand,
and we rejoice
in our hope
of sharing the glory
of God.[28]

PASSING THE PEACE

*In preparation for the offertory and Holy Communion, all
may greet those around them as a sign of their desire to be
at peace with all people. This sign of peace may be*

expressed by a handshake or an embrace, accompanied by such words as: "The peace of God be with you," and the response: "And also with you."

All who are able may rise for the passing of the peace. The following words paraphrased from Matthew or other words may be used to introduce this act of reconciliation.

LEADER
So if you are about to offer your gift
to God at the altar and there remember
that your sister or brother
has something against you,
leave your gift
in front of the altar,
go at once and make peace
with your brother or sister,
and then come back
and offer your gift.[29]

PEOPLE
In response to Christ's command,
we reach out to each other in love.

Leaders of the service may move among the congregation to share the signs of peace.

During this period, an opportunity may be given to those present to make their commitment to Christian disciple-ship or to renew their commitment to the Christian life.

OFFERTORY

The people may be seated.

As part of the offering of life and labor, significant announce-ments concerning the mission of the church may be made at this time.

A leader may introduce the offertory and give an invita-tion to Holy Communion, using her or his own words or one of the following.

A

LEADER

**We shall bring to Christ's
table with our offerings
the bread and wine
for the supper.
Christ invites to this table
all who profess
the Christian faith,
who endeavor to be at
peace with their neighbors,
and who seek
the mercy of God.**

B

LEADER

**As we prepare the table
for Christ's supper,
let us recall the words
of the apostle Paul:
So then, my sisters
and brothers,
because of God's great
mercy to us
I appeal to you:
Offer yourselves
as a living sacrifice to God,
dedicated to God's service
and pleasing to God.**

PEOPLE

This is the true worship
that we should offer.[30]

*Music may be offered to God's glory while the tithes and
offerings are being received. Silence is also appropriate.
The people may express their dedication and thanksgiving
to God through music, prayers, dance, and other acts.*

*The people who are able may stand as representatives
bring the gifts to the table. The communion elements may
be brought to the table with the other gifts.*

A

*This doxology may be
sung. Musical settings are
on pages 452 and 461.*

ALL

**Praise God from whom
all blessings flow;
Praise Christ,
all creatures here below;
Praise Holy Spirit,
the Comforter;
One God, Triune,
whom we adore.
Amen.**

B

*A doxology, such as the
following to the tune "Old
Hundredth," may be sung.*

ALL

**Praise God from whom
all blessings flow;
Praise Christ the Word
in flesh born low;
Praise Holy Spirit evermore;
One God, Triune,
whom we adore.
Amen.**

AND

A prayer of dedication may be said.

LORD'S PRAYER

Standing, sitting, or kneeling, all may sing or say the prayer received from Jesus Christ.

LEADER
Let us pray as Christ our Savior has taught us.

A	**B**	**C**
ALL	ALL	ALL
Our Father in heaven, hallowed be your name, your kingdom come, your will be done, on earth as in heaven. Give us today our daily bread. Forgive us our sins as we forgive those who sin against us. Save us from the time of trial and deliver us from evil. For the kingdom, the power, and the glory are yours now and for ever. Amen.[31]	**Our Father, who art in heaven, hallowed be thy name. Thy kingdom come. Thy will be done on earth as it is in heaven. Give us this day our daily bread. And forgive us our trespasses, as we forgive those who trespass against us. And lead us not into temptation, but deliver us from evil. For thine is the kingdom, and the power, and the glory, for ever and ever. Amen.**	**Our Father, who art in heaven, hallowed be thy name. Thy kingdom come. Thy will be done on earth as it is in heaven. Give us this day our daily bread. And forgive us our debts, as we forgive our debtors. And lead us not into temptation, but deliver us from evil. For thine is the kingdom, and the power, and the glory, for ever. Amen.**

If Holy Communion is not to be celebrated, the service may be concluded with a hymn, a benediction, and a postlude.

INVITATION

All who are able may stand. In these or other words informed by scripture, a leader may remind the congregation that Christ is the host, and they are guests at the table.

A

LEADER
Jesus said:
I am the bread of life.
You who come to me
shall not hunger;
you who believe in me
shall never thirst.[32]

PEOPLE
In company with all who
hunger for spiritual food,
we come to this table
to know the risen Christ
in the sharing
of this life-giving bread.

B

LEADER
Luke, the evangelist,
wrote of our risen Savior,
who at the table
with two of the disciples
took bread and blessed
and broke it
and gave it to them.
Their eyes were opened,
and they recognized
the risen Christ
in the breaking
of the bread.

PEOPLE
In company
with all believers
in every time
and beyond time,
we come to this table
to know the risen Christ
in the breaking
of the bread.

COMMUNION PRAYER

All who are able may stand.

PASTOR
God be with you.

PEOPLE
And also with you.

PASTOR
Lift up your hearts.

PEOPLE
We lift them to God.

PASTOR
Let us give thanks to God Most High.

PEOPLE
It is right to give God thanks and praise.

The pastor leads the congregation in thankfully recalling God's great acts of salvation, using the outline on page 72 or one of these prayers.

A

PASTOR
**Eternal God,
who has created the
heavens and the earth,
giving breath
to every living thing,
we thank you
for all the gifts of creation
and for the gift of life itself.
We thank you
for making us
in your own image,
for forgiving us
when we act as though you
have no claim on us,
and for keeping us
in your steadfast care.**

**We rejoice in Jesus Christ,
the only one eternally
begotten by you,
who was born
of your servant Mary
and shared the joys
and sorrows of life
as we know it.**

**We remember Christ's death,
we celebrate Christ's
resurrection, and,**

B

PASTOR
**Holy God,
our loving Creator,
close to us as breathing
and distant
as the farthest star,
we thank you
for your constant love
for all you have made.**

**We thank you for all
that sustains life,
for all people of faith
in every generation
who have given themselves
to your will, and
especially for Jesus Christ,
whom you have sent
from your own being
as our Savior.**

**We praise you
for Christ's birth, life,
death, and resurrection,
and for the calling forth
of your church
for its mission in the world.**

**Gifted by the presence
of your Holy Spirit,**

in the beloved community
of your church,
we await Christ's return
at the end of history.

We take courage
from the abiding presence
of your Holy Spirit
in our midst.
We offer you our praise
for women and men
of faith in every age
who stand as witnesses
to your love and justice.
With all the prophets,
martyrs, and saints, and
all the company of heaven,
we glorify you:

*Musical settings are on
pages 454 and 463. All may
say or sing:*
ALL
Holy, holy, holy God
of love and majesty,
the whole universe speaks
of your glory,
O God Most High.

Blessed is the one who comes
in the name of our God!
Hosanna in the highest!

*The people may be seated
or kneel. As the following
words are spoken, the
pastor may indicate the
communion elements.*

PASTOR
We remember
that on the night

we offer ourselves to you
as we unite our voices
with the entire family
of your faithful people
everywhere:

*Musical settings are on
pages 454 and 463. All may
say or sing:*
ALL
Holy, holy, holy God
of love and majesty,
the whole universe speaks
of your glory,
O God Most High.

Blessed is the one who comes
in the name of our God!
Hosanna in the highest!

*The people may be seated
or kneel. As the following
words are spoken, the
pastor may indicate the
communion elements.*

PASTOR
Merciful God,
as sisters and brothers
in faith,
we recall anew these words
and acts of Jesus Christ.
Now as they were eating,
Jesus took bread, and
blessed, and broke it,
and gave it to the disciples
and said: "Take, eat:
This is my body."

Jesus took a cup,
and after giving thanks,
gave it to the disciples

of betrayal and desertion,
Jesus took bread,
gave you thanks,
broke the bread,
and gave it to the disciples,
saying: "This is my body
which is broken for you.
Do this
in remembrance of me."

In the same way,
Jesus also took the cup,
after supper, saying:
"This cup is the new
covenant in my blood.
Do this, as often
as you drink it,
in remembrance of me."

By eating this bread
and drinking this cup,
we proclaim Christ's death,
celebrate Christ's
resurrection, and await
Christ's coming again.[33]

PEOPLE
Amen.
Come, Christ Jesus!

PASTOR
Gracious God,
we ask you to bless this
bread and cup and all of us
with the outpouring
of your Holy Spirit.
Through this meal,
make us the body of Christ,
the church,
your servant people,
that we may be salt,
and light, and leaven

and said: "Drink of it,
all of you;
for this is my blood
of the covenant,
which is poured out for many
for the forgiveness of sins."[34]

We remember Christ's
promise not to drink of the
fruit of the vine again
until the heavenly banquet
at the close of history,
and we say boldly
what we believe:

All may say or sing:
ALL
Christ has died.
Christ is risen.
Christ will come again.

PASTOR
Come, Holy Spirit, come.
Bless this bread,
and bless this fruit
of the vine.
Bless all of us in our eating
and drinking at this table
that our eyes may be opened,
and we may recognize the
risen Christ in our midst,
in each other,
and in all
for whom Christ died.

PEOPLE
Amen.

**for the furtherance
of your will in all the world.**
PEOPLE
Amen.
Come, Holy Spirit.

*If option A or B of the communion prayer has been used,
the service continues with breaking bread and pouring wine.*

🄲
*The pastor, following the outline below or a similar outline,
may offer the prayer of great thanksgiving in his or her
own words.*

- *Give thanks for God's goodness to us shown in the
  creation of the world and in the events of history.*
- *Remember people of faith through whom God has
  spoken to the human family as witnessed in scripture.*
- *Give thanks for the birth, life, death, and resurrection
  of Jesus Christ.*
- *Recall Jesus' words at the institution of the supper in
  the upper room.*
- *Remind us that our participation in Holy Communion
  is a sacrifice of praise which includes the offering of our
  lives to God.*
- *Briefly proclaim faith in Christ who has died, is raised,
  and will return at the close of history.*
- *Give thanks for the gift of the Holy Spirit whose
  presence is invoked.*

BREAKING BREAD AND POURING WINE

*The bread is broken and the wine is poured as visible and
audible reminders of the sacrificial self-giving of Jesus
Christ. These actions call to mind the cost as well as the
joy of Christian discipleship.*

PASTOR
while taking the bread and breaking it
**Through the broken bread
we participate in the body of Christ.**

PASTOR
while pouring the wine and raising the cup
**Through the cup of blessing
we participate in the new life Christ gives.**

RESURRECTION ACCLAMATION

*Because Holy Communion is the memorial feast of the risen
Christ, not a fast held for a deceased Jesus, the following
words may be said immediately before the people receive
the bread and cup. During the season of Lent, the alleluia
may be omitted. The pastor may speak of the presence of
Christ in her or his own words.*

A
PASTOR

(**Alleluia!**)

**Fear not,
I am the first and the last,
and the living one.**

PEOPLE
I died, and behold I am
alive for evermore.[35]

(Alleluia!)

B
PASTOR

(**Alleluia!**)

**Christ our Passover
is offered for us.**

PEOPLE
Therefore let us
keep the feast.

(Alleluia!)

SHARING THE ELEMENTS

PASTOR
**The gifts of God for the people of God.
Come, for all things are ready.**

*In giving the bread and cup, the pastor and those assisting may
use their own words or one of these, and the people respond.*

A
while giving the bread
PASTOR
**The body of Christ,
the living bread.**
PEOPLE
Amen!

B
while giving the bread
PASTOR
**Eat this, for it is the body
of Christ, broken for you.**
PEOPLE
Amen!

while giving the cup

PASTOR
**The blood of Christ,
the saving cup.**

PEOPLE
Amen!

while giving the cup

PASTOR
**Drink this,
for it is the blood of Christ,
shed for you.**

PEOPLE
Amen![36]

*After the distribution of the bread and cup, the elements
may be covered, according to local custom.*

*Words of dismissal may precede the prayer of thanks-
giving if people have moved from their seats to receive
communion.*

PRAYER OF THANKSGIVING

*All who are able may stand. A leader may give thanks in
his or her own words or may use one of the following.*

LEADER
Let us pray.

Ⓐ
ALL
**Eternal God,
you have called your people
from east and west
and north and south
to feast at the table
of Jesus Christ.
We thank you
for Christ's presence
and for the spiritual food
of Christ's body and blood.
By the power
of your Holy Spirit,
keep us faithful
to your will.
Go with us to the streets,
to our homes,
and to our places**

Ⓑ
ALL
**We give thanks,
almighty God,
that you have refreshed us
at your table
by granting us the presence
of Jesus Christ.
Strengthen our faith,
increase our love
for one another,
and send us forth
into the world
in courage and peace,
rejoicing in the power
of the Holy Spirit;
through Jesus Christ
our Savior.
Amen.**[37]

**of labor and leisure
that whether we are
gathered or scattered,
we may be the servant
church of the servant
Christ, in whose name
we rejoice to pray.
Amen.**

*The benediction and recessional hymn may follow, or, if
there is no recessional by the choir, the hymn of parting
may precede the benediction.*

BENEDICTION

*All who are able may stand. A leader may use one of these
or may dismiss the congregation with other words of comfort and challenge and with a blessing in words informed
by scripture, and the people respond.*

A

LEADER
**May God bless you
and keep you.**

PEOPLE
Amen.

LEADER
**May God's face
shine upon you
and be gracious to you.**

PEOPLE
Amen.

LEADER
**May God look upon you
with kindness
and give you peace.**[38]

PEOPLE
Amen.

LEADER
Let us go forth

B

LEADER
**Holy One,
now let your servant
go in peace;
your word has been
fulfilled:**

PEOPLE
My own eyes have
seen the salvation
which you have prepared
in the sight
of every people:

LEADER
**A light to reveal you
to the nations;**

PEOPLE
And the glory
of your people Israel.[39]

**into the world,
rejoicing in the power
of the Holy Spirit.**

PEOPLE
Thanks be to God!

HYMN OF PARTING

POSTLUDE

The congregation may be seated and remain until the postlude is concluded.

Brief Order for the Service of Word and Sacrament

INTRODUCTION

This order may be used in its fullest form in a private home or other places where a small congregation is gathered. It is not intended as an order for the Sunday celebration of the Service of Word and Sacrament by the congregation gathered for weekly worship. Depending on the situation, additional music, including a prelude and a postlude, may be incorporated into the order.

When the service is used in an abbreviated form, the affirmation of faith, the passing of the peace, and the commissioning may be omitted, as may all sections for which no text is supplied, except the reading of scripture.

When this order is used on the same occasion as the Order for Healing for Use with an Individual, that order may be used through the prayers of intercession. Then begin here with the communion prayer. While the brief order which begins on page 90 is specifically prepared for use with those who are sick, this order may also be used with the sick.

In using this Brief Service of Word and Sacrament, as in all services of the church, it is appropriate that lay people be included as leaders.

In some local churches, communion elements that have been consecrated during the regular Sunday service are used for services such as this one. In the communion prayer, there is an option that allows for the consecration of the elements during this service.

OUTLINE

Greeting
Sentences of Adoration
Invitation
Confession of Sin
Assurance of Pardon
Hymn of Adoration
Reading of Scripture
Sermon
Affirmation of Faith
Prayers of the People
Offertory
Passing the Peace
Communion Prayer
Breaking Bread and Pouring Wine
Prayer of Our Savior
Sharing the Elements
Prayer of Thanksgiving
Commissioning
Benediction

GREETING

After the people have gathered, a leader may greet them informally or lead them in one of the following.

Ⓐ
LEADER
**In the name
of God:
Creator,
Redeemer,
and Comforter.**

PEOPLE
Amen.

Ⓑ
LEADER
**Peace be
to this house and
to all for whom
this is home.**

PEOPLE
And also to you.

Ⓒ
LEADER
**In the name
of the Father,
the Son, and
the Holy Spirit.**

PEOPLE
Amen.

SENTENCES OF ADORATION

These or other words based on scripture may be spoken to introduce the service.

LEADER
**The Holy One says:
Why spend money on what does not satisfy?
Why spend your wages and still be hungry?
Listen to me
and do what I say,
and you will enjoy the best food of all.
Listen now, my people,
and come to me;
come to me,
and you will have life!**[40]

Hear also these words of Jesus Christ:

Ⓐ
LEADER
**I am the
bread of life;
anyone who
comes to me
shall not hunger;**

Ⓑ
LEADER
**"Hurry down,
Zacchaeus,
because I must
stay in your
house today."**

Ⓒ
LEADER
**Where two
or three gather
in my name,
there am I in the
midst of them.**[43]

anyone who believes in me shall never thirst.[41]	**Zacchaeus hurried down and welcomed Jesus with great joy. Jesus said to him: "Salvation has come to this house today."**[42]

This response may follow option A, B, or C.

PEOPLE
Amen.
Come, Christ Jesus.

INVITATION

A leader may summarize the scriptural background of the communion meal, using one of the following or her or his own words.

A

LEADER
In Luke's Gospel we read that Jesus, at the table with two of the disciples, took bread and blessed and broke it, and gave it to them, and their eyes were opened, and they recognized the risen Christ in the breaking of the bread.

In the Acts of the Apostles we read that as the church was gathered, often in the homes of believers, Christians devoted themselves

B

LEADER
This table is open to all who confess Jesus as the Christ and seek to follow Christ's way. Come to this sacred table not because you must, but because you may. Come not because you are fulfilled, but because in your emptiness you stand in need of God's mercy and assurance.

Come not to express an opinion, but to seek a presence and to pray for a spirit.

to the apostles' teaching
and community,
to the breaking of bread,
and to prayers.

PEOPLE
Jesus Christ,
the Bread of Life,
we gather at your table
to know you
in the breaking of the bread.

Come to this table, then,
sisters and brothers,
as you are.
Partake and share.
It is spread for you and me
that we might again know
that God has come to us,
shared our common lot,
and invited us
to join the people
of God's new age.[44]

CONFESSION OF SIN

The one presiding may lead the gathering in a prayer of confession in his or her own words, invite each person to share petitions asking for forgiveness, invite all to join in a unison prayer of confession, use the following, or combine these.

LEADER
**Jesus,
I am not worthy to have you come under my roof.**

PEOPLE
But only say the word,
and your servant will be healed.[45]

LEADER
Let us confess our sins.

ALL
**God of all mercy,
we confess before you and each other
that we have been unfaithful to you.
We lack love for our neighbors,
we waste opportunities to do good,
and we look the other way
when you cry out to us in the suffering
of our brothers and sisters in need.
We are sincerely sorry for our sins,
both those we commit deliberately
and those that we allow to overtake us.**

**We ask your forgiveness
and pray for strength
that we may follow in your way
and love all your people
with that perfect love which casts out all fear;
through Jesus Christ our Redeemer.
Amen.**

ASSURANCE OF PARDON

*In her or his own words or using one of the following, a
leader may assure all present of God's mercy toward all
who sincerely repent of their sins.*

A

LEADER
**Hear these
comforting words:
If you repent
and believe in God's
redeeming mercy,
your sins are forgiven.
Trust in God's promises
and begin anew your life
with God and all people,
in the name of Jesus Christ.**

PEOPLE
Amen.

B

LEADER
**Jesus looked up
and said to a sinner:
Where are your accusers?
Has no one condemned you?
Neither do I condemn you;
go, and do not sin again.**[46]

PEOPLE
Thanks be to God.

HYMN OF ADORATION

A hymn or doxology may be sung.

READING OF SCRIPTURE

*One or more lessons from the Old and New Testaments
may be read. A psalm may be read or sung. It is appropriate
to include a Gospel lesson among the readings.*

SERMON

A brief sermon may be preached, a group study of one of the lessons may be held, silence may be observed for meditation on one or more of the lessons, or any combination of these may be undertaken.

AFFIRMATION OF FAITH

A creed, statement of faith, church covenant, or biblical affirmation may be used. Forms of the Statement of Faith of the United Church of Christ, historic creeds, and other affirmations are in the Resource Section, beginning on page 509.

PRAYERS OF THE PEOPLE

Prayers of thanksgiving, petition, and intercession may be offered. Bidding prayers may be particularly suitable.

OFFERTORY

An offering may be received, and the bread and wine may be presented as an offering of the people.

PASSING THE PEACE

In preparation for Holy Communion, the congregation, including the leaders, may greet each other with a sign of reconciliation and peace, such as a handshake or embrace, and say these or similar words.

LEADER
The peace of Christ be with you.

PEOPLE
And also with you.

COMMUNION PRAYER

The pastor may use this prayer, a similar prayer, or one in her or his own words following the outline on page 49.

PASTOR
God be with you.

PEOPLE
And also with you.

PASTOR
Lift up your hearts.

PEOPLE
We lift them to God.

PASTOR
Let us give thanks to God Most High.

PEOPLE
It is right to give God thanks and praise.

PASTOR
**Holy God,
we praise and bless you for creation and the gift of life
and for your abiding love which brings us close to you,
the source of all blessing.
We thank you for revealing your will for us
in the giving of the law
and in the preaching of the prophets.**

**We thank you especially
that in the fullness of time you sent Jesus,
born of Mary,
to live in our midst,
to share in our suffering,
and to accept the pain of death
at the hands of those whom Jesus loved.**

**We rejoice that in a perfect victory over the grave
you raised Christ with power
to become sovereign in your realm.**

**We celebrate the coming of the Holy Spirit
to gather your church
by which your work may be done in the world
and through which we share the gift of eternal life.**

**With the faithful
in every place and time,
we praise with joy your holy name:**

ALL
**Holy, holy, holy God
of love and majesty,
the whole universe speaks of your glory,
O God Most High.**

PASTOR
**We remember that on the night
of betrayal and desertion,
Jesus took bread,
gave you thanks,
broke the bread,
and gave it to the disciples, saying:
"This is my body
which is broken for you.
Do this in remembrance of me."**

**In the same way,
Jesus also took the cup, after supper, saying:
"This cup is the new covenant in my blood.
Do this,
as often as you drink it,
in remembrance of me."**[47]

A *for use to consecrate the elements*	B *for use when the elements have been consecrated*
PASTOR **Consecrate, therefore, by your Holy Spirit, these gifts of bread and wine, and bless us that as we receive them at this table, we may offer you our faith and praise, we may be united with Christ and with one another, and we may continue faithful in all things.**	PASTOR **Bless us, therefore, by your Holy Spirit that as we receive the consecrated bread and fruit of the vine at this table, we may offer you our faith and praise, we may be united with Christ and with one another, and we may continue faithful in all things.**

The response, or one similar, may follow either option.

ALL
**In the strength Christ gives us,
we offer ourselves to you, eternal God,
and give thanks
that you have called us to serve you.
Amen.**

BREAKING BREAD AND POURING WINE

PASTOR
while taking the bread and breaking it
**Through the broken bread
we participate in the body of Christ.**

PASTOR
while pouring the wine and raising the cup
**Through the cup of blessing
we participate in the new life Christ gives.**

PRAYER OF OUR SAVIOR

*Standing, sitting, or kneeling, all may say the prayer
received from Jesus Christ. They may hold hands, if able.*

LEADER
Let us pray as Christ our Savior has taught us.

A
ALL
**Our Father
in heaven,
hallowed be
your name,
your kingdom
come, your will
be done, on earth
as in heaven.
Give us today
our daily bread.
Forgive us our sins
as we forgive those
who sin against us.**

B
ALL
**Our Father,
who art in heaven,
hallowed be
thy name.
Thy kingdom
come. Thy will
be done on earth
as it is in heaven.
Give us this day
our daily bread.
And forgive us
our trespasses,
as we forgive those**

C
ALL
**Our Father,
who art in heaven,
hallowed be
thy name.
Thy kingdom
come. Thy will
be done on earth
as it is in heaven.
Give us this day
our daily bread.
And forgive us
our debts,
as we forgive**

| Save us from the time of trial and deliver us from evil. For the kingdom, the power, and the glory are yours now and for ever. Amen.[48] | who trespass against us. And lead us not into temptation, but deliver us from evil. For thine is the kingdom, and the power, and the glory, for ever and ever. Amen. | our debtors. And lead us not into temptation, but deliver us from evil. For thine is the kingdom, and the power, and the glory, for ever. Amen. |

SHARING THE ELEMENTS

When communion is offered to a person who is critically ill and unable to receive in the usual manner, the bread alone or the wine alone may be received. In some circumstances, communion is best given with the bread and wine combined on a spoon or the bread dipped in wine and touched to that person's lips. If the person is unable to receive the bread and wine at all, it is appropriate to assure that person of God's love and grace which are not set aside by the inability to complete an intention of faith. The pastor may offer the bread and cup in his or her own words or may use the following.

PASTOR
Come, for all things are ready.

while giving the bread
Eat this, for it is the body of Christ, broken for you.

PEOPLE
Amen.

PASTOR
while giving the cup
Drink this, for it is the blood of Christ, shed for you.

PEOPLE
Amen.[49]

PASTOR
after all have received
**Our Savior Jesus Christ keep and preserve you
to everlasting life.**

PRAYER OF THANKSGIVING

LEADER
Let us pray.

ALL
**We thank you, God, for inviting us to this table
where we have known the presence of Christ
and have received all Christ's gifts.
Strengthen our faith,
increase our love for one another,
and let us show forth your praise in our lives;
through Jesus Christ our Savior.
Amen.**

COMMISSIONING

*Great sensitivity should be exercised when commissioning
a person who is ill and unable to resume normal activity.*

🅐 *for use in any setting*

LEADER
**You are the light
of the world.
A city set on a hill
cannot be hid.
Nor does anyone light a lamp
and put it under a bushel,
but on a stand,
and it gives light
to all in the house.
May your light so shine
before all people,
that they may see your
good works and give glory
to God who is in heaven.**[50]

🅑 *for use with those
not confined*

LEADER
**Go forth into the world
to serve God with gladness;
be of good courage;
hold fast to that
which is good;
render to no one evil for evil;
strengthen the fainthearted;
support the weak;
help the afflicted;
honor all people;
love and serve God,
rejoicing in the power
of the Holy Spirit.**[51]

BENEDICTION

A leader may use one of these or other words of blessing.

A

LEADER
**The blessing
of God Almighty:
Creator,
Christ,
and Holy Spirit
be with you all.**

PEOPLE
Amen.

B

LEADER
**May God
bless you
and keep you.
May God's face
shine upon you
and be gracious
to you.
May God look
upon you
with kindness
and give you
peace.**[52]

PEOPLE
Amen.

C

LEADER
**Hear the promise
of Jesus Christ:
Peace I leave
with you;
my peace
I give to you;
not as the
world gives
do I give to you.
Let not your
hearts be
troubled,
neither let them
be afraid.**[53]

**The grace
of Jesus Christ
be with you all.**

PEOPLE
Amen.

Brief Order for the Service of Word and Sacrament for One Who Is Sick

INTRODUCTION

This order is intended for use with sick and shut-in individuals in their homes, with their children, in hospitals, in hospices, or in nursing homes. It is to be used when people are unable to participate in services with the congregation.

When this order is used on the same occasion as the Order for Healing for Use with an Individual, that order may be used through the prayers of intercession. Then begin here with the communion prayer.

In using this brief service, as in all services of the church, it is appropriate that lay people be included as leaders.

In some local churches, communion elements which have been consecrated in the regular Sunday service are used for services such as this one. In the communion prayer there is an option which allows for the consecration of the elements during this service.

OUTLINE

Greeting
Prayers of Confession, Other Prayers, and Assurance
Reading of Scripture
Communion Prayer
Lord's Prayer
Sharing the Elements
Prayer of Thanksgiving
Benediction

GREETING

*After those people who plan to participate with the person
who is ill have gathered, a leader may greet them informally or may use one of these.*

Ⓐ
LEADER
**Hear the words of Jesus:
I am the bread of life;
anyone who comes to me
shall not hunger;
anyone who believes in me
shall never thirst.**[54]

Ⓑ
LEADER
**Hear the words of Jesus:
For where two or three
come together in my name,
I am there with them.**[55]

PRAYERS OF CONFESSION, OTHER PRAYERS, AND ASSURANCE

*The one presiding may lead those gathered in prayers of
confession or may invite those present to offer in their
own words petitions asking for forgiveness. After the
prayer of confession, the one presiding assures all present
of God's mercy to all who sincerely repent of their sins.*

*Prayers of thanksgiving and intercession may also be
offered by a leader or the people.*

READING OF SCRIPTURE

*One or more lessons speaking to the condition of the person
may be read. It is appropriate to offer brief comments
related to the lessons and the situation.*

COMMUNION PRAYER

*The pastor may use the following or a similar prayer or
may offer a communion prayer in his or her own words
following the outline on page 49.*

PASTOR

**Holy God,
we praise and bless you
for creation and the gift of life
and for your abiding love
which brings us close to you,
the source of all blessing.
We thank you for revealing your will for us
in the giving of the law
and in the preaching of the prophets.**

**We thank you especially
that in the fullness of time you sent Jesus,
born of Mary,
to live in our midst,
to share in our suffering,
and to accept the pain of death
at the hands of those whom Jesus loved.**

**We rejoice that in a perfect victory over the grave
you raised Christ with power
to become sovereign in your realm.**

**We celebrate the coming of the Holy Spirit
to gather your church
by which your work may be done in the world
and through which we share the gift of eternal life.**

**With the faithful in every place and time,
we praise with joy your holy name:**

**Holy, holy, holy God of love and majesty,
the whole universe speaks of your glory,
O God Most High.**

**We remember that on the night
of betrayal and desertion,
Jesus took bread, gave you thanks, broke the bread,**

Here the bread is broken.

**and gave it to the disciples, saying:
"This is my body which is broken for you.
Do this in remembrance of me."**

In the same way,
Jesus also took the cup, after supper, saying:

Here the wine is poured and the cup raised.

"This cup is the new covenant in my blood.
Do this, as often as you drink it,
in remembrance of me."[56]

Ⓐ *for use to consecrate the elements*	Ⓑ *for use when the elements have been consecrated*
PASTOR	
Consecrate, therefore,	
by your Holy Spirit,	PASTOR
these gifts of bread and wine,	**Bless us, therefore,**
and bless us	**by your Holy Spirit**
that as we receive them	**that as we receive the**
at this table,	**consecrated bread and fruit**
we may offer you our faith	**of the vine**
and praise,	**at this table,**
we may be united with Christ	**we may offer you our faith**
and with one another,	**and praise,**
and we may continue	**we may be united with Christ**
faithful in all things.	**and with one another,**
In the strength	**and we may continue**
Christ gives us,	**faithful in all things.**
we offer ourselves to you,	**In the strength**
eternal God,	**Christ gives us,**
and give thanks	**we offer ourselves to you,**
that you have called us	**eternal God,**
to serve you.	**and give thanks**
Amen.	**that you have called us**
	to serve you.
	Amen.

LORD'S PRAYER

All present may say the prayer received from Jesus Christ.
If able, they may hold hands.

LEADER
Let us pray as Christ our Savior has taught us.

A

ALL

**Our Father
in heaven,
hallowed be
your name,
your kingdom
come, your will
be done, on earth
as in heaven.
Give us today
our daily bread.
Forgive us our sins
as we forgive those
who sin against us.
Save us from the
time of trial
and deliver us
from evil.
For the kingdom,
the power,
and the glory
are yours now
and for ever.
Amen.**[57]

B

ALL

**Our Father,
who art in heaven,
hallowed be
thy name.
Thy kingdom
come. Thy will
be done on earth
as it is in heaven.
Give us this day
our daily bread.
And forgive us
our trespasses,
as we forgive those
who trespass
against us.
And lead us not
into temptation,
but deliver us
from evil.
For thine
is the kingdom,
and the power,
and the glory,
for ever and ever.
Amen.**

C

ALL

**Our Father,
who art in heaven,
hallowed be
thy name.
Thy kingdom
come. Thy will
be done on earth
as it is in heaven.
Give us this day
our daily bread.
And forgive us
our debts,
as we forgive
our debtors.
And lead us not
into temptation,
but deliver us
from evil.
For thine
is the kingdom,
and the power,
and the glory,
for ever.
Amen.**

SHARING THE ELEMENTS

When communion is offered to a person who is critically ill and unable to receive in the usual manner, the bread alone or the wine alone may be received. In some circumstances, communion is best given with the bread and wine combined on a spoon or the bread dipped in wine and touched to the person's lips. If the person is unable to receive the bread and wine at all, it is appropriate to assure the person of God's love and grace which are not set aside by the inability to complete an intention of faith.

The pastor may offer the bread and cup in his or her own words or may use the following.

PASTOR
while giving the bread
Eat this,
for it is the body of Christ,
broken for you.

PASTOR
while giving the cup
Drink this,
for it is the blood of Christ,
shed for you.[58]

PRAYER OF THANKSGIVING

LEADER
Let us pray.

ALL
We thank you, God, for inviting us to this table
where we have known the presence of Christ
and have received all Christ's gifts.
Strengthen our faith,
increase our love for one another,
and let us show forth your praise in our lives;
through Jesus Christ our Savior.
Amen.

BENEDICTION

LEADER
May God bless you and keep you.
May God's face shine upon you
and be gracious to you.
May God look upon you with kindness
and give you peace.[59]
Amen.

Introduction to Orders for Services of the Word

INTRODUCTION

Christian worship in the Protestant tradition emerged from the two major concerns of the sixteenth century reformers: that preaching should be restored to its rightful place in Christian worship and that both the bread and the cup should be made available once again to every Christian. These concerns reflect a basic understanding that corporate Christian worship is primarily a fusion of the service of the synagogue and the sacrament of the upper room. From earliest times, the full and central Sunday worship of Christian people was a Service of Word and Sacrament.

There also emerged in ancient Christian practice a series of daily offices, or spiritual exercises, using scripture and prayer to nourish Christian life. In some traditions these offices included a sermon. Eventually they became a pattern for Sunday worship without Holy Communion.

The sixteenth century reformers intended to reinstate the full service of sermon and supper, which the medieval church had lost, on each Sunday or Lord's Day. They did not succeed. John Calvin declared that any Sunday service without Holy Communion was "defective." Nevertheless, he realized that for sixteenth century Christians it was difficult to go from having little or no access to the sacrament to celebrating it every Sunday. Consequently, monthly or quarterly communion became normative in many Protestant churches.

Within the United Church of Christ and the ecumenical movement of the late twentieth century, there is a definite movement toward making the weekly Service of Word and Sacrament normative. In some situations, however, a distinct Service of the Word, without Holy Communion, remains the desire of many local churches. It is important to develop resources that have historical integrity for these churches. Furthermore, it is appropriate to provide within a Service of the Word some expression of those particular worship practices valued by those in the free church tradition of Reformation Christianity.

The judgment that any Sunday service that does not include Holy Communion is inadequate or unacceptable worship must be avoided. The *ante-communion* or Service of the Word leading to Holy Communion has its own unity, instructs people in the faith, and offers acceptable worship to God. It was the weekly worship that nourished early pilgrims preparing to make deeper commitments to Christ and the church. After these non-communicants were dismissed, the service moved into the mass, a word meaning "after the dismissal." Over the years, this sequence has been interpreted by some to imply that the Service of the Word is merely a weak prologue leading to the more important Eucharist, or Holy Communion. In reality, the Service of the Word possesses an integrity that gives it intrinsic meaning alongside the service of the upper room.

The sixteenth century reformers celebrated this integrity and restored the power of the read and preached word to weekly worship. Reformed worship did not replace communion with preaching, but sought to upgrade the medieval mass to a full Service of Word and Sacrament. Reformed worship did not create a Service of the Word by adding a sermon to the daily offices used in the discipline of monastic life. For many in the free church tradition, a Service of the Word sets out the full salvation story and is a recognition of the sacramental power of preaching. It can stand alone or be part of the Service of Word and Sacrament.

The offertory in a Service of the Word may be located in one of two places. One placement follows the Order for the Service of Word and Sacrament. The intercessions or prayers of the people are voiced after the sermon and in response to it. The offertory follows the sermon and the prayers and, as a gathering of the gifts of the people, constitutes a sacramental form of dedication and renewal.

The second placement moves from the scripture readings directly into a prayer service that is followed by the offertory. While this order has the disadvantage of separating the sermon from the lessons, it allows the sermon to build upon both the witness of scripture and the contemporary human struggle to walk with God.

By placing the sermon after the prayers of confession and intercession and the recommitment expressed in the offertory, the preached word leads worship back to the promises of God. A service arranged this way usually closes with a prayer of thanksgiving, perhaps the Prayer of Our Savior, a hymn, and a benediction. The sermon is not placed near the end because it is the most important part of worship, but because this is one way that mature Christians explore the meaning of the gospel together. In churches where children do not remain for the sermon, this order allows them to share a more complete worship experience including the offertory.

A Service of the Word may completely omit the confession and assurance sequence or place it after the word has been read or preached rather than at the beginning of the service. It is clear that the earliest Christian services did not always contain major penitential elements. A convincing argument may also be made that people are only ready to confess their sin and receive God's pardon after hearing the word and finding themselves wanting.

A Service of the Word may or may not include a creed or statement of faith. Most early orders did not include such public declarations in corporate worship each week. They assumed that the salvation story was retold in each communion prayer or prayer of great thanksgiving. In the sixteenth century, however, the renewed concern for catechism often led to the placement of a creed immediately after the scripture lessons or the sermon in response to the word.

The orders in this book preserve the integrity of a Service of the Word and incorporate the concerns flowing from the free church tradition.

Order for the
Service of the Word I

PRELUDE

*The service may begin with music as the congregation
gathers. The hymn or introit may follow, according to
local custom.*

CALL TO WORSHIP

*A leader may use one of the following or may offer other words
appropriate to the season.*

A

LEADER
**Morning has broken.
Let us give thanks
for the gift of life
and for the presence
of the Holy One among us.
Let us worship God
together.**

PEOPLE
Thanks be to God!

B

LEADER
**Our help is in the name
of God,
who made heaven
and earth.
Let us worship God.**

HYMN OF ADORATION

All who are able may stand. This may be a processional.

INTROIT

An introit related to the season may be said or sung.

PRAYER OF CONFESSION

*All may be seated. A leader may offer a prayer based on
scripture, may use his or her own words, or may use one
of the following prayers.*

LEADER
**Let us confess our sins
before God and one another.**

A

ALL

**Almighty and merciful God,
you created and are
creating still.
In your presence our limits
lie stark before us.
We confess our unclean
lips, our cold hearts,
our turning away
from neighbors,
our broken promises,
and our unrepentant hours.
Forgive us, O Holy One.**

**We confess that we have
squandered the gifts
you have given.
We have neglected the land.
We have grasped for goods.
We have used each other.
We have loved power more
than people.
Forgive us, O Holy One.**

**Cleanse from us
the illusion of innocence.
Come into our hearts,
and make us new again.
We pray in the name
of Jesus.
Amen.**

B

LEADER

**Most merciful God,
we confess that we are
in bondage to sin
and cannot free ourselves.
We have sinned against you
in thought, word, and deed
by what we have done
and by what we have
left undone.
We have not loved you
with our whole heart.
We have not loved
our neighbors as ourselves.
For the sake
of Jesus Christ,
have mercy on us.
Forgive us, renew us,
and lead us,
so that we may delight
in your will
and follow in your ways,
to the glory
of your holy name.
Amen.**[60]

SILENCE

Silence may be observed for reflection and prayer.

ASSURANCE OF PARDON

A leader may speak of God's pardon or mercy in her or his own words or may use one of the following.

A

LEADER
**In Jesus Christ,
God knows and receives us
as we are.
Listen, give thanks,
and live.**

B

LEADER
**Almighty God,
who is great in mercy
and promises forgiveness
of sin to all
who truly repent
and are sincere in faith,
have mercy on you,
pardon and deliver you
from all sin,
confirm and strengthen you
in all goodness,
and bring you
to everlasting life.**

PEOPLE
Amen.
Thanks be to God.

PASSING THE PEACE

*As a sign of their reconciliation with God and each other,
all may greet those around them with an embrace or a
handshake, accompanied by such words as: "The peace of
God be with you," and the response: "And also with you."*

*All who are able may rise for the passing of the peace.
Leaders of the service may move among the congregation
to share the signs of peace.*

PSALM OR RESPONSIVE READING

A psalm may be sung or read responsively or in unison.

GLORIA

*All who are able may stand for a gloria or another hymn
of praise.*

Ⓐ

This gloria may be said or sung. Musical settings are on pages 451 and 460.

ALL
**Glory to God the Creator,
and to the Christ,
and to the Holy Spirit:
as it was in the beginning,
is now,
and will be for ever.
Amen.**

Ⓑ

A gloria such as the following may be read or sung, or another hymn of praise may be sung.

ALL
**Glory to God
in the highest,
and peace
to God's people on earth.**

**Holy One, heavenly God,
sovereign God
and Creator,
we worship you,
we give you thanks,
we praise you
for your glory.**

**Lord Jesus Christ,
God's only begotten one,
Lord God,
Lamb of God,
you take away the sin
of the world:
have mercy on us;
you are seated
at the right hand
of Majesty:
receive our prayer.**

**For you alone
are the Messiah,
you alone are the Lord,
you alone are
the Most High,
Jesus Christ,
with the Holy Spirit,
in the glory
of the triune God.
Amen.**

READING OF SCRIPTURE

The people may be seated as the scripture lessons are introduced. It is recommended that the schedule of readings found in the ecumenical lectionary be used. If it is not, care should be taken to maintain a balance in readings from the Old Testament, the Epistles, and the Gospels.

A collect for illumination, a seasonal collect, or an extemporaneous prayer asking for attentive hearts may precede the first reading. A brief introduction to the theme of each lesson may be offered. In order to distinguish the lesson from the commentary, the reader may announce the lesson.

OLD TESTAMENT LESSON

READER
before the lesson
Listen for the word of God in _____ .

After the lesson, a psalm may be said or sung, followed by a gloria, unless one has been said or sung earlier, or the following or a similar announcement may be made.

READER
Here ends the Old Testament lesson.

EPISTLE LESSON

READER
before the lesson
Listen for the word of God in _____ .

READER
following the lesson
Here ends the Epistle lesson.

GOSPEL LESSON

In some local churches, standing, for those who are able, for the reading of the Gospel is customary as it is a sign of respect for Jesus Christ, who addresses the congregation in words remembered by the early church. The responses before and after this lesson may be said or sung.

READER
before the lesson
Listen to the Gospel of Jesus Christ according to _____ .

PEOPLE
Glory to you, O Christ.

READER
following the lesson
This is the good news.

PEOPLE
Praise to you, O Christ.

SERMON

AFFIRMATION OF FAITH

All who are able may stand for a form of the Statement of Faith of the United Church of Christ, a creed, or a church covenant. Forms of the statement of faith, historic creeds, and other affirmations are in the Resource Section, beginning on page 509.

HYMN, ANTHEM, OR OTHER MUSIC

PRAYERS OF THE PEOPLE

The people may be seated. Leaders may announce special concerns for prayers and invite the people to indicate needs or to name causes for thanksgiving. Intercessions may include prayers for:

- *The church universal, including ecumenical councils, specific churches in other places, the United Church of Christ and its leaders, and this local church.*
- *The nations and all in authority.*
- *Justice and peace in all the world.*
- *The health of those who suffer in body, mind, or spirit.*
- *The needs of families, single people, and the lonely.*
- *Reconciliation with adversaries.*
- *The local community and all other communities.*
- *All who are oppressed or in prison.*

A litany of prayers and responses, with silences, may be

used; a pastoral prayer may be offered; petitions may be offered by anyone present, ending with a phrase to which all may respond, such as those below. A longer period of silence may precede or follow the prayers.

A

LEADER
Christ, in your mercy,

PEOPLE
Hear our prayer.

B

LEADER
Holy Spirit, our Comforter,

PEOPLE
Receive our prayer.

LORD'S PRAYER

Standing, sitting, or kneeling, all may sing or say the prayer received from Jesus Christ.

A

ALL
**Our Father
in heaven,
hallowed be
your name,
your kingdom
come, your will
be done, on earth
as in heaven.
Give us today
our daily bread.
Forgive us our sins
as we forgive those
who sin against us.
Save us from the
time of trial
and deliver us
from evil.
For the kingdom,
the power,
and the glory
are yours now
and for ever.
Amen.**[61]

B

ALL
**Our Father,
who art in heaven,
hallowed be thy
name. Thy
kingdom come.
Thy will be done
on earth as it is
in heaven. Give
us this day our
daily bread. And
forgive us our
trespasses, as we
forgive those
who trespass
against us. And
lead us not into
temptation, but
deliver us from
evil. For thine is
the kingdom,
and the power,
and the glory,
for ever and ever.
Amen.**

C

ALL
**Our Father,
who art in heaven,
hallowed be
thy name.
Thy kingdom
come. Thy will
be done on earth
as it is in heaven.
Give us this day
our daily bread.
And forgive us
our debts,
as we forgive
our debtors.
And lead us not
into temptation,
but deliver us
from evil.
For thine
is the kingdom,
and the power,
and the glory,
for ever.
Amen.**

CONCERNS OF THE CHURCH

The people may be seated. A leader and the people may announce information concerning the program, ministry, and people of the church.

OFFERTORY

A leader may use his or her own words or one of the following to introduce the offertory.

A

LEADER
**Let everyone give,
not grudgingly
or of necessity,
but from the fullness
of our gratitude to God.**

B

LEADER
**Let us give,
as each is able,
according to the blessings
God has given each of us.**

Music may be offered to God's glory while the tithes and offerings are being received. Silence is also appropriate. The people may express their dedication and thanksgiving to God through music, prayers, dance, and other acts.

The people who are able may stand as representatives bring the gifts to the table.

A

This doxology may be sung. Musical settings are on pages 452 and 461.

ALL
**Praise God from whom
all blessings flow;
Praise Christ,
all creatures here below;
Praise Holy Spirit,
the Comforter;
One God, Triune,
whom we adore.
Amen.**

B

A doxology, such as the following to the tune "Old Hundredth," may be sung.

ALL
**Praise God from whom
all blessings flow;
Praise Christ the Word
in flesh born low;
Praise Holy Spirit evermore;
One God, Triune,
whom we adore.
Amen.**

AND

A prayer of dedication may be said.

HYMN

COMMISSIONING AND BENEDICTION

A

LEADER

**The blessing of the God
of Sarah and of Abraham;
the blessing of Jesus Christ,
born of Mary;
the blessing
of the Holy Spirit,
who broods over us
as a mother over her children;
be with you all.
Amen.**[62]

B

LEADER

**Go forth into the world
to serve God with gladness;
be of good courage;
hold fast to that
which is good;
render to no one evil for evil;
strengthen the fainthearted;
support the weak;
help the afflicted;
honor all people;
love and serve God,
rejoicing in the power
of the Holy Spirit.**[63]

**The grace of Jesus Christ,
the love of God,
and the communion
of the Holy Spirit,
be with you all.**[64]
Amen.

POSTLUDE

*The congregation may be seated and remain until the
postlude is concluded.*

Order for the
Service of the Word II

CONCERNS OF THE CHURCH

Leaders and the people may announce information concerning the program, ministry, and people of the church now or at the offertory.

PRELUDE

The service may begin with music as the congregation gathers. The call to worship or hymn may follow, according to local custom.

CALL TO WORSHIP

All who are able may stand. A leader may offer one of the following or other words appropriate to the season.

A

LEADER
**Rejoice,
for God is among us.
Give thanks,
for in Christ
we are a new people.
Sing praise,
for we come
to worship God.**

B

LEADER
**Come from the east
and the west,
the north and the south,
and worship the God
of our fathers and mothers,
the God of Jesus Christ.
Amen.**

**The grace of Jesus Christ
and the love of God
and the communion
of the Holy Spirit
be with us all.**[65]

PEOPLE
Amen.

HYMN OF ADORATION

All who are able may stand. This may be a processional hymn.

INVOCATION

*All who are able may stand. A leader may offer a prayer in
her or his own words or may use one of these, asking for
the worshipers to be made responsive to the presence of God.*

Ⓐ

LEADER
Christ is with us.

PEOPLE
Christ is in our midst.

LEADER
Let us pray.

Ⓑ

LEADER
God be with you.

PEOPLE
And also with you.

LEADER
Let us pray.

AND

Ⓐ

ALL
**O God,
distant yet near,
we gather as witnesses
to your promise that if we
seek you with all our hearts,
we will find you.
Be among us this day.
Hear the confessions
of our mouths
and the yearnings
of our hearts.
Help us change the
narrowness of our vision
and the pettiness
of our living.
Make us new again
with your holy grace.
Grant us the maturity
to accept your many gifts
in humility
and to use them
with faithfulness.
Grant to us your spirit**

Ⓑ

ALL
**Gracious God,
gentle in your power and
strong in your tenderness,
you have brought us forth
from the womb
of your being
and breathed into us
the breath of life.
We know that we do not
live by bread alone
but by every word
that comes from you.
Feed our deep hungers
with the living bread
that you give us
in Jesus Christ.
May Jesus' promise,
"Where two or three are
gathered in my name,
there am I
in the midst of them,"[66]
be fulfilled in us.
Make us a joyful company**

that our worship may have
integrity and energy,
ever witnessing to your holy
presence in our lives.
We praise and give thanks
to you, Eternal Presence;
through Jesus Christ
we pray.
Amen.

of your people
so that with the faithful
in every place and time
we may praise
and honor you,
God Most High.
Amen.

PRAYER OF OUR SAVIOR

*Standing, sitting, or kneeling, all may sing or say the
prayer received from Jesus Christ.*

LEADER
Let us pray as Christ our Savior has taught us.

A

ALL
**Our Father
in heaven,
hallowed be
your name,
your kingdom
come, your will
be done, on earth
as in heaven.
Give us today
our daily bread.
Forgive us our sins
as we forgive those
who sin against us.
Save us from the
time of trial
and deliver us
from evil.
For the kingdom,
the power,
and the glory
are yours now
and for ever.**

B

ALL
**Our Father,
who art in heaven,
hallowed be
thy name.
Thy kingdom
come. Thy will
be done on earth
as it is in heaven.
Give us this day
our daily bread.
And forgive us
our trespasses,
as we forgive those
who trespass
against us.
And lead us not
into temptation,
but deliver us
from evil.
For thine
is the kingdom,
and the power,**

C

ALL
**Our Father,
who art in heaven,
hallowed be
thy name.
Thy kingdom
come. Thy will
be done on earth
as it is in heaven.
Give us this day
our daily bread.
And forgive us
our debts,
as we forgive
our debtors.
And lead us not
into temptation,
but deliver us
from evil.
For thine
is the kingdom,
and the power,
and the glory,**

| Amen.[67] | and the glory, for ever and ever. Amen. | for ever. Amen. |

PSALM OR RESPONSIVE READING

A psalm may be sung or read responsively or in unison.

GLORIA

All who are able may stand for a gloria or another hymn of praise.

Ⓐ

This gloria may be said or sung. Musical settings are on pages 451 and 460.

ALL

**Glory to God the Creator,
and to the Christ,
and to the Holy Spirit:
as it was in the beginning,
is now,
and will be for ever.
Amen.**

Ⓑ

A gloria such as the following may be read or sung, or another hymn of praise may be sung.

ALL

**Glory to God
in the highest,
and peace
to God's people on earth.**

**Holy One, heavenly God,
sovereign God and Creator,
we worship you,
we give you thanks,
we praise you
for your glory.**

**Lord Jesus Christ,
God's only begotten one,
Lord God,
Lamb of God,
you take away the sin
of the world:
have mercy on us;
you are seated at the right
hand of Majesty:
receive our prayer.**

**For you alone
are the Messiah,
you alone are the Lord,
you alone are
the Most High,
Jesus Christ,
with the Holy Spirit,
in the glory
of the triune God.
Amen.**

PRAYER FOR ILLUMINATION
OR COLLECT FOR THE DAY

*The people may be seated. A leader may offer a prayer for
illumination in her or his own words asking for open
hearts and attentive minds, may use a seasonal collect, or
may use one of these.*

A
LEADER
**Eternal God,
in the reading
of the scripture,
may your word be heard;
in the meditations
of our hearts,
may your word be known;
and in the faithfulness
of our lives,
may your word be shown.
Amen.**

B
LEADER
**Almighty God,
you have revealed yourself
to us as one God;
give us grace to continue
steadfast in the living
of our faith
and constant in our
worship of you,
for you live and reign,
one God, now and for ever.
Amen.**

READING OF SCRIPTURE

*It is recommended that the schedule of readings found in
the ecumenical lectionary be used. If it is not, care should
be taken to maintain a balance in readings from the Old
Testament, the Epistles, and the Gospels.*

A brief introduction to the theme of each lesson may be

*offered. In order to distinguish the lesson from the com-
mentary, the reader may announce: "A reading from
_____" and may conclude: "Here ends the lesson."*

SERMON

HYMN, ANTHEM, OR OTHER MUSIC

PRAYERS OF THE PEOPLE

*The people may be seated. Leaders may announce special
concerns for prayers and invite the people to indicate
needs or to name causes for thanksgiving. Intercessions
may include prayers for:*

- *The church universal, including ecumenical councils,
  specific churches in other places, the United Church
  of Christ and its leaders, and this local church.*
- *The nations and all in authority.*
- *Justice and peace in all the world.*
- *The health of those who suffer in body, mind, or spirit.*
- *The needs of families, single people, and the lonely.*
- *Reconciliation with adversaries.*
- *The local community and all other communities.*
- *All who are oppressed or in prison.*

*A litany of prayers and responses, with silences, may be
used; a pastoral prayer may be offered; petitions may be
offered by anyone present, ending with a phrase to which
all may respond, such as those below. A longer period of
silence may precede or follow the prayers.*

A	**B**
LEADER	LEADER
Merciful God,	**Healing Spirit,**
PEOPLE	PEOPLE
Hear our prayer.	Receive our prayer.

PASSING THE PEACE

As a sign of their reconciliation with God and each other, all may greet those around them with an embrace or a handshake, accompanied by such words as: "The peace of God be with you," and the response: "And also with you."

All who are able may rise for the passing of the peace. Leaders of the service may move among the congregation to share the signs of peace.

OFFERTORY

As part of the offering of life and labor, significant announcements concerning the mission of the church may be made.

Music may be offered to God's glory while the tithes and offerings are being received. Silence is also appropriate. The people may express their dedication and thanksgiving to God through music, prayers, dance, and other acts.

Upon presentation of the offerings, a leader may offer a prayer of dedication, and a doxology may be sung. See pages 452 and 461 for musical settings of a doxology.

HYMN

COMMISSIONING AND BENEDICTION

Ⓐ

LEADER
Let us go forth into the new seasons of our lives.

PEOPLE
We go forth into growing and changing and living.

LEADER
Let us go with caring awareness for the world and all that is in it.

Ⓑ

LEADER
God's peace go with you into the worlds in which you live; be nurtured by the time of gathering, be faithful in the time apart. Love and serve each other in the name of the faithful God,

PEOPLE
We go to discover the needs
and opportunities around us.

LEADER
**Let us go forth in peace
and be led out in joy.**

ALL
**We go in God's
continuing presence,
with the power to love
and the strength to serve.
Amen.**[68]

**who calls us
to be God's people;
and the blessing of God,
Creator, Redeemer,
and Sanctifier,
be with us always.
Amen.**

POSTLUDE

The congregation may be seated and remain until the postlude is concluded.

Order for the Service of the Word III

OUTLINE

Concerns of the Church
Prelude
Hymn of Adoration
Call to Worship
Invocation
Sentences of Praise
Psalm or Responsive Reading
Gloria
Reading of Scripture
Prayers of the People
Offertory
Hymn
Sermon
Prayer of Thanksgiving
Lord's Prayer
Hymn
Benediction
Postlude

CONCERNS OF THE CHURCH

Leaders and the people may announce information concerning the program, ministry, and people of the church now or at the offertory.

PRELUDE

The service may begin with music as the congregation gathers. The hymn or call to worship may follow, according to local custom.

HYMN OF ADORATION

All who are able may stand. This may be a processional hymn.

CALL TO WORSHIP

All who are able may stand. A leader may use words appropriate for the season or may use one of these.

A	B
LEADER	LEADER
God knows us	**The Holy One bends low**
and our hungers.	**at home with the humble,**
God loves us like a father	**taking up residence**
and nurtures us	**in the contrite heart**
like a mother.	**and forming all people**
God draws us to each other	**in God's image.**
and claims us	**Come, let us worship.**
as the people of God.	**Let us offer thanksgiving**
Knowing this,	**and praise to God.**
let us worship God.	

INVOCATION

All who are able may stand. A leader may offer a prayer in her or his own words or may use one of the following, asking for the worshipers to be made responsive to the presence of God.

A

ALL
**O God of the morning
and of the evening hours,
let your Spirit come on us
here gathered.
This is the holy place
where we, your people,
call on you in faith,
joining heart and voice
in thanksgiving and praise
to your name.
Amen.**

B *for use in the morning*

ALL
**We come before you,
O God,
and wait for the kindling
flame of your Holy Spirit,
calling us into fuller
and richer lives.
You have blessed us
by the night's rest
and by morning's light.
Open us to your claim
on us.
Show us your way.
Let us live in the spirit
of Jesus Christ our Savior.
Amen.**

SENTENCES OF PRAISE

All who are able may stand as one or more of these sentences are said, or other sentences appropriate for the day or liturgical season are offered.

A

LEADER
**Blessed is God,
who reveals to us the presence of the Christ
and who incorporates us into divine love.**

B

LEADER
**God has brought the people of the covenant
from the land of bondage into freedom.**

C

LEADER
**In the beginning was the Word,
and the Word was with God,
and the Word was God.**[69]

PSALM OR RESPONSIVE READING

A psalm may be sung or read responsively or in unison.

GLORIA

All who are able may stand for a gloria or another hymn of praise.

A

This gloria may be said or sung. Musical settings are on pages 451 and 460.

ALL

**Glory to God the Creator,
and to the Christ,
and to the Holy Spirit:
as it was in the beginning,
is now,
and will be for ever.
Amen.**

B

A gloria such as the following may be read or sung, or another song of praise may be sung.

ALL

**Glory to God in the highest,
and peace
to God's people on earth.**

**Holy One, heavenly God,
sovereign God and Creator,
we worship you,
we give you thanks,
we praise you
for your glory.**

**Lord Jesus Christ,
God's only begotten one,
Lord God, Lamb of God,
you take away the sin
of the world:
have mercy on us;
you are seated at the right
hand of Majesty:
receive our prayer.**

**For you alone
are the Messiah,
you alone are the Lord,
you alone are
the Most High,**

> **Jesus Christ,**
> **with the Holy Spirit,**
> **in the glory**
> **of the triune God.**
> **Amen.**

READING OF SCRIPTURE

The people may be seated. It is recommended that the schedule of readings found in the ecumenical lectionary be used. If it is not, care should be taken to maintain a balance in readings from the Old Testament, the Epistles, and the Gospels.

A brief introduction to the theme of each lesson may be offered. In order to distinguish the lesson from the commentary, the reader may announce: "A reading from _____" and may conclude: "Here ends the lesson."

The reading of scripture may begin with the following or other words of preparation.

LEADER
God offers to us,
through prophets and apostles,
words of life which through faith become the word of life.
Listen then for that word in these lessons.

PRAYERS OF THE PEOPLE

The people may be seated for the prayers. Leaders may announce special concerns for prayers and invite the people to indicate needs or to name causes for thanksgiving. Intercessions may include prayers for:

- *The church universal, including ecumenical councils, specific churches in other places, the United Church of Christ and its leaders, and this local church.*
- *The nations and all in authority.*
- *Justice and peace in all the world.*
- *The health of those who suffer in body, mind, or spirit.*
- *The needs of families, single people, and the lonely.*

- *Reconciliation with adversaries.*
- *The local community and all other communities.*
- *All who are oppressed or in prison.*

A litany of prayers and responses, with silences, may be used; a pastoral prayer may be offered; petitions may be offered by anyone present, ending with a phrase to which all may respond, such as those below. A longer period of silence may precede or follow the prayers.

A

LEADER
Holy Spirit,

PEOPLE
Be with us as we pray.

B

LEADER
Healing Spirit,

PEOPLE
Receive our prayer.

OFFERTORY

As part of the offering of life and labor, significant announcements concerning the mission of the church may be made. Music may be offered to God's glory while the gifts are being received. Silence is also appropriate. The people may express their dedication and thanksgiving to God through music, prayers, dance, and other acts.

The people who are able may stand as representatives bring the gifts to the table.

A

A doxology, such as the following to the tune "Old Hundredth," may be sung.

ALL
**Praise God from whom
all blessings flow;
Praise Christ the Word
in flesh born low;
Praise Holy Spirit evermore;
One God, Triune,
whom we adore.
Amen.**

B

This doxology may be sung. Musical settings are on pages 452 and 461.

ALL
**Praise God from whom
all blessings flow;
Praise Christ,
all creatures here below;
Praise Holy Spirit,
the Comforter;
One God, Triune,
whom we adore.
Amen.**

A leader may offer a prayer of dedication, using one of these or his or her own words.

A

LEADER
**Bless these tithes and
offerings, O God,
returned to you.
Multiply and use them
to bring the word
and the touch of Jesus
to this place
and throughout the world,
in the name of Jesus Christ.
Amen.**

B

LEADER
**Holy One, blessed are you,
who entrust
to our care and use
the richness of creation.
Through our tithes
and offerings, we return
to you a portion of that
which you have given us.
May they be a means
of serving you
in the mission to which
you have called us;
through Jesus Christ.
Amen.**

HYMN

SERMON

PRAYER OF THANKSGIVING

_A leader may offer a prayer of thanksgiving for the oppor-
tunity to hear and understand God's word in her or his own
words or may use this prayer._

LEADER
**Thanks be to you, O God,
for from the beginning
you have entrusted us with your word
and have called us
to give heart, mind, voice, and love
to serving its truth,
even as Jesus Christ brought it to life among us.
Amen.**

LORD'S PRAYER

Standing, sitting, or kneeling, all may sing or say the prayer received from Jesus Christ.

LEADER
Let us pray as Christ our Savior has taught us.

A	B	C
ALL	ALL	ALL
Our Father in heaven, hallowed be your name, your kingdom come, your will be done, on earth as in heaven. Give us today our daily bread. Forgive us our sins as we forgive those who sin against us. Save us from the time of trial and deliver us from evil. For the kingdom, the power, and the glory are yours now and for ever. Amen.[70]	**Our Father, who art in heaven, hallowed be thy name. Thy kingdom come. Thy will be done on earth as it is in heaven. Give us this day our daily bread. And forgive us our trespasses, as we forgive those who trespass against us. And lead us not into temptation, but deliver us from evil. For thine is the kingdom, and the power, and the glory, for ever and ever. Amen.**	**Our Father, who art in heaven, hallowed be thy name. Thy kingdom come. Thy will be done on earth as it is in heaven. Give us this day our daily bread. And forgive us our debts, as we forgive our debtors. And lead us not into temptation, but deliver us from evil. For thine is the kingdom, and the power, and the glory, for ever. Amen.**

HYMN

BENEDICTION

A leader may use one of the following or may dismiss the

congregation with other words of comfort and challenge and with a blessing informed by scripture.

⟨A⟩

LEADER
**May God's Holy Spirit
lead you.
May God's strength
protect you.
May God's peace
be with you.
Go now
in the name of God,
by the grace of Christ,
and with the presence
of the Holy Spirit.
Amen.**

⟨B⟩

LEADER
**Let us go
and meet the world
which God loves
and for which Christ died.
Let us proclaim that
God is worthy of our trust
and Christ of our discipleship.
Let us live as heirs of Christ
and as the people of God
in the midst of God's world.
Amen.**

POSTLUDE

The congregation may be seated and remain until the postlude is concluded.

Services of Baptism and Affirmation of Baptism

Order for Baptism

A person is incorporated into the universal church, the body of Christ, through the sacrament of baptism. The water, words, and actions of the sacrament are visible signs that convey the Christian's burial and resurrection with Jesus Christ (Romans 6:3-4). The invocation of the Holy Spirit upon the water and upon the candidates for baptism is an affirmation that it is God who takes the initiative in the sacrament. "Baptism is both God's gift and our human response to that gift." It is "a sign and seal of our common discipleship. Through baptism, Christians are brought into union with Christ, with each other and with the church of every time and place."[1]

In the United Church of Christ people are baptized either as children or adults. Baptism with water and the Holy Spirit is the mark of their acceptance into the care of Christ's church, the sign and seal of their participation in God's forgiveness, and the beginning of their new growth into full Christian faith and life.

When an infant or young child is baptized, one or both parents and/or one or more sponsors promise to assume certain responsibilities for the Christian nurture of the baptized child. One of the parents or sponsors should be a member in good standing of a Christian church. Those who are baptized at an early age are given an opportunity in their youth to make a personal profession of faith through confirmation.

Parents, in consultation with the pastor, may choose sponsors for infants and young children who are to be baptized. Other candidates for baptism may also be given this opportunity to have sponsors. At the time of the baptismal service, the sponsors, who accompany new Christians on their journeys of faith, may accompany the candidates and present them for baptism. They may make promises identical to the promises of the parents concerning their role. At the end of the Order for Baptism, they may be among those introducing the newly baptized to the congregation, perhaps by moving with them throughout the congregation.

Baptism is not only a personal celebration in the lives of the individual candidates and their families, but also a central celebration in the life of the local church which embodies the universal church in a particular place. For this reason, baptism should take place in the presence of the community of faith gathered for public worship. In officiating at a service of baptism, the pastor acts as a representative of the church universal. When urgent circumstances make it necessary to undertake baptism apart from the worshiping congregation, leaders of the local church should participate in the ceremony with the pastor. If an ordained minister is not available in such circumstances, a lay person may administer the sacrament.

Baptism should occur only once in a person's life. If there is a question about whether baptism has taken place, a conditional phrase may be added as a person is baptized, such as "If you are not already baptized . . ."

It is important to consider the meaning conveyed in the location of the baptism in the church building. A baptismal service held in a narthex or near a door to the sanctuary emphasizes initiation or entry into the church. Baptism held in the center of the sanctuary in the midst of the congregation stresses incorporation into the community of faith. Baptism held at the chancel, near the pulpit and table, accents the connections between baptism, God's word, and communion. A baptismal service held in a place visually cut off from the people communicates that baptism is peripheral to church life.

Water is an essential element of baptism. Its presence and use should be boldly dramatized in the service. The mode of baptism remains a matter of choice. The candidates, or their parents and sponsors, in consultation with the pastor, may elect sprinkling, immersion, or pouring.

Baptism is most properly incorporated into a Service of Word and Sacrament, where it follows the sermon and precedes Holy Communion. By baptism, a person becomes a member of Christ's church and is welcome at Christ's table. For the newly baptized, the journey is from the font to the feast of the table.

Some churches use a lighted paschal candle during baptism. *Paschal*, derived from the Hebrew "to pass over," refers to the lamb sacrificed for its blood which was used as a sign for death to pass over the houses of the people of Israel before the Exodus. Thus their children were saved. In Christian worship, a large paschal candle is used to symbolize Jesus, the one whose death and resurrection bring salvation and eternal life to God's people and so deliver them, as the Israelites had been delivered.

This order includes instructions for incorporating confirmation and reception of members.

OUTLINE

This order may be incorporated into a Service of Word and Sacrament or a Service of the Word following the sermon. A hymn may precede this order. When used with the Order for Confirmation or Order for Reception of Members, begin with the prayer of baptism and end with the act of praise.

> **Invitation**
> **Welcome**
> **Address**
> **Questions of the Candidates**
> **Congregational Assent**
> **Affirmation of Faith**
> **Prayer of Baptism**
> **Act of Baptism**
> **Act of Praise**
> **Prayer for the Baptized**
> **Benediction**

A Service of Word and Sacrament or a Service of the Word continues, omitting the affirmation of faith.

Water in adequate supply may be in the baptistry, a font, a bowl, or a pitcher, depending upon local custom. If it is the practice of the local church to use a paschal candle, it may stand near the place of baptism and be lighted.

INVITATION

The pastor and others who will lead the baptismal service may invite those who desire baptism for themselves or their children to come to the place where baptism will be celebrated. They may go out into the congregation to escort the candidates to the place for baptism. The invitation may be given informally, in words that reflect the growing relationship between the local church and the candidates.

As an expression of a special ministry of hospitality to children to be baptized, all children present may be invited to stand near children who are to be baptized.

A baptismal hymn may be sung.

WELCOME

The pastor and people may introduce the baptismal service, using one of these statements or similar words.

A

PASTOR
Members and friends in Christ, we gather now to celebrate the gift of grace in the sacrament of baptism.

PEOPLE
There is one body and one Spirit. There is one hope in God's call to us.

B

PASTOR
Dear friends, as we come to this font of living water, let us recall the meaning of baptism.

For just as the body is one and has many members, and all the members of the body,

C *for use when children are baptized*

PASTOR
They were bringing children to Jesus that Jesus might touch them; and the disciples rebuked them. But when Jesus saw it, Jesus was indignant,

PASTOR
**There is one Lord,
one faith,
one baptism,
one God and
Creator of us all.**[2]

**though many,
are one body,
so it is
with Christ.**

PEOPLE
For by one Spirit
we were all
baptized into
one body
—Jews or Greeks,
slaves or free—
and all were
made to drink
of one Spirit.

PASTOR
**Now you are the
body of Christ
and individually
members of it.**[3]

and said to them,

PEOPLE
"Let the children
come to me,
do not hinder
them; for to such
belongs the realm
of God.
Truly, I say
to you, whoever
does not receive
the realm of God
like a child shall
not enter it."

PASTOR
**And Jesus took
them in his arms
and blessed them,
laying his hands
upon them.**[4]

ADDRESS

*The pastor may address those gathered, using one of these
options or other words based on scripture.*

A
PASTOR
**Jesus came to John
to be baptized by him.
But John tried to make
him change his mind.
"I ought to be baptized
by you," John said,
"yet you have come to me!"**

PEOPLE
Jesus said,
"Let it be so for now.
For in this way,

B
PASTOR
**Jesus said:
Unless we are born anew,
we cannot see
the reign of God;
unless we are born of water
and the Spirit,
we cannot enter
God's new order.**[7]

**Paul the apostle said:
All of us who have been
baptized into Christ Jesus**

we shall do all
that God requires."
So John agreed.

PASTOR
As soon as Jesus
was baptized, he came up
out of the water.
Then heaven was opened
to him, and
he saw the Spirit of God
coming down like a dove
and lighting on him.

PEOPLE
Then a voice said
from heaven,
"This is my own dear Son,
with whom I am well pleased."[5]

PASTOR
At another time Jesus said:
Go and make disciples
of all nations,
baptizing them
in the name of the Father
and of the Son
and of the Holy Spirit.[6]

were baptized
into Christ's death.
We were buried therefore
with Christ by baptism
into death,
so that as Christ was raised
from the dead,
to the glory of God,
we too might walk
in newness of life.[8]

AND

Ⓐ *for baptism of infants*
and young children

PASTOR
The sacrament of baptism
is an outward and visible
sign of the grace of God.
Inasmuch as the promise
of the gospel is not only to
us but also to our children,
baptism with water and the
Holy Spirit is the mark

Ⓑ *for baptism of older*
children, youth, and adults

PASTOR
Baptism is the sacrament
through which we are
united to Jesus Christ
and given part
in Christ's ministry
of reconciliation.
Baptism is the visible sign
of an invisible event:

of their acceptance into the
care of Christ's church,
the sign and seal
of their participation
in God's forgiveness,
and the beginning of their
growth into full Christian
faith and discipleship.[9]

the reconciliation
of people to God.
It shows the death of self
and the rising to a life
of obedience and praise.
It shows also the pouring
out of the Holy Spirit
on those whom
God has chosen.
In baptism, God works in
us the power of forgiveness,
the renewal of the Spirit,
and the knowledge
of the call
to be God's people always.[10]

This response may follow either option.

PEOPLE
This is the water of baptism.
Out of this water we rise with new life,
forgiven of sin
and one in Christ,
members of Christ's body.

QUESTIONS OF THE CANDIDATES

*If there are no infants or young children to be baptized,
continue with the questions for older children and adults
on page 138.*

INFANTS AND YOUNG CHILDREN

*These questions may be used when the candidates are
unable to speak for themselves. If more than one child
is to be baptized, all parents and sponsors may
respond in unison.*

PASTOR
addressing the parent(s)
Do you desire to have your child(ren) baptized
into the faith and family of Jesus Christ?

PARENT(S)
I/We do.

PASTOR
addressing the parent(s) and sponsor(s), if any
Will you encourage *this child/these children*
to renounce the powers of evil
and to receive the freedom of new life in Christ?

PARENT(S) AND SPONSOR(S)
I/We will, with the help of God.

PASTOR
Will you teach *this child/these children*
that *he/she/they* **may be led to profess**
Jesus Christ as Lord and Savior?

PARENT(S) AND SPONSOR(S)
I/We will, with the help of God.

PASTOR
Do you promise, by the grace of God,
to be Christ's disciple(s),
to follow in the way of our Savior,
to resist oppression and evil,
to show love and justice,
and to witness to the work and word of Jesus Christ
as best you are able?

PARENT(S) AND SPONSOR(S)
I/We do, with the help of God.

PASTOR
Do you promise, according to the grace given you,
to grow with *this child/these children* **in the Christian faith,**
to help *this child/these children*
to be *a faithful member/faithful members*
of the church of Jesus Christ,
by celebrating Christ's presence,
by furthering Christ's mission in all the world,
and by offering the nurture of the Christian church
so that *she/he/they* **may affirm** *her/his/their* **baptism?**

PARENT(S) AND SPONSOR(S)
I/We do, with the help of God.

If there are no older children or adults to be baptized, continue with the congregational assent on page 139.

continue with the congregational assent on page 139.

OLDER CHILDREN AND ADULTS
These questions may be used when candidates are able to speak for themselves. If more than one person is to be baptized, they may respond to the questions in unison.

PASTOR
addressing the candidate(s)

———————,
    name(s)

**do you desire to be baptized
into the faith and family of Jesus Christ?**

CANDIDATE(S)
I do.

PASTOR
addressing the sponsor(s), if any
**Are you ready with God's help
to guide and encourage ———————
by counsel and example,**   name(s)
**in prayer and with love,
to follow the way of Jesus Christ?**

SPONSOR(S)
I am.

PASTOR
addressing the candidate(s)
**Do you renounce the powers of evil
and desire the freedom of new life in Christ?**

CANDIDATE(S)
I do.

PASTOR
Do you profess Jesus Christ as Lord and Savior?

CANDIDATE(S)
I do.

PASTOR
Do you promise,
by the grace of God,
to be Christ's disciple,
to follow in the way of our Savior,
to resist oppression and evil,
to show love and justice,
and to witness to the work and word of Jesus Christ
as best you are able?

CANDIDATE(S)
I promise, with the help of God.

PASTOR
Do you promise,
according to the grace given you,
to grow in the Christian faith
and to be a faithful member
of the church of Jesus Christ,
celebrating Christ's presence
and furthering Christ's mission in all the world?

CANDIDATE(S)
I promise, with the help of God.

CONGREGATIONAL ASSENT

All who are able may stand as the congregation is asked to make promises.

PASTOR
Jesus Christ calls us
to make disciples of all nations
and to offer them the gift of grace in baptism.

Do you, who witness and celebrate this sacrament,
promise your love, support, and care
to the one(s) about to be baptized,
as *he/she/they* **live(s) and grow(s) in Christ?**

PEOPLE
We promise our love, support, and care.

AFFIRMATION OF FAITH

All who are able may stand. Responses are made in unison by each worshiper, including the candidate(s) for baptism.

PASTOR
**Let us unite with the church
in all times and places
in confessing our faith in the triune God.**

Ⓐ
PASTOR
Do you believe in God?

PEOPLE
I believe in God.

PASTOR
**Do you believe
in Jesus Christ?**

PEOPLE
I believe in Jesus Christ.

PASTOR
**Do you believe
in the Holy Spirit?**

PEOPLE
I believe in the Holy Spirit.

Ⓑ
An ancient baptismal creed, another creed, or a statement of faith may be used in full or in an abbreviated version. The style should allow congregational response. Forms of the United Church of Christ Statement of Faith, historic creeds, and other affirmations of faith are in the Resource Section, beginning on page 509.

When incorporating baptism and confirmation or reception of members, begin the Order for Baptism here.

PRAYER OF BAPTISM

The congregation may be seated. A prayer may be offered, using the pastor's own words, option A with B, or B alone.

PASTOR
Christ be with you.

PEOPLE
And also with you.

PASTOR
Let us pray.

Ⓐ
PASTOR
We thank you, God,
for the gift of creation
called forth by your saving Word.
Before the world had shape and form,
your Spirit moved over the waters.
Out of the waters of the deep,
you formed the firmament
and brought forth the earth
to sustain all life.

In the time of Noah,
you washed the earth
with the waters of the flood,
and your ark of salvation bore a new beginning.

In the time of Moses,
your people Israel passed
through the Red Sea waters
from slavery to freedom
and crossed the flowing Jordan
to enter the promised land.

In the fullness of time,
you sent Jesus Christ,
who was nurtured
in the water of Mary's womb.

Jesus was baptized by John
in the water of the Jordan,
became living water to a woman
at the Samaritan well,
washed the feet of the disciples,
and sent them forth
to baptize all the nations
by water and the Holy Spirit.

The water may be visibly poured.

The following prayer, option B, may be used alone or with option A.

B

PASTOR

**Bless by your Holy Spirit,
gracious God, this water.
By your Holy Spirit
save those who confess
the name of Jesus Christ
that sin may have no power over them.
Create new life in** *the one/all*
**baptized this day
that** *she/he/they* **may rise in Christ.
Glory to you, eternal God,
the one who was, and is, and shall always be,
world without end.
Amen.**

ACT OF BAPTISM

NAMING OF A CHILD

When a child is baptized, as each child is handed into the arms of the pastor, the parent(s) may be asked to name the child.

PASTOR

By what name will your child be called?

PARENT(S)

_____.
     name

The pastor, administering the water by pouring, sprinkling, or immersion, says one of these.

A

PASTOR

_____,
    name

**you are baptized
in the name of the Father,
and of the Son,
and of the Holy Spirit.**

PEOPLE
Amen.

B

PASTOR

_____,
    name

**I baptize you
in the name of the Father,
and of the Son,
and of the Holy Spirit.**

PEOPLE
Amen.

The pastor may lay hands on the head of the baptized and say these or similar words.

PASTOR
The Holy Spirit be upon you,

——————,
name

**child of God,
disciple of Christ,
member of the church.**

ACT OF PRAISE

A doxology or another act of praise may follow the baptism.

If this order is being used in conjunction with one of the Orders for Affirmation of Baptism, return to the Order for Confirmation at the prayer on page 150 or the Order for Reception of Members at the address on page 162.

PRAYER FOR THE BAPTIZED

A prayer for the baptized may be said, using one of the following or the pastor's own words.

A

PASTOR
**We give you thanks,
O Holy One, mother and
father of all the faithful,
for** *this your child/these your children* **and for the grace
acknowledged here today
in water
and the Holy Spirit.**

**Embrace us all as sons and
daughters in the one
household of your love.**

**Grant us grace to receive,
nurture, and befriend** *this
new member/these new members*
of the body of Christ.

B *includes optional
words for use when a child
is baptized*

PASTOR
Let us pray for *the one/those*
baptized today.

**Gracious God,
you have filled the world
with joy by giving us
the gift of Jesus.
Bless** *this newly baptized person/
these newly baptized people.*
May *she/he/they*
**be filled with joy;
may** *he/she/they* **never
be ashamed to confess
a personal faith in you.**

ALL
**Give to the newly baptized:
strength for life's journey,
courage in time of suffering,
the joy of faith,
the freedom of love,
and the hope of new life;
through Jesus Christ,
who makes us one.
Amen.**

Bless the parent(s)

and sponsor(s)

of *this child/these children*.
May *she/he/they* **always
show** *her/his/their*
**gratitude for the life
you have given
by loving and caring
for** _____.
            name(s)

**Bless these your
faithful people.
Unite them in the peace
of Christ and the company
of the Holy Spirit.**
PEOPLE
Amen.

BENEDICTION

*Those leading the service may greet the newly baptized,
the parents, and the sponsors informally. A lighted candle
or another gift signifying discipleship may be given to each
newly baptized person. The pastor, sponsors, or others
may move through the congregation with the newly baptized and introduce the person(s) as a sign of entry and
incorporation into the living community of faith.*

PASTOR
Go in the peace of Christ.

ALL
Thanks be to God.

*Those who have participated in the Order for Baptism
may return to their places in the congregation.*

***A Service of Word and Sacrament or a Service of the
Word continues, omitting the affirmation of faith.***

Order for Confirmation: Affirmation of Baptism

INTRODUCTION

A person is incorporated into the universal church, the body of Christ, through the sacrament of baptism. When an infant or very young child is baptized, the baptismal promises are made by one or more parents and/or sponsors. These adult Christians assume certain responsibilities for the Christian nurture of the baptized child. Those who consent to this ministry of nurture are members in good standing of a Christian church in order that they may honor their promises fully. The entire congregation also assumes the role of sponsors as its members promise to provide a supportive Christian community in which a child may grow in awareness and understanding concerning the meaning of life in Christ.

As a child who was baptized in infancy approaches adolescence, the local church offers that person the opportunity to give public assent to the baptismal promises. Confirmation celebrates this occasion of affirmation of baptism in the life of the individual and of the local church.

Before a service of confirmation is scheduled, the appropriate leaders of the local church shall be satisfied that the participants have been instructed properly in the Christian faith and personally desire to affirm their baptism. This order is designed to be used within a Service of Word and Sacrament or a Service of the Word. The service shall be held in the presence of the worshiping congregation. When urgent circumstances make it necessary to hold the service apart from the worshiping congregation, appropriate leaders of the local church shall participate in the ceremony with the pastor.

Parents and sponsors stand with those who are affirming their baptism as an expression of continuing support and concern for their Christian pilgrimage. If a young person who has not been baptized but has shared in a preparatory class with peers wishes to participate with classmates rather than receive baptism on a separate occasion, he or she may be baptized as indicated in the instructions.

OUTLINE

This order may be incorporated into a Service of Word and Sacrament or a Service of the Word following the sermon.

Invitation
Sentences
Questions of the Candidates
Affirmation of Faith
Prayer of the Candidates
Prayers of the Congregation
Act of Confirmation
Prayer of Confirmation
Address
Question about Participation
Welcome
Greeting of Christian Love
Prayer
Benediction

A Service of Word and Sacrament or a Service of the Word continues, omitting the affirmation of faith.

INVITATION

*After the sermon has been preached, appointed represen-
tatives and the pastor may gather in the chancel for
confirmation. An elected leader of the church may invite
all who have indicated willingness to affirm their baptism
by confirmation to come forward, using the following or
similar words.*

LEADER
We invite to come forward *the one/those*
who wish(es) to affirm *his/her/their* **baptism
by being confirmed.**

*The name(s) of the individual(s) may be read, and the
candidate(s) may come and stand, if able.*

LEADER
**Friends in Christ,
we all are received into the church
through the sacrament of baptism.**
This person has/ These people have **found nurture and support
in the midst of the family of Christ.
Through prayer and study**
she/he/they   has/have **been led
by the Holy Spirit
to affirm** *her/his/their* **baptism
and to claim in our presence**
her/his/their **covenantal relationship
with Christ and the members of the church.**
He/She/They   is/are **here
for service to Jesus Christ,
using the gifts
which the Holy Spirit bestows.**

SENTENCES

*One of the following or other passages from scripture may
be read.*

A

LEADER

Hear the words of Jesus: I am the vine, you are the branches. Anyone who abides in me, and I in that person, is the one who bears much fruit. If you abide in me, and my words abide in you, ask whatever you will, and it shall be done for you. If you keep my commandments, you will abide in my love. These things I have spoken to you, that my joy may be in you, and that your joy may be full.[11]

B

LEADER

God's message is near you, on your lips and in your heart, that is, the word of faith that we preach. If you confess with your lips that Jesus is Lord and believe that God raised Jesus from the dead, you will be saved. For it is by our faith that we are put right with God; it is by our confession that we are saved.[12]

C

LEADER

You are no longer strangers and sojourners, but you are equally citizens with the saints and members of the household of God, built upon the foundation of the apostles and prophets, Christ Jesus alone being the cornerstone, in whom the whole structure is joined together and grows into a holy temple in Christ; in whom you also are built into it for a dwelling place of God in the Spirit.[13]

QUESTIONS OF THE CANDIDATES

These questions parallel the questions asked of candidates for baptism. If there is more than one candidate, they may be asked together and respond in unison.

The first question includes words for candidate(s) being baptized as well as one(s) affirming baptism. With more than one candidate, it may be necessary to address the question using each set of words.

PASTOR

———————————,
　　　name(s)
do you desire to *affirm your baptism/be baptized*
into the faith and family of Jesus Christ?

CANDIDATE(S)
I do.

PASTOR
**Do you renounce the powers of evil
and desire the freedom of new life in Christ?**

CANDIDATE(S)
I do.

PASTOR
Do you profess Jesus Christ as Lord and Savior?

CANDIDATE(S)
I do.

PASTOR
**Do you promise, by the grace of God,
to be Christ's disciple,
to follow in the way of our Savior,
to resist oppression and evil,
to show love and justice,
and to witness to the work and word of Jesus Christ
as best you are able?**

CANDIDATE(S)
I promise, with the help of God.

PASTOR
**Do you promise,
according to the grace given you,
to grow in the Christian faith
and to be a faithful member
of the church of Jesus Christ,
celebrating Christ's presence
and furthering Christ's mission in all the world?**

CANDIDATE(S)
I promise, with the help of God.

AFFIRMATION OF FAITH

All who are able may stand. The responses are made in unison by each worshiper, including the candidate(s).

PASTOR
**Let us unite with the church
in all times and places
in confessing our faith in the triune God.**

🅰

PASTOR
Do you believe in God?

PEOPLE
I believe in God.

PASTOR
**Do you believe
in Jesus Christ?**

PEOPLE
I believe in Jesus Christ.

PASTOR
**Do you believe
in the Holy Spirit?**

PEOPLE
I believe in the Holy Spirit.

🅱

An ancient baptismal creed, another creed, a statement of faith, or the local church covenant may be used in full or in an abbreviated version. The style should allow congregational response. Forms of the United Church of Christ Statement of Faith, historic creeds, and other affirmations are in the Resource Section, beginning on page 509.

The congregation may be seated.

If there is a candidate for baptism, use the Order for Baptism, beginning with the prayer of baptism on page 140. Following the act of praise on page 143, return to this point of the Order for Confirmation.

If no one is to be baptized, the service continues with the prayer of the candidates which follows.

PRAYER OF THE CANDIDATES

The candidates who are able may stand or kneel.

PASTOR AND CANDIDATE(S)
O God, my God,
known to me in Jesus Christ,
I give myself to you as your own,
to love and serve you faithfully
all the days of my life.
Amen.[14]

PRAYERS OF THE CONGREGATION

PASTOR
Let us pray in silence.

A period of silent prayer follows.

PASTOR
Let us pray together.

ALL
Almighty God,
who in baptism
received these your servants into the church,
forgave their sins,
and promised them eternal life,
increase in them the gifts
of your Holy Spirit.
Grant love for others,
joy in serving you,
peace in disagreement,
patience in suffering,
kindness toward all people,
goodness in evil times,
faithfulness in temptation,
gentleness in the face of opposition,
self-control in all things.
Thereby strengthen them
for their ministry in the world;
through Jesus Christ our Savior.
Amen.

If the Lord's Prayer is not to be said elsewhere in the
service, it may be said at this time.

ACT OF CONFIRMATION

Parents and baptismal and/or confirmation sponsors, if any, may come forward and stand, if able, near the confirmands. Candidates who are able may kneel. The pastor and other leaders of the local church may place hands upon each candidate individually. One of the following or similar words may be said.

A
PASTOR

————————————,
name

**the God of peace
sanctify you.
I pray that you will be
preserved blameless
to the coming of our Savior
Jesus Christ.**

CANDIDATE(S) AND PEOPLE
Amen.

B
PASTOR

————————————,
name

**the God of mercies
multiply grace and peace
in you, enable you truly
and faithfully to keep
your vows, defend you
in every time of danger,
preserve you to the end,
and finally bring you
to rest with all the saints
in glory everlasting.**

CANDIDATE(S) AND PEOPLE
Amen.

OR

C
PASTOR
**Strengthen, O God,
this your servant**

————————————
name

**with your heavenly grace
that** *he/she* **may continue
yours for ever;
and daily increase in** *him/her*
**your Holy Spirit, until you
receive** *him/her* **at last
in your eternal home.**

CANDIDATE(S) AND PEOPLE
Amen.

D
PASTOR
**O God, in the grace
of Jesus Christ you have
accepted this your servant**

————————————
name

**through the water
of baptism.
Nourish in** *her/him* **the
power of your Holy Spirit
that** *she/he* **may serve you
in the world.**

CANDIDATE(S) AND PEOPLE
Amen.

PRAYER OF CONFIRMATION

PASTOR
We rejoice,
O merciful God,
with *this person/these people*
in the gift of the Holy Spirit,
and in the Spirit's power
to awaken us to new truth
and to inspire us to venture
into fullness of life.

We give you thanks
that *she/he/they   has/have* **been moved**
to affirm *her/his/their* **baptism.**
Help *him/her/them* **to live**
not for *himself/herself/themselves*
but for Christ and those whom Christ loves.
Keep *her/him/them* **steady**
and abounding in hope,
never giving up,
pressing toward the goal of life with you
in Jesus Christ.

CANDIDATE(S) AND PEOPLE
Amen.

The newly confirmed individual(s) who are able may rise
and stand in place.

ADDRESS

PASTOR
By your baptism
you were made one with us
in the body of Christ, the church.
Today we rejoice in your pilgrimage of faith
which has brought you
to this time and place.
We celebrate your presence
in this household of faith.

QUESTION ABOUT PARTICIPATION

PASTOR
**Do you promise to participate in the life and mission
of this family of God's people,
sharing regularly in the worship of God
and enlisting in the work of this local church
as it serves this community and the world?**

CANDIDATE(S)
I promise, with the help of God.

WELCOME

*Members of the local church who are able may stand and
say the following or other words of welcome.*

PASTOR
Let us, the members of _____,
                                   local church
**express our welcome
and affirm our mutual ministry in Christ.**

PEOPLE
We promise you our continuing friendship and prayers
as we share the hopes and labors
of the church of Jesus Christ.
By the power of the Holy Spirit
may we continue to grow together
in God's knowledge and love
and be witnesses of our risen Savior.

GREETING OF CHRISTIAN LOVE

*The congregation may be seated. The pastor and represen-
tatives of the local church may greet each newly confirmed
person individually with these or other words and may
offer the hand of Christian love.*

PASTOR AND REPRESENTATIVES
**In the name of Jesus Christ,
and on behalf of** _____,
                            local church
we extend to you the hand of Christian love.

PRAYER

PASTOR
Let us pray.

A

PASTOR
**Eternal God,
we praise you
for calling us
to be your
servant people
and for gathering
us into the body
of Christ.
We thank you
for sending to us**
*this believer/these
believers* **that
we may work
together in
serving the needs
of others.**

**Confirm in us
the power
of your covenant
that we may live
in your Spirit,
share regularly
in worship,
and so love each
other that we
may have among
us the same mind
which was
in Christ Jesus,
to whom be all
honor and glory.**

ALL
Amen.[15]

B

PASTOR
**Almighty and
everliving God,
may your hand
ever be over
your servant(s)
confirmed today.
May your
Holy Spirit
ever be with**
her/him/them.
So lead
him/her/them
**in the knowledge
and obedience
of your Word
that** *he/she/they*
**may serve you
in this life
and dwell
with you
in the life
to come;
through Jesus
Christ.**

ALL
Amen.[16]

C

PASTOR
**O God,
we praise you
for calling us
to faith and
for gathering us
into the church,
the body
of Christ.
We thank you
for your people
gathered in this
local church
and rejoice
that you have
increased
our community
of faith.**

**Together may we
live in the Spirit,
building one
another up
in love,
sharing in the life
and worship of
the church, and
serving the world
for the sake
of Jesus Christ.**

ALL
Amen.[17]

BENEDICTION

PASTOR
Go in the peace of Christ.

PEOPLE
Thanks be to God.

Those who have participated in the Order for Confirmation may return to their places in the congregation.

At the conclusion of this order, a Service of Word and Sacrament or a Service of the Word continues, omitting the affirmation of faith.

Order for Reception of Members: Affirmation of Baptism

INTRODUCTION

A person is incorporated into the universal church, the body of Christ, through the sacrament of baptism. Baptism with water and the Holy Spirit is the mark of acceptance of individuals into the care of Christ's church, the sign and seal of their participation in God's forgiveness, and the beginning of their new growth into full Christian faith and life. Baptism is not only a personal celebration in the lives of the individual candidates and their families, but also a central celebration in the life of the local church which embodies the universal church in a particular place. For this reason, baptism takes place in the presence of the community of faith gathered for public worship. Public worship is also the setting for affirmation of baptism.

While baptism occurs only once in a person's life, there are times when Christians feel called to affirm their baptism. For adolescents, this usually occurs in confirmation. A congregation may be offered an opportunity for affirmation of baptism. One such opportunity is the service of water in the Order for the Great Vigil of Easter, beginning on page 238. When Christians unite with a local church, they affirm their baptism. This order asks those being received as members to respond to questions parallel to those of baptism as they affirm their baptism.

In the United Church of Christ, people unite with a local church by baptism and confirmation or by profession of faith and baptism. They also unite by reaffirmation or re-profession of faith or letter of transfer or certification from other Christian churches.

Before the Order for Reception of Members is scheduled, the appropriate leaders of the local church shall be satisfied that the participants have been instructed properly in the Christian faith and personally desire to affirm their baptism. If people are uniting by letter of transfer or certification from other Christian churches, it is the responsibility of the leaders to verify that the documents are in order.

This order is designed to be used within a Service of Word and Sacrament or a Service of the Word. The service shall be held in the presence of the worshiping congregation. When urgent circumstances make it necessary to hold the service apart from the worshiping congregation, appropriate leaders of the local church shall participate in the ceremony with the pastor. There are instructions in this order for the Order for Baptism to be used for adults who have not been baptized and wish to unite with the local church by profession of faith. Confirmation may or may not follow.

OUTLINE

This order may be incorporated into a Service of Word and Sacrament or a Service of the Word following the sermon.

Invitation
Sentences
Questions of the Candidates
Affirmation of Faith
Address
Question about Participation
Welcome and Reception
Greeting of Christian Love
Prayer
Benediction

A Service of Word and Sacrament or a Service of the Word continues, omitting the affirmation of faith.

INVITATION

After the sermon has been preached, appointed represen-tatives and the pastor may gather in the chancel. An elected leader of the church may invite all who have indicated willingness to affirm their baptism by joining this local church to come forward, using the following or similar words.

LEADER
We invite to come forward *the one/those*
who wish(es) to affirm *his/her/their* **baptism**
by uniting with us in this household of faith.

The name(s) of the individual(s) may be read and the candidate(s) may come forward and stand, if able. If member(s) are being received from other churches by letter of transfer, that information may be presented.

LEADER
Friends in Christ,
we all are received into the church
through the sacrament of baptism.
This person has/ These people have **found nurture and support**
in the midst of the family of Christ.
Through prayer and study
she/he/they   has/have **been led**
by the Holy Spirit
to affirm *her/his/their* **baptism**
and to claim in our presence
her/his/their **covenantal relationship**
with Christ and the members of the church.
He/She/They   is/are **here**
for service to Jesus Christ,
using the gifts
which the Holy Spirit bestows.

SENTENCES

One of the following or other passages from scripture may be read.

Ⓐ
LEADER
**Hear the words
of Jesus:
I am the vine,
you are the
branches.
Anyone who
abides in me, and
I in that person,
is the one who
bears much fruit.
If you abide in
me, and my words
abide in you,
ask whatever you
will, and it shall
be done for you.
If you keep my
commandments,
you will abide
in my love.
These things I
have spoken to
you, that my joy
may be in you,
and that your joy
may be full.**[18]

Ⓑ
LEADER
**God's message is
near you,
on your lips and
in your heart,
that is, the
word of faith
that we preach.
If you confess
with your lips
that Jesus is Lord
and believe that
God raised Jesus
from the dead,
you will be saved.
For it is by our
faith that we are
put right
with God;
it is by our
confession that
we are saved.**[19]

Ⓒ
LEADER
**You are no
longer strangers
and sojourners,
but you are
equally citizens
with the saints
and members
of the household
of God,
built upon the
foundation of the
apostles and
prophets,
Christ Jesus
alone being the
cornerstone,
in whom the
whole structure
is joined together
and grows into
a holy temple
in Christ;
in whom you also
are built into it
for a dwelling
place of God
in the Spirit.**[20]

QUESTIONS OF THE CANDIDATES

*These questions parallel the questions asked of candidates
for baptism. If there is more than one candidate, they may
be asked together and respond in unison.*

*The first question includes words for candidate(s) being
baptized as well as one(s) affirming baptism. With more
than one candidate, it may be necessary to address the
question using each set of words.*

PASTOR

———————————,
 name(s)
do you desire to *affirm your baptism/be baptized*
into the faith and family of Jesus Christ?

CANDIDATE(S)
I do.

PASTOR
Do you renounce the powers of evil
and desire the freedom of new life in Christ?

CANDIDATE(S)
I do.

PASTOR
Do you profess Jesus Christ as Lord and Savior?

CANDIDATE(S)
I do.

PASTOR
Do you promise, by the grace of God,
to be Christ's disciple,
to follow in the way of our Savior,
to resist oppression and evil,
to show love and justice,
and to witness to the work and word of Jesus Christ
as best you are able?

CANDIDATE(S)
I promise, with the help of God.

PASTOR
Do you promise,
according to the grace given you,
to grow in the Christian faith
and to be a faithful member
of the church of Jesus Christ,
celebrating Christ's presence
and furthering Christ's mission in all the world?

CANDIDATE(S)
I promise, with the help of God.

AFFIRMATION OF FAITH

All who are able may stand. The responses are made in unison by each worshiper, including the candidate(s).

PASTOR
**Let us unite with the church
in all times and places
in confessing our faith in the triune God.**

A

PASTOR
Do you believe in God?

PEOPLE
I believe in God.

PASTOR
**Do you believe
in Jesus Christ?**

PEOPLE
I believe in Jesus Christ.

PASTOR
**Do you believe
in the Holy Spirit?**

PEOPLE
I believe in the Holy Spirit.

B

An ancient baptismal creed, another creed, a statement of faith, or the local church covenant may be used in full or in an abbreviated version. The style should allow congregational response. Forms of the United Church of Christ Statement of Faith, historic creeds, and other affirmations are in the Resource Section, beginning on page 509.

The congregation may be seated.

If there is a candidate for baptism, use the Order for Baptism, beginning with the prayer of baptism on page 140. Following the act of praise on page 143, return to this point of the Order for Reception of Members.

If no one is to be baptized, the service continues here.

ADDRESS

The following or similar words may be addressed to all people uniting with the church by baptism, reaffirmation or re-profession of faith, or by transfer or certification from other Christian churches.

PASTOR
**By your baptism you were made one with us
in the body of Christ, the church.
Today we rejoice in your pilgrimage of faith
which has brought you to this time and place.
We give thanks for every community of faith
that has been your spiritual home,
and we celebrate your presence
in this household of faith.**

QUESTION ABOUT PARTICIPATION

PASTOR
**Do you promise to participate in the life and mission
of this family of God's people,
sharing regularly in the worship of God
and enlisting in the work of this local church
as it serves this community and the world?**

CANDIDATE(S)
I promise, with the help of God.

WELCOME AND RECEPTION

*Members of the local church who are able may stand and
say the following or other words of welcome.*

PASTOR
Let us, the members of _____ ,
                              local church
**express our welcome
and affirm our mutual ministry in Christ.**

PEOPLE
We welcome you with joy
in the common life of this church.
We promise you our friendship and prayers
as we share the hopes and labors
of the church of Jesus Christ.
By the power of the Holy Spirit
may we continue to grow together
in God's knowledge and love
and be witnesses of our risen Savior.

GREETING OF CHRISTIAN LOVE

The congregation may be seated. The pastor and representatives of the local church may greet each new member personally with these or other words and may offer the hand of Christian love.

PASTOR AND REPRESENTATIVES
**In the name of Jesus Christ,
and on behalf of _____ ,**
local church
**we extend to you the hand of Christian love,
welcoming you into the company of this local church.**

PRAYER

PASTOR
Let us pray.

A
PASTOR
**Eternal God,
we praise you
for calling us
to be your
servant people
and for gathering
us into the body
of Christ.
We thank you
for sending to us**
*this believer/these
believers* **that
we may work
together in
serving the needs
of others.**

**Confirm in us
the power
of your covenant
that we may live**

B
PASTOR
**Almighty and
everliving God,
may your hand
ever be over
your servant(s)
who made a
commitment
to membership
here today.
May your
Holy Spirit
ever be with**
her/him/them.
So lead
him/her/them
**in the knowledge
and obedience
of your Word
that** *he/she/they*
**may serve you
in this life**

C
PASTOR
**O God,
we praise you
for calling us
to faith and for
gathering us into
the church, the
body of Christ.
We thank you
for your people
gathered in this
local church
and rejoice
that you have
increased
our community
of faith.**

**Together may we
live in the Spirit,
building one
another up**

in your Spirit,
share regularly
in worship,
and so love each
other that we
may have among
us the same mind
which was
in Christ Jesus,
to whom be all
honor and glory.

ALL
Amen.[21]

and dwell
with you
in the life
to come;
through Jesus
Christ.

ALL
Amen.[22]

in love,
sharing in the life
and worship
of the church,
and serving
the world
for the sake
of Jesus Christ.

ALL
Amen.[23]

BENEDICTION

PASTOR
Go in the peace of Christ.

PEOPLE
Thanks be to God.

Those who have participated in the Order for Reception of Members may return to their seats.

At the conclusion of this order, a Service of Word and Sacrament or a Service of the Word continues, omitting the affirmation of faith.

Services of a Church's Life

Order for
Lighting Advent Candles

An Advent wreath with Advent candles is a tradition that helps Christians focus attention on the coming of the Christ at Bethlehem and at the close of history. As Advent is the beginning of the liturgical year, this season may be used to retell the biblical stories of the life of Jesus.

The lighting of Advent candles may take place at an appropriate point in a Service of Word and Sacrament or a Service of the Word. The candles could be lighted during the opening acts or at the time of the reading of scripture.

The suggestions offered here may encourage worship leaders to create new traditions for their local churches. Children and youth should be included in the preparation of the Advent wreath and as leaders in lighting the candles.

Purple, the liturgical color of the season of Advent, usually is shown in the four candles surrounding a larger white Christ candle in the center of the Advent wreath, although local church traditions vary.

A theme should continue through Advent to Christmas. The theme of light is often used in the northern hemisphere because Advent is experienced at the darkest time of the year. Jesus is the Light of the World and thus brings God's hope. Traditions regarding the order of the themes of hope, peace, love, and joy may differ in some local churches.

This is also a good time to integrate worship and the educational program of the church. Common themes for the worship and the educational program enhance the celebration of Christ's birth.

This order, which illustrates one approach to the use of the Advent wreath, is adapted and used by permission of United

Church Press. It was published in 1977 as "Celebrating Advent in the Congregational Service of Worship" in *Advent: A Congregational Life/Intergenerational Experience*, copyright 1977 United Church Press.

OUTLINE

This order may be incorporated into a Service of Word and Sacrament or a Service of the Word as part of the opening acts or at the time of the reading of scripture.

The outline is followed each Sunday of Advent.

> **Introductory Sentences**
> **Reading of Scripture**
> **Lighting of the Candle(s)**
> **Prayer**
> **Hymn**

A Service of Word and Sacrament or a Service of the Word may continue.

FIRST SUNDAY: HOPE

During this order, one candle of the Advent wreath is lighted. It may be any candle in the wreath except the central Christ candle.

INTRODUCTORY SENTENCES

LEADER
**Today is the beginning of Advent—
the preparation time
for celebrating Christ's birth.
We are here because God's promises
to our ancestors came true
when Jesus was born.
God's promise is kept each Sunday
when we worship
because Christ is in our midst.
God will keep the promise
to come again in glory.**

READING OF SCRIPTURE

Read Isaiah 60:2.

LIGHTING OF THE CANDLE

LEADER
**We light this candle
to proclaim the coming
of the light of God
into the world.
With the coming of this light there is *hope*.
Because of Christ we not only have hope,
but we believe that good is stronger than evil.
God wants us to work for good in this world.**

Light one candle in the wreath.

PRAYER

LEADER
**O God, we thank you
that Jesus brought hope into our world.
By the good news of the Bible
you are still bringing hope to people.
Help us to be ready to welcome Jesus Christ
so that we may think good thoughts
and do good deeds
and so that we may be a people of hope
in our world.**

ALL
Amen.

HYMN

SECOND SUNDAY: PEACE

*The candle lighted on the first Sunday may be relighted
when other candles are lighted in preparation for the service. During this order, a second Advent candle, other
than the central Christ candle, is lighted.*

INTRODUCTORY SENTENCES

LEADER
**We gather around the Advent wreath today
knowing that we are not perfect—
that we all make mistakes and do bad things.
Only Jesus obeyed God fully.
Jesus helps us to live as God wants us to live.
Jesus gives us peace.**

READING OF SCRIPTURE

Read Isaiah 9:6-7.

LIGHTING OF THE CANDLE

LEADER
**We light this candle
to proclaim the coming
of the light of God
into the world.
With the coming of this light there is *peace*,
for Christ is called the "Prince of Peace."
Christ's name is also Emmanuel, "God with us."
The presence of Christ with us gives us peace day by day.**

Light the second candle in the wreath.

PRAYER

LEADER
**Eternal God, we thank you
that through all the years
you have given peace to your people.
Help us to have your peace in our lives.
We pray that, in this Advent season,
we may, by what we do,
show your presence to the sick, to the hungry,
and to the lonely,
so that they too may have peace.**

ALL
Amen.

HYMN

THIRD SUNDAY: LOVE

*The candles lighted on previous Sundays may be relighted
when other candles are lighted in preparation for the
service. During this order, a third Advent candle, other
than the central Christ candle, is lighted.*

INTRODUCTORY SENTENCES

LEADER
**As we gather around the Advent wreath today,
we rejoice that Christmas is a time of prayer
and of open hearts when we sing songs of joy.
Christmas is a time of worship—
the moment when the busiest of us pause in wonder.
Christmas happens when God comes to us
in love through Jesus Christ
and fills us with love for all humankind.**

READING OF SCRIPTURE

Read 1 John 4:9-11.

LIGHTING OF THE CANDLE

LEADER
**We light this candle to proclaim the coming
of the light of God into the world.
With the coming of this light there is *love*.
Such great love helps us to love God and one another.**

Light the third candle in the wreath.

PRAYER

LEADER
**O God, we thank you
that Jesus showed your love for every person—
babies and children, old people and young,
sick people and those who were strong,
rich people and those who were poor.
Come to us in this Advent season,
and give us love in our hearts for all people.**

ALL
Amen.

HYMN

FOURTH SUNDAY: JOY

The candles lighted on previous Sundays may be relighted when other candles are lighted in preparation for the service. During this order the fourth Advent candle, one other than the central Christ candle, is lighted.

INTRODUCTORY SENTENCES

LEADER
Soon we shall celebrate the birth of Jesus.
We worship God with joy in our hearts
as we are reminded of the words the angel said
on that first Christmas Day:
"Behold, I bring you good news of a great joy
which will come to all the people."[1]

READING OF SCRIPTURE

Read John 15: 9-11.

LIGHTING OF THE CANDLE

LEADER
We light this candle to proclaim the coming
of the light of God into the world.
With the coming of this light there is *joy*,
joy that is ours not only at Christmas but always.

Light the fourth candle in the wreath.

PRAYER

LEADER
O Holy One, as Christmas draws near,
there is a sense of excitement in the air.
We can feel a joy in our lives
and see it in those around us.

**Still, for some of us this is a sad time
because of unhappy things
that have happened in our lives.
Help us to have the joy
that does not depend on earthly happiness
but on you.
Help us to be filled with your joy
so that we may share it with a joyless world.**

ALL
Amen.

HYMN

CHRISTMAS: GOOD NEWS

*All candles in the Advent wreath remain unlighted through-
out the service until they are lighted during this order.*

INTRODUCTORY SENTENCES

LEADER
**Good evening [morning]!
On this Christmas Eve [Day] we are gathered
as God's people to celebrate again
what Christ's coming means to the world.
We join with Christians all over the world
who are celebrating tonight [today].**

READING OF SCRIPTURE

*A different person may read each passage: Isaiah 9:6;
Luke 2:10, 14; and Romans 5:5.*

LIGHTING OF THE CANDLES

LEADER
**Tonight [Today] we relight the four Advent candles
and recall what the good news means.**

A leader lights a candle while saying each word: **hope, peace, love, joy.**

LEADER
**Jesus Christ is the greatest gift
who makes all these other gifts possible.
So, we light the Christ candle now,
as we think about what Christ's coming means
to each one of us.**

A leader lights the central Christ candle.

PRAYER

LEADER
**We thank you, God,
for your gift of Jesus Christ to the entire world.
We thank you that Christ's coming
makes hope, peace, love, and joy possible
for every person in every nation.
Encourage us to do our part
to bring goodwill and peace to our families,
our churches, our neighborhoods, and the world.
Now let your Spirit put us in touch with you,
the living God, through the words and music
we hear tonight [today].
In the name of Jesus Christ we pray.**

ALL
Amen.

HYMN

Order for Ash Wednesday

INTRODUCTION

Ash Wednesday begins the season of Lent for many in the Christian church. The forty days of fasting (not counting Sundays) may begin with the imposition of the ashes on the foreheads of the faithful.

During the moving ancient ceremony, the ashes—from which Ash Wednesday gets its name—were placed on the foreheads of the faithful with the words from Genesis: "Remember that you are dust, and to dust you shall return." While this service was widely used after the seventh century, there is evidence that such a service originated in Gaul in the sixth century and was at first "confined to public penitents doing penance for grave and notorious sin, whom the clergy tried to comfort and encourage by submitting themselves to the same public humiliation."[2]

While the imposition of ashes is not widely used in the tradition of the United Church of Christ, the service of penitence and confession is used before the celebration of Holy Communion. Very often the service provides periods of extended silence for personal prayers and reflection.

Ashes may be placed on the forehead of each worshiper as part of the act of confession and as a sign of mortality and penitence. Traditionally, ashes are prepared before the service by burning palm or olive branches and grinding the ashes together with a little water or oil. The leader's thumb is used to transfer the mixture from a shallow bowl to each participant's forehead. A towel or napkin is provided for cleaning the hands of the leader.

The Order for Ash Wednesday is designed to begin a service. Following this order, a Service of Word and Sacrament or a Service of the Word begins, omitting the portions of that order which have occurred during the Order for Ash Wednesday.

This order is adapted from an order in both *The Book of Common Prayer* and the *Lutheran Book of Worship.*

The following scripture passages may be used on Ash Wednesday: Psalm 51:1-13; Psalm 103; Joel 2:12-19; 2 Corinthians 5:20b-6:2; and Matthew 6:1-6, 16-21.

OUTLINE

This order begins a Service of Word and Sacrament or a Service of the Word.

Prelude
Greeting
Sentences
Hymn of Adoration
Confession of Sin, including Imposition of Ashes

A hymn may be sung. A Service of Word and Sacrament or a Service of the Word follows, beginning with the reading of scripture and omitting the elements that have occurred during this order.

PRELUDE

The service may begin with music as the congregation gathers in a penitential atmosphere.

GREETING

All who are able may stand. This or another Lenten greeting may be used.

LEADER
**Let us look to Jesus,
the pioneer and perfecter of our faith,
who for the joy that was waiting
endured the cross.**[3]

SENTENCES

All who are able may stand. The leader may offer these and/or other words based on scripture.

LEADER
**Jesus came to preach good news to the poor,
to proclaim release to the captives
and recovery of sight to the blind,
to liberate those who are oppressed,
and to proclaim the year of God's favor.**[4]

HYMN OF ADORATION

CONFESSION OF SIN

The people may be seated. A leader may use these or other words to invite confession.

LEADER
**As disciples of Jesus Christ,
we are called to struggle against everything
that leads us away from the love of God and neighbor.
Repentance, fasting, prayer, study, and works of love
help us return to that love.**

**I invite you, therefore,
to commit yourselves to love God and neighbor
by confessing your sin
and by asking God for strength
to persevere in your Lenten discipline.**

Silence may be observed for reflection and prayer.

*The one presiding may lead the people in confession.
A period of silence also may be included following
each response.*

LEADER
Let us pray.

PEOPLE
Most holy and merciful God:
We confess to you and to one another,
and to the whole communion of saints
in heaven and on earth,
that we have sinned by our own fault
in thought, word, and deed,
by what we have done,
and by what we have left undone.

LEADER
**We have not loved you
with all our heart, and mind, and strength.
We have not loved our neighbors as ourselves.
We have not forgiven others
as we have been forgiven.**

PEOPLE
Have mercy on us, O God.

LEADER
**We have been deaf to your call
to serve as Christ served us.
We have not been true
to the mind of Christ.
We have grieved your Holy Spirit.**

PEOPLE
Have mercy on us, O God.

LEADER
**We confess to you, O God,
all our past unfaithfulness.
The pride, hypocrisy, and impatience in our lives,**

PEOPLE
We confess to you, O God.

LEADER
**Our self-indulgent appetites and ways
and our exploitation of other people,**

PEOPLE
We confess to you, O God.

LEADER
**Our anger at our own frustration
and our envy of those more fortunate than ourselves,**

PEOPLE
We confess to you, O God.

LEADER
**Our intemperate love of worldly goods and comforts
and our dishonesty in our daily life and work,**

PEOPLE
We confess to you, O God.

LEADER
**Our negligence in prayer and worship
and our failure to commend the faith that is in us,**

PEOPLE
We confess to you, O God.

LEADER
**Accept our repentance, O God,
for the wrongs we have done.
For our neglect of human need and suffering
and our indifference to injustice and cruelty,**

PEOPLE
Accept our repentance, O God.

LEADER
**For all false judgments,
for uncharitable thoughts toward our neighbors,**

**and for our prejudice and contempt
toward those who differ from us,**

PEOPLE
Accept our repentance, O God.

LEADER
**For our waste and pollution of your creation
and our lack of concern for those who come after us,**

PEOPLE
Accept our repentance, O God.

LEADER
**Restore us, O God,
and let your anger depart from us.**

PEOPLE
Favorably hear us, O God, for your mercy is great.
Amen.

Silence may be observed for confession and prayer.

*In her or his own words, a leader may invite those who
wish to receive ashes to come forward. Recipients who are
able may kneel or stand. The leader may apply ashes to
the forehead of each person with these or other words.*

A
LEADER
**Remember that
you are dust,
and to dust
you shall return.**

B
LEADER
**Turn away from your sins
and believe the good news.**

*After all who wish to receive ashes have received them, the
prayers of confession may be concluded with these or
other words.*

LEADER
**Accomplish in us, O God,
the work of your salvation,**

PEOPLE
That we may show forth your glory.

LEADER
By the cross and passion of our Savior,
PEOPLE
Bring us with all your saints
to the joy of Christ's resurrection.
ALL
Amen.

LEADER
addressing the congregation
**Almighty God does not desire the death of sinners,
but rather that they may turn
from their wickedness and live.
Therefore we implore God to grant us true repentance
and the Holy Spirit
that those things which we do this day
may be pleasing to God,
that the rest of our lives may be lived faithfully,
and that at the last we may come to God's eternal joy;
through Jesus the Christ.**
ALL
Thanks be to God!

*At the conclusion of this order, a hymn may be sung. A
Service of Word and Sacrament or a Service of the Word
follows, beginning with the reading of scripture and omitting elements that have occurred during this order.*

Order for
Palm/Passion Sunday

INTRODUCTION

Passion Sunday (*Judica me*), by the medieval period, was observed on the fifth Sunday in Lent, that is, the Sunday before Palm Sunday. In western Europe during the nineteenth century, the entire week was called "Passion Week." It was characterized by services in which Christ's suffering and death were liturgically anticipated and remembered. The most ancient witnesses, however, associate this practice not with the fifth Sunday in Lent but with the Saturday immediately before Palm Sunday. For this and other reasons, the liturgical reform movement today, with remarkable consensus, has chosen to see Palm/Passion Sunday as a unit. The distinction between Christ's triumphal entry into Jerusalem and the events of Christ's suffering and death is fully honored, with the greater emphasis being placed on the latter.

Palm/Passion Sunday is the gateway to Holy Week. It is appropriate that both Christ's triumphal entry into Jerusalem and the full account of Christ's passion, death, and burial be commemorated in the principal worship of the congregation on this day. Where this is not done, Christians are deprived of adequate preparation for the events of Holy Week, and those who attend only Sunday worship will experience a distorted transition from the triumph of Palm Sunday to the victory of an Easter devoid of the reality of Christ's suffering and death on the cross.

The triumphal entry into Jerusalem is best commemorated in an introduction to the service which includes a congregational procession into the sanctuary. Where this is done, arrangements should be made to accommodate those whose abilities do not include walking easily. When a full procession is not feasible, the ceremony may be held in the chancel with the choir and worship leaders representing the congregation in the procession.

The reading of the passion of Jesus Christ is an ancient practice worthy of the time it requires. If the full lesson is read in dramatic form by rehearsed participants, the congregation is enabled to visualize the historic events in the fullness of their power. A brief sermon may further explain an aspect of the passion message.

This order is to be used with a Service of Word and Sacrament or a Service of the Word. It replaces the beginning of the service and adds another Gospel lesson.

OUTLINE

This order replaces the beginning of a Service of Word and Sacrament or a Service of the Word.

> **Gathering**
> **Greeting**
> **Prayer**
> **Reading of the Palm Sunday Gospel**
> **Blessing of the Palms**
> **Hymn of Adoration**
> **Collect for Illumination**
> **Reading of Scripture**

A Service of Word and Sacrament or a Service of the Word follows, beginning at the point after the reading of scripture and omitting the elements that have occurred during this order.

GATHERING

*The people may assemble informally in a special place
outdoors, in a parish hall, or in the usual place of worship.
Palm branches or cuttings of evergreen or other trees may
be distributed to all as they arrive or may be placed where
they are visible to all present and may be distributed after
the blessing. The church bell may be sounded to announce
the beginning of the service.*

GREETING

*The one presiding may give necessary instructions and may
lead a responsive greeting with these or similar words.*

A

LEADER
Hosanna!

PEOPLE
Hosanna in the highest!

ALL
Praise be to God!

B

LEADER
**Lift your heads and behold
Emmanuel, "God with us."**

PEOPLE
Behold our God
who comes riding
on an ass,
the ruler who dares to be
last rather than first.

PRAYER

LEADER
Christ is with us.

PEOPLE
Christ is in our midst.

LEADER
Let us pray.

PEOPLE
Merciful God,
as we enter Holy Week
and gather at your house of prayer,
turn our hearts again to Jerusalem,
to the life, death, and resurrection of Jesus Christ,

that united with Christ
and all the faithful
we may one day enter in triumph
the city not made by human hands,
the new Jerusalem,
eternal in the heavens,
where with you
and the Holy Spirit,
Christ lives in glory for ever.
Amen.

READING OF THE PALM SUNDAY GOSPEL

*The account of Jesus' entry into Jerusalem may be read.
The people may stand or sit depending upon physical
arrangements, individuals' abilities, and local custom. The
ecumenical lectionary suggests the following cycle of
Gospel lessons.*

YEAR A: Matthew 21:1-11
YEAR B: Mark 11:1-11 or John 12:12-16
YEAR C: Luke 19:28-40

BLESSING OF THE PALMS

*The one presiding may lead the congregation in a prayer
of thanksgiving and blessing using these or similar words.*

LEADER
God be with you.

PEOPLE
And also with you.

LEADER
Let us give thanks to God Most High.

PEOPLE
It is right to give God thanks and praise.

LEADER
Let us pray.

ALL
O God, who in Jesus Christ
triumphantly entered Jerusalem,
heralding a week of pain and sorrow,
be with us now
as we follow the way of the cross.
In these events of defeat and victory,
you have sealed the closeness
of death and resurrection,
of humiliation and exaltation.
We thank you for these branches
that promise to become for us
symbols of martyrdom and majesty.
Bless them and us
that their use this day may announce in our time
that Christ has come
and that Christ will come again.
Amen! Come, Christ Jesus!

If the palms were not distributed earlier, they may be distributed at this time. If there is to be a procession into or around the sanctuary, the following words may be used to introduce it.

LEADER
Let us go forth in peace.

PEOPLE
In the name of Christ.
Amen.

HYMN OF ADORATION

A suitable hymn may be sung as all enter the sanctuary or as the choir and worship leaders process to their places.

COLLECT FOR ILLUMINATION

The people may be seated. This collect or another asking for open hearts and attentive minds may be used prior to the first lesson.

LEADER
Blessed is the one who comes in the name of our God.

PEOPLE
Hosanna in the highest!

LEADER
Let us pray.

PEOPLE
Eternal God,
whose whisper silences the shouts of the mighty,
quiet within us every voice but your own.
Speak to us now
through the suffering and death of Jesus Christ
that by the power of your Holy Spirit
we may receive grace to show forth Christ's love
in lives committed to your service.

ALL
Amen.

READING OF SCRIPTURE

It is fitting on Passion Sunday that in addition to the Old Testament and Epistle lessons, chosen according to the lectionary suggestions, the Gospel of Christ's passion be read in dramatic form as the final lesson. With the congregation seated, a narrator and individuals or groups assigned the parts of the speakers in the lesson may recite it in full, reading with dramatic effect. Several rehearsals may be needed.

The ecumenical lectionary suggests the following cycle of passion lessons to be read following the selected Old Testament and Epistle lessons.

YEAR A: Matthew 26:14 through Matthew 27:66

YEAR B: Mark 14:1 through Mark 15:47

YEAR C: Luke 22:14 through Luke 23:56

A Service of Word and Sacrament or a Service of the Word follows, beginning at the point after the reading of scripture and omitting the elements that have occurred.

Order of the Table
for Maundy Thursday

INTRODUCTION

Maundy is the English form of the Latin word meaning *commandment*. Jesus' new commandment to "love one another even as I have loved you" is the focus of Maundy Thursday. This love is demonstrated in Jesus' example of servanthood and the gift of Jesus' self in Holy Communion. The theme of servanthood is sometimes included in the observance of Maundy Thursday through a service of foot-washing. The Order for Tenebrae follows the conclusion of a Maundy Thursday service of the table in some local churches.

Although some local churches traditionally celebrate the institution of Holy Communion in their usual place of worship, others prefer a less formal setting. This service is intended to be informal and intimate. It may be held in the auditorium or dining hall of the church building and includes a common meal. The service may take place around the tables where the meal is served.

The tables may be clustered around a primary table. The pastor, her or his family who are present, and a deacon or other representative of the church and his or her family may sit at the primary table. A representative may be appointed to each of the other tables. Families are encouraged to sit together, without making single people feel excluded.

A simple table setting is appropriate. A small glass may be at each place setting at every table, and candles may be placed on each table. A small loaf of bread and a pitcher of wine or grape juice for each table may be placed in a central position on the primary table. It is helpful for each participant to have an order of service placed at each plate.

Plan a simple meal which requires no servers except at the beginning. Placing the food and beverage on the table as the people gather allows all to participate fully in the meal and the service.

OUTLINE

Arrival and Informal Greeting
Greeting
Prayer
Meal
Introduction
Hymn
Reading of Scripture
Meditation
Silence
Invitation
Communion Prayer
Prayer of Our Savior
Sharing the Elements
Prayer of Thanksgiving
Hymn of Thanksgiving
Dismissal and Benediction

ARRIVAL AND INFORMAL GREETING

If possible have subdued lighting. As the people arrive, the candles may be lighted. People may be encouraged to greet one another and to gather around tables set in advance for the meal.

GREETING

At the appointed time, the pastor or another representative may greet those gathered in the name of Jesus Christ, welcome them to the service, and lead them in a litany.

LEADER
**We are gathered in the presence of God,
who asks us to choose
between life and death,
between blessing and curse.**

PEOPLE
We are gathered like the people of Israel,
who were challenged to choose the way of life.

LEADER
Like them, we often follow the ways of death.

PEOPLE
Yet, like them, we have the freedom each day
to begin anew by the grace of God.

LEADER
**By our presence here,
we are saying that we choose life.**

ALL
**Let us praise the God of love and life
who has called us to this place.
Amen.**

PRAYER

A leader may offer a prayer of thanksgiving for the day and the meal.

MEAL

A simple meal may be shared and the tables cleared, leaving individual glasses and candles.

INTRODUCTION

A leader may offer words of greeting and introduction.

HYMN

Words may be printed on an order of service.

READING OF SCRIPTURE

The lessons for Maundy Thursday may be read. The ecumenical lectionary suggests Psalm 116:12-19 and:

YEAR A: Exodus 12:1-14, 1 Corinthians 11:23-26, John 13:1-15

YEAR B: Exodus 24:3-8, 1 Corinthians 10:16-17, Mark 14:12-26

YEAR C: Jeremiah 31:31-34, Hebrews 10:16-25, Luke 22:7-20

MEDITATION

A leader may offer a brief sermon on the lessons.

SILENCE

The people may be invited to prepare themselves for Holy Communion by joining in silence, reflection, and confession at the tables.

INVITATION

LEADER

This table is open to all who confess Jesus as the Christ and seek to follow Christ's way.

Come to this sacred table
not because you must,
but because you may.
Come not because you are fulfilled,
but because in your emptiness
you stand in need of God's mercy and assurance.
Come not to express an opinion,
but to seek a presence
and to pray for a spirit.
Come to this table, then,
sisters and brothers, as you are.
Partake and share.
It is spread for you and me
that we might again know
that God has come to us,
shared our common lot,
and invited us to join the people of God's new age.[5]

COMMUNION PRAYER

The pastor may offer a prayer of consecration and thanksgiving using his or her own words or one of the prayers from the Services of Word and Sacrament. Elements of the prayer are outlined on page 49.

PRAYER OF OUR SAVIOR

SHARING THE ELEMENTS

The deacons or other representatives may come to the primary table and receive a pitcher and a loaf for each table. At the tables, each person may break the bread and pass it, then may fill a glass and pass the pitcher. A familiar hymn, such as "Let Us Break Bread Together," may be sung during the passing of the elements. According to the custom of the church, individuals may partake as the elements reach them or may hold each element so that all may partake together.

PRAYER OF THANKSGIVING

LEADER

**O God, by coming to your table
we receive more gifts than we deserve.
We give thanks for Jesus Christ,
through whom we receive life
and in whom we are bound in covenant.
Renew us so we may willingly serve as Christ served.
Amen.**

HYMN OF THANKSGIVING

*All may sing the last stanza of "Let Us Break Bread
Together" or another hymn of thanksgiving.*

DISMISSAL AND BENEDICTION

*A leader may dismiss the people with words of comfort
and challenge and a blessing informed by scripture.*

Order for Footwashing

INTRODUCTION

In footwashing the church recalls the example of Jesus' humility as Good Friday drew near and Jesus performed this menial domestic chore for the protesting disciples. It was the custom in the ancient world that provision be made for the feet of guests to be bathed when they arrived at the home of their host. This task was ordinarily done by servants or people of low rank in the larger family. The Gospel of John (13:1-17), where the story is recounted, does not tell why this act of hospitality was omitted when Jesus and the disciples arrived for the meal. It is clear that no one but Jesus volunteered to rise from the table and perform the servile but gracious act. Jesus waited for others to remedy the oversight, but none did. It was *during* the meal that Jesus rose from the table and began the task in silence.

The church observes footwashing because Jesus offered it as an example whereby Christians may mutually observe the place of humility and service in the Christian life. It is not itself the only or highest example of humility and service, but symbolically it demonstrates them in great power.

A service of footwashing may be held at any time, but it is traditionally included in the evening service of Maundy Thursday in Holy Week.

Careful preparation is necessary. It is important that people be given notice of the nature of the service and that participants be encouraged to use footwear that is easily removed. The service may be observed in a room where people can be seated in a manner to permit access for the washing. It is recommended that basins be arranged for approximately every ten people, along with an adequate supply of towels. If footwashing is held in a sanctuary containing pews, an area at the front of the sanctuary may be arranged for a small number at a time to participate. If footwashing takes place with representatives only, with one person washing the feet of a few people chosen for that purpose, it is suggested that the washing be done in such a way as to be seen by the entire congregation.

Footwashing may take place within a Service of Word and Sacrament or a Service of the Word, or it may be held as a full service.

OUTLINE

This order may be used alone. When it is incorporated into a Service of Word and Sacrament or a Service of the Word, the portion of the Order for Footwashing before the introduction may be omitted. An affirmation of faith and a hymn may precede this order.

> **Call to Worship**
> **Hymn**
> **Confession of Sin**
> **Assurance of Pardon**
> **Telling the Story**
> **Sermon**
> **Hymn**
> **Introduction**
> **Footwashing**
> **Prayer of Thanksgiving**

A Service of Word and Sacrament or a Service of the Word may continue, or a hymn and benediction may close the order.

If footwashing is to be included within another service, following the sermon all who are able may stand and unite in an affirmation of faith and a hymn. The lesson from John may be read in part or full. The Order for Footwashing may begin with the introduction on page 203.

CALL TO WORSHIP

All who are able may stand. A leader may open the service with these or other words.

A

LEADER
**Make a joyful noise
to the Holy One,
all the lands!
Serve God with gladness!
Come into God's presence
with singing!**

PEOPLE
For the Holy One is good;
God's steadfast love endures
for ever,
and God's faithfulness
to all generations.[6]

B

LEADER
**Create in me a clean heart,
O God,
and put a new and right
spirit within me.**

PEOPLE
Cast me not away
from your presence,
and take not your
Holy Spirit from me.

LEADER
**Purge me from my sin,
and I shall be pure;**

PEOPLE
Wash me,
and I shall be clean indeed.[7]

HYMN

All who are able may stand as a hymn about service, humility, penitence, or related themes is sung.

CONFESSION OF SIN

All may be seated or those who are able may kneel. The person presiding may lead the people in confession, using these or other words.

LEADER
**If we say we have no sin,
we deceive ourselves,
and the truth is not in us.**

PEOPLE
If we confess our sins,
God is faithful and just
and will forgive our sins
and cleanse us from all unrighteousness.[8]

LEADER
**Brothers and sisters in Christ,
let us confess our sins in silence
and ask God for the forgiveness we need.**

Extended silence may follow for reflection and prayer.

LEADER
Let us pray.

A

ALL
**Gracious God,
we have denied
your intentions for us.
We have preferred our way
to Christ's way.
We have served ourselves
and things we have made.
We have disobeyed your
commandment to love
others as we love ourselves.
Forgive us,
and awaken us to faith
and to a life of service;
through Jesus Christ,
who came not to be served,
but to serve,
and who served you
even to death,
for our redemption.
Amen.**

B

ALL
**Have mercy on me, O God,
according to your
loving-kindness;
in your great compassion
blot out my offenses.
Wash me through
and through
from my wickedness and
cleanse me from my sin.
For I know my
transgressions, and
my sin is ever before me.
Amen.**[9]

ASSURANCE OF PARDON

A

LEADER
**While we were yet helpless,
at the right time
Christ died for the ungodly.**

PEOPLE
The love of God for us
is shown in this:
While we were yet sinners,
Christ died for us.[10]

B

LEADER
**We have, then,
my sisters and brothers,
complete freedom to go
into the most holy place,
God's very presence,
by means of the death
of Jesus.**

PEOPLE
We have a great priest
in charge of the house
of God.

LEADER
**So let us come near to God
with a sincere heart
and a sure faith;**

PEOPLE
With hearts that have been
purified from a guilty
conscience,
and with bodies washed
with clean water.[11]

TELLING THE STORY

*The people may sit or those who are able may stand. The
reading may be spoken by one voice, used as a responsive
reading, or presented dramatically by a narrator and two
others taking the roles of Jesus and of Peter.*

NARRATOR (LEADER)
**It was now the day before the Passover festival.
Jesus and his disciples were at supper.
So Jesus rose from the table,
took off his outer garment,
and tied a towel around his waist.**

**Then Jesus poured some water into a washbasin
and began to wash the disciples' feet
and dry them with the towel around his waist.**

**Jesus came to Simon Peter,
who said to him:**

PETER (PEOPLE)
Are you going to wash my feet, Lord?

NARRATOR (LEADER)
Jesus answered Peter:

JESUS (PEOPLE)
You do not understand now what I am doing,
but you will understand later.

NARRATOR (LEADER)
Peter declared:

PETER (PEOPLE)
Never at any time will you wash my feet!

NARRATOR (LEADER)
Jesus answered:

JESUS (PEOPLE)
If I do not wash your feet,
you will no longer be my disciple.

NARRATOR (LEADER)
Simon Peter answered:

PETER (PEOPLE)
Lord, do not only wash my feet, then!
Wash my hands and head, too!

NARRATOR (LEADER)
Jesus said:

JESUS (PEOPLE)
Anyone who has taken a bath is completely clean
and does not have to wash,
other than the feet.

NARRATOR (LEADER)
**After washing their feet,
Jesus put the outer garment back on,
returned to his place at the table,
and said:**

JESUS (PEOPLE)
Do you understand what I have just done to you?

You call me Teacher and Lord,
and it is right that you do so,
because that is what I am.

I, your Lord and Teacher,
have just washed your feet.
You, then, should wash one another's feet.
I have set an example for you,
so that you will do just what I have done for you.

Silence may be observed for reflection before the lesson is concluded.

NARRATOR (LEADER)
Jesus said:

JESUS (PEOPLE)
I am telling you the truth:
No slave is greater
than the master who is served,
and no messenger is greater
than the one who sends the message.
Now that you know this truth,
how happy you will be
if you put it into practice.[12]

SERMON

HYMN

All who are able may stand.

INTRODUCTION

All who are able may stand as a leader introduces footwashing in the following or similar words. Following this introduction, others may assist in directing the people in the procedures to be carried out.

LEADER

Friends in Christ,
we are reminded by the scriptures,
in diverse words and symbols,
of what God intends for us.
The water of our baptism is a cleansing sign
of our dying and rising with Christ.

The bread and wine of Holy Communion are saving food,
announcing to us again Christ's sacrifice and victory
for our salvation.

Now, at Christ's command,
we share the water of humility,
and stoop,
as once Christ stooped,
to wash the feet of others.

Ⓐ *for use when all partici-*
pate in footwashing

LEADER
With Peter,
we also open ourselves
to another
and allow our feet
to be washed.

PEOPLE
How happy we will be
if we put into practice
the truth of humility.

Ⓑ *for use when only*
representatives participate
in footwashing

LEADER
How happy we will be
if we put into practice
the truth of humility.

PEOPLE
With God's help,
may we each practice
humility.

FOOTWASHING

The people may be seated for the footwashing. Those who
wish to participate may remove their footwear and place
it under their chairs. If the footwashing is to be done by
representatives only, those chosen to have their feet
washed may move to the front of the congregation, be
seated in chairs provided, remove their footwear, and
place it under their chairs.

To begin the footwashing, a deacon or another appointed person kneels before the person in the next seat, places that person's feet in the basin one at a time, lifts and dries each foot, and rises. The person whose feet have been washed also may rise, exchange the peace with the one who did the washing, and likewise turn to the person sitting next, kneel, and repeat the footwashing. People who have had their feet washed and have washed the feet of another may be seated and replace their footwear. The feet of the one who began the footwashing are to be washed before the cycle is completed. Adjustments will need to be made for those whose abilities do not include some of these physical movements.

If this is to be done by representatives only, the one presiding or another appointed officer of the church may wash the feet of each of the representatives and may also greet each in an exchange of peace.

PRAYER OF THANKSGIVING

When the footwashing is completed, all who are able may stand. The one presiding may lead the people in this or another prayer of thanksgiving.

LEADER
Let us pray.

ALL
**O God, we give you thanks
for the gift of Jesus Christ,
the only one begotten by you before all worlds.
We thank you for the splendor
of Christ's life of service.
We thank you for symbols of love and humility.
We ask that you will strengthen us
for the service to which you call us,
that we may find in lowering ourselves, in washing,
and in all other acts of mercy,
the fullness of life
that we see in Jesus Christ,**

**who with you and the Holy Spirit,
lives in exaltation,
one God, for ever and ever.
Amen.**

When this order is observed alone, the service may be concluded with a hymn and a benediction. When it is incorporated within a Service of Word and Sacrament or a Service of the Word, that service continues, omitting the affirmation of faith.

Order for Tenebrae

INTRODUCTION

Tenebrae is the Latin term for *shadows*. It is a service of lessons accompanied by the gradual extinguishing of lights. Although many local churches observe the ceremony at the conclusion of the Maundy Thursday Service of Word and Sacrament, it is historically associated with the evenings of Wednesday, Thursday, and Friday of Holy Week. The readings on these evenings commemorated the events of the following day. On Wednesday, they commemorated the Last Supper, the betrayal, and the arrest; on Thursday, Christ's passion, trial, and death; and on Friday, Christ's burial and the destitution of the disciples. In the service presented here, these events are combined in one ceremony.

Tenebrae may be held as a full service, or the readings and extinguishing of lights may be incorporated within another service.

It is recommended that twelve candles, representing the twelve disciples, and a larger candle, representing Christ, be placed where they may be seen by all. No other candles should be lighted for this service. A careful rehearsal for all who share the leadership of the service is essential to its effectiveness. When Tenebrae follows Holy Communion on Maundy Thursday, it is appropriate that the readers and candles be arranged around an extended communion table. On other occasions, the readers may be at a lectern or near the candle to be extinguished following the reading. Regardless of their position, it is of great importance that the congregation be able to hear and understand the readings from scripture.

OUTLINE

This order may be used alone. When it is incorporated into another service, only the readings and extinguishing of lights need to be used. In a Service of Word and Sacrament, the readings and extinguishing of lights may follow the post-communion prayer of thanksgiving. Then the instructions for departure are also followed.

> **Prelude**
> **Sentences**
> **Hymn of Adoration**
> **Collect**
> **Lighting of the Candles**
> **Confession of Sin**
> **Prayer for Mercy**
> **Assurance of Pardon**
> **Hymn, Anthem, or Other Music**
> **Readings and Extinguishing of Lights**
> **Lord's Prayer**
> **Departure**

A continuing vigil may begin at the conclusion of the Order for Tenebrae.

When Tenebrae is observed as a full service, the complete order below may be used. When it is incorporated within another service, only the readings and extinguishing of lights need to be used, with consideration given to the instructions for departure.

All candles may remain unlighted until "O Gracious Light" or an anthem is sung at the time designated for lighting them.

PRELUDE

The service may begin with music as the congregation gathers.

SENTENCES

All who are able may stand for one or both of these.

A

LEADER
**Jesus said:
I am the light of the world.**

PEOPLE
Anyone who follows me will not walk in darkness,
but will have the light of life.[13]

B

LEADER
**If I say,
"Let the darkness cover me,
and the light around me turn to night,"
darkness is not dark to you, O God.**

PEOPLE
The night is as bright as the day;
darkness and light to you are both alike.[14]

HYMN OF ADORATION

All who are able may stand as a hymn on the theme of God's light is sung.

COLLECT

All who are able may stand while this or another opening prayer is said.

LEADER
God be with you.

PEOPLE
And with you also.

LEADER
Let us pray.

ALL
Gracious God,
you give us the sun to illumine the day
and the moon and stars to shine by night.
Kindle in us the flame of your love
that our lives may shed abroad the radiance of your light
and the world may be full of the splendor of your glory;
through Jesus Christ,
the Sun of Righteousness.
Amen.

LIGHTING OF THE CANDLES

The people may be seated. The candles to be used in the service may be lighted during the singing of "O Gracious Light" ("Phos Hilaron"*) or another hymn. The text here is adapted from the ancient version of the* "Phos Hilaron."

ALL
O gracious Light,
Pure brightness of the eternal Creator in heaven,
O Jesus Christ, holy and blessed!

Now as we come to the setting of the sun,
And our eyes behold your vesper light,
We sing your praises, Holy God, One in Trinity.

You are worthy at all times
To be praised by happy voices,
O Christ of God, O giver of life,
And to be glorified through all the worlds.

CONFESSION OF SIN

The people may be seated or those who are able may kneel. A leader may invite the people to confess in silence or may incorporate a unison prayer and silence. This or another call to confession and prayer may be used.

LEADER
Brothers and sisters,
we are called to be children of the day
and not children of the night.

PEOPLE
Let us approach the throne of grace
that we may receive mercy.

LEADER
Let us pray.

ALL
Gracious God,
our sins are too heavy to carry,
too real to hide,
and too deep to undo.
Forgive what our lips tremble to name,
what our hearts can no longer bear,
and what has become for us
a consuming fire of judgment.
Set us free from a past that we cannot change;
open to us a future in which we can be changed;
and grant us grace
to grow more and more
in your likeness and image;
through Jesus Christ,
the light of the world.
Amen.

PRAYER FOR MERCY

The Kyrie, Trisagion, *or another prayer for mercy may be said or sung. Musical settings are on pages 449, 450, and 459.*

A

LEADER
Lord, have mercy.

PEOPLE
Christ, have mercy.

LEADER
Lord, have mercy.

B

LEADER
**Holy God,
Holy and mighty,
Holy Immortal One,**

ALL
Have mercy upon us.

ASSURANCE OF PARDON

LEADER
**This is the message we have heard from Christ
and proclaim to you:
God is light.**

PEOPLE
If we walk in the light
as Christ is in the light,
we have communion with one another,
and the blood of Jesus Christ cleanses us
from all sin.[15]

HYMN, ANTHEM, OR OTHER MUSIC

*A hymn, anthem, or other music about Christ's passion
may be offered.*

READINGS AND EXTINGUISHING OF LIGHTS

*The people may be seated. When used in a Service of
Word and Sacrament, this ceremony may follow the post-
communion hymn. When used in a Service of the Word, it
may replace the reading of scripture.*

*As a dramatic portrayal of the desertion of Christ by the
disciples, twelve people extinguish the candles and leave
the room in sequence. These same people may read the
assigned lessons. Diverse numbers of readings and
candles may be used. If twelve readings are chosen, one*

candle may be extinguished after each reading. If fewer than twelve readings are chosen, those without lessons may extinguish their candles in silence, one at a time. The Christ candle may be extinguished or momentarily hidden.

The schedule of readings includes eight lessons taken from all four Gospels. If twelve lessons are desired, then other appropriate ones may be added. An alternative schedule may also be developed by dividing into twelve sections the long passion narrative in the Gospel of John (Chapters 13-19).

When this order is used on Maundy Thursday following Holy Communion, it is suggested that the candles and twelve representatives be placed about an extended communion table. The lessons may be read while the representatives are seated. After each lesson, the reader may extinguish a candle and leave the room.

FIRST READING
Shadow of Betrayal   Matthew 26:20-25
Candle one is extinguished; the reader may leave the room.

SECOND READING
Shadow of Desertion   Matthew 26:31-35
Candle two is extinguished; the reader may leave the room.

THIRD READING
Agony of the Soul   Luke 22:39-44
Candle three is extinguished; the reader may leave the room.

FOURTH READING
Unshared Vigil   Mark 14:32-41
Candle four is extinguished; the reader may leave the room.

FIFTH READING
"Father, the hour is come"   John 17:1-6
Candle five is extinguished; the reader may leave the room.

SIXTH READING
"That they may all be one"   John 17:15-22
Candle six is extinguished; the reader may leave the room.

SEVENTH READING
Arrest in the Garden   John 18:1-5
Candle seven is extinguished; the reader may leave the room.

EIGHTH READING
Shadow of the Cross   Mark 15:16-20
Candle eight is extinguished; the reader may leave the room.

In silence, the remaining four candles representing the disciples are extinguished in sequence by four people who may also leave the room.

FINAL READING
The Word was God   John 1:1-4,14,10,12; 3:19,
       paraphrased

A person may read these or other appropriate verses from a location near the central Christ candle.

READER
**Before the world was created,
the Word already existed;
the Word was with God,
and the Word was the same as God.
From the beginning the Word was with God.
Through the Word
God made all things;
not one thing in all creation was made without the Word.
The Word was the source of life,
and this life brought light to humanity.**

**The Word became a human being
and, full of grace and truth,
lived among us.**

**The Word was in the world;
and though God made the world through the Word,
the world did not recognize the Word.
Some, however, did receive the Word
and believed in the Word.
So the Word gave them the right
to become God's children.**

This is how the judgment works:
The light has come into the world,
but people love the shadows rather than the light,
because their deeds are evil.[16]

At the conclusion of the reading, the reader may extinguish the Christ candle or may remove it from the vision of the people. A loud noise may be made as this is done to signify Christ's death. After a pause, the candle may be relighted or returned to its place to stand as a symbolic promise of the resurrection.

LORD'S PRAYER

Standing, sitting, or kneeling, all may sing or say the prayer received from Jesus Christ.

DEPARTURE

All may leave the darkened church in silence. The continuity of events leading to Easter is best symbolized if the benediction is omitted at this service. A vigil may begin at the conclusion of this order in churches where one is observed from Maundy Thursday until the first service of Easter.

Order for Good Friday

INTRODUCTION

The Order for Good Friday is intended to rehearse the passion story of our Savior Jesus Christ. While the mood is solemn, it is also one of hope, looking forward to the great Easter celebration.

Some traditions prepare a service so that the seven last words of Jesus from the cross form the theme for the meditations.

In some traditions, a rough-hewn cross is carried into the chancel during the service.

The service offered here is taken from the ancient Christian tradition of the fourth and fifth centuries.[17] The structure of the prayers of intercession seeks to capture the need of the penitent to hear the story of the passion and also to pray for the whole of society. In the ancient services, much of the time the congregation was invited to stand to help participants understand the suffering of Jesus on the cross. Many times lay members shared in the leadership by reading the passion story to create dramatic interest.

OUTLINE

Sentences
Invocation
Reading of Scripture
Silence
Hymn
Reading of the Passion Story
Hymn
Sermon
Prayer
Prayer of Our Savior
Meditation about the Cross
Hymn
Benediction

*The service is often without instrumental music except to
support singing by the congregation. The leaders may
enter in silence.*

SENTENCES

*All who are able may stand. A leader may offer the
following and/or other sentences from scripture.*

LEADER
**Blessed be our God,
for ever and ever.
Amen.**

INVOCATION

All who are able may stand.

LEADER
Let us pray.
ALL
**Almighty God,
we ask you to look with mercy on your family
for whom our Savior Jesus Christ was willing
to be betrayed,
to be given over to the hands of sinners,
and to suffer death on the cross;
who now lives and reigns with you
and the Holy Spirit,
one God, for ever and ever.
Amen.**

READING OF SCRIPTURE

*The people may be seated as Hosea 6:1-6, Isaiah 52:13-
53:12, or other scripture passages are read.*

SILENCE

Silence may be observed for reflection and prayer.

HYMN

All who are able may stand as "O Sacred Head, Now Wounded" or another hymn is sung.

READING OF THE PASSION STORY

The passion story may be read by one person, or a different person may read each part.

PART I
Mark 9:30-37; 10:17-23, 46-52

PART II
Mark 11:1-11, 14:1-25
John 13:2-17

PART III
John 12:20-28, 13:31-14:10
Matthew 26:36-56

PART IV
John 17:1-10, 17:16-23
Luke 22:54-71
Matthew 27:3-10

PART V
Mark 15:1-14
Luke 23:4-11
Matthew 27:11-31

PART VI (SEVEN LAST WORDS)
Luke 23:26-32
Matthew 27:33, 34, 37
Luke 23:35, 36; 23:34, 39-43
John 19:25-27
Luke 23:44-45
Matthew 27:46
John 19:28-30
Luke 23:46

PART VII
Matthew 27:51-66

HYMN

All who are able may stand for a hymn on a passion theme.

SERMON

PRAYER

A leader may guide the people in a bidding prayer, with silence for the prayers of the people. Some or all of the following sections may be used.

LEADER
**Let us pray, brothers and sisters,
for the holy church of God
throughout the world
that God may guide it
and gather it together
so that we may worship God
in peace and tranquility.**

Silent prayer.

LEADER
**Almighty and eternal God,
you have shown your glory
to all nations in Jesus Christ.
Guide the work of the church.
Help it to persevere in faith,
to proclaim your name,
and to offer salvation to people everywhere.
We ask this through Christ our Savior.**

PEOPLE
Amen.

LEADER
**Let us pray for our pastor(s) and other ordained ministers,
for all servants of the church,
and for all the people of God.**

Silent prayer.

LEADER
**Almighty and eternal God,
your Spirit guides the church and makes it holy.
Strengthen and uphold our pastor(s) and our leaders;
keep them in health and safety
for the good of the church,
and help each of us to do faithfully the work
to which you have called us.
We ask this through Christ our Savior.**

PEOPLE
Amen.

LEADER
**Let us pray for those preparing for baptism,
that God may make them responsive to God's love
and give them new life in Jesus Christ.**

Silent prayer.

LEADER
**Almighty and eternal God,
you continually bless the church with new members.
Increase the faith and understanding
of those preparing for baptism.
Give them a new birth as your children.
Keep them in the faith and communion
of your holy church.
We ask this through Christ our Savior.**

PEOPLE
Amen.

LEADER
**Let us pray for those who do not believe in Christ,
that the light of the Holy Spirit may show them
the way of salvation.**

Silent prayer.

LEADER
**Almighty and eternal God,
enable those who do not acknowledge Christ
to receive the truth of the gospel.**

Help us, your people,
to grow in love for one another,
to grasp more fully the mystery of your Godhead,
and so to become more perfect witnesses of your love
in the sight of all people.
We ask this through Christ our Savior.

PEOPLE
Amen.

LEADER
Let us pray for those who do not believe in God,
that they may find the God
who is the author and goal of our existence.

Silent prayer.

LEADER
Almighty and eternal God,
you created humanity
so that all might long to know you
and have peace in you.
Grant that,
in spite of the hurtful things
that stand in their way,
all may recognize in the lives of Christians
the tokens of your love and mercy
and gladly acknowledge you
as the one true God of us all.
We ask this through Christ our Savior.

PEOPLE
Amen.

LEADER
Let us pray for those who serve in public office,
that God may guide their minds and hearts,
so that all of us may live in true peace and freedom.

Silent prayer.

LEADER
Almighty and eternal God,
you are the champion of the poor and oppressed.

In your goodness,
watch over those in authority
so that people everywhere may enjoy
justice, peace, freedom,
and a share in the goodness of your creation.
We ask this through Christ our Savior.

PEOPLE
Amen.

LEADER
Let us pray that the almighty and merciful God
may heal the sick,
comfort the dying,
give safety to travelers,
free those unjustly deprived of liberty,
and rid the world of falsehood, hunger, and disease.

Silent prayer.

LEADER
Almighty and eternal God,
you give strength to the weary
and new courage to those who have lost heart.
Hear the prayers of all who call on you
in any trouble
that they may have the joy
of receiving your help in their need.
We ask this through Christ our Savior.

PEOPLE
Amen.

PRAYER OF OUR SAVIOR

Standing, sitting, or kneeling, all may sing or say the prayer received from Jesus Christ.

MEDITATION ABOUT THE CROSS

If a cross is a focal point for the congregation, the following may be said.

LEADER
**Behold the cross
on which hung the salvation of the whole world.**

PEOPLE
Come, let us worship the Christ,
the child of God.

LEADER
**Behold the cross
on which hung the salvation of the whole world.**

PEOPLE
Come, let us worship the Christ,
the child of God.

LEADER
**Behold the cross
on which hung the salvation of the whole world.**

PEOPLE
Come, let us worship the Christ,
the child of God.

Silence may be observed for meditation and prayers.

HYMN

A hymn may be sung on the theme of the merciful Christ.

BENEDICTION

LEADER
**We adore you,
O Christ,
and we bless you.**

PEOPLE
By your holy cross you have redeemed the world.

*The leaders may leave in silence. The people may depart
quietly as they finish their private meditation and prayers.*

Order for the Great Vigil of Easter

INTRODUCTION

The Great Vigil of Easter, scheduled anytime after sunset on Holy Saturday and before sunrise on Easter Sunday, is an ancient liturgy of the church with deep roots in scripture. It is a full liturgy, rich in symbolism and dramatic in form. It is a complex and lengthy service that requires careful advance planning, considerable participation by the congregation, and a thorough rehearsal for all its leaders.

The Great Vigil of Easter seeks to proclaim the cosmic significance of God's saving acts in history through four integrally related services held on the same occasion. It appeals to the total person through various human senses. Music plays an important role in the effectiveness of the vigil. Consequently, the church's music leaders and choirs will need adequate time to prepare. In this vigil a cantor usually sings parts that otherwise might be read.

The vigil begins with the service of light. By the use of fire, candles, words, movement, and music, it seeks to portray the pilgrim people of God following the *pillar of fire* given in Jesus Christ, the light of the world. A tall Easter or paschal candle, plain or decorated, is used in procession to represent Jesus Christ. Individual candles may also be lighted from the Easter candle to dramatize "a flame divided but undimmed." Planning for the procession should include consideration of those who do not move easily.

The vigil continues with a Service of the Word. From two to twelve lessons from the Old Testament are read in the minimally lighted church. The lessons seek to portray a panoramic view of all that God has done for the human family in preparation for the coming of Jesus Christ. They are read at length, unhurriedly, in the spirit of those who patiently watch and wait in the true sense of the word *vigil*—with alertness. At the end of the readings from the

Old Testament, the Service of the Word reaches a climactic moment when the gloria or another hymn of the church is sung to herald Christ's resurrection. In some traditions, the church bell and the organ, silent since Maundy Thursday evening, are used again for the first time during the singing of this major hymn. The Epistle and Gospel lessons are then read, and a sermon may be preached.

The service of water follows. This is a service of the sacrament of baptism or the renewal of baptismal vows. Water plays a prominent role in this service. It may be used to sprinkle the entire congregation as a reminder of the baptism each Christian has experienced.

The Great Vigil of Easter concludes with a celebrative service of bread and wine. In the joyous hours of Easter morning, the people of God festively share the sacrament of Holy Communion, not as followers of a deceased Jesus but as followers of the risen Jesus Christ whose return is awaited at the end of history. This portion of the vigil follows an order for the Service of Word and Sacrament.

In churches where the Great Vigil of Easter is a new observance, it is suggested that a Lenten study program or other means be used to interpret the history and purpose of the vigil for the people and to elicit their active involvement in the planning of the four component services.

The Great Vigil of Easter may be celebrated in an abbreviated form, lasting between one and one and one-half hours, or a fuller form may exceed two hours. Detailed suggestions and directions require careful reading and preparation.

The Order for the Great Vigil of Easter is based on ancient texts and contemporary editions of the vigil used in the churches of Eastern Orthodoxy, the Roman Catholic Church, the Episcopal Church, the Lutheran churches, and the United Methodist Church in the United States.

OUTLINE

Service of Light
  Lighting of New Fire
  Greeting
  Blessing of New Fire
  Lighting of the Paschal Candle
  Easter Proclamation

Service of the Word
  Greeting
  Old Testament Readings
  Act of Praise
  New Testament Readings
  Sermon
  Hymn

Service of Water
  Greeting
  Blessing of Water
  Renewal of Baptismal Vows
  Blessing of the People

Service of Bread and Wine
  Greeting
  Passing the Peace

*A Service of Word and Sacrament continues, beginning
with the offertory.*

SERVICE OF LIGHT

LIGHTING OF NEW FIRE

The people may assemble in silence outdoors or within the darkened church. A small fire may be started on the ground or in an urn or kettle that will safely contain it. When the ceremony is held indoors, the people may face the rear of the sanctuary toward an entrance where the ceremony is held. When the fire is ready, the leader may proceed with the greeting.

GREETING

All who are able may stand as a leader greets the people in these or other words.

LEADER
**Grace to you from Jesus Christ,
who was, and is, and is to come.**

**Sisters and brothers in Christ,
on this most holy night
when our Savior Jesus Christ passed
from death to life,
we gather with all the church
throughout the world
in vigil and prayer.
This is the Passover of Jesus Christ:
Through light and the word,
through water and the bread and wine,
we recall Christ's death and resurrection,
we share Christ's triumph over sin and death,
and with invincible hope
we await Christ's coming again.**

**Hear the word of God:
In the beginning was the Word,
and the Word was with God,
and the Word was God.
In the Word was life,**

and the life was the light of all humanity.
The light shines in the darkness,
and the darkness has not overcome it.[18]

BLESSING OF NEW FIRE

*A leader, located near the flame, may offer the following
or a similar prayer.*

LEADER
**Let us pray.
Eternal God, giver of light and life,
bless this new flame,
that by its radiance and warmth
we may respond to your love and grace,
and be set free from all that separates us
from you and from each other;
through Jesus Christ,
the Sun of Righteousness.
Amen.**

LIGHTING OF THE PASCHAL CANDLE

*A leader, using a taper, may take flame from the fire and
light the paschal candle, saying these or similar words.*

LEADER
**May the light of Christ,
rising in glory,
illumine our hearts and minds.**

FIRST RAISING OF THE PASCHAL CANDLE
*Immediately after the words above, the bearer may raise
the paschal candle, and the following words may be said
or sung responsively.*

CANTOR OR READER
Christ our light.

PEOPLE
Thanks be to God.

If individual candles are provided for the congregation, the process of lighting them may begin after the first raising of the paschal candle. The one bearing the paschal candle, and all other leaders, may process toward the table. When the ceremony is held outdoors, the entire congregation may share in the processional into the church. When the ceremony is held indoors, the smaller procession may move from the entrance to the chancel. As the procession moves forward, all candles other than those on the table may also be lighted.

Second Raising of the Paschal Candle

If the congregation is processing into the church from outdoors, the second raising of the candle may be held at the entrance door. If the people are already in the sanctuary, the paschal candle may be elevated midway of the aisle.

CANTOR OR READER
Christ our light.

PEOPLE
Thanks be to God.

Third Raising of the Paschal Candle

The paschal candle may be raised the third time at its stand in the center of the chancel, between the table and the congregation.

CANTOR OR READER
Christ our light.

PEOPLE
Thanks be to God.

The paschal candle may be placed in its stand.

Easter Proclamation

While all who are able remain standing, holding their candles, a cantor may stand between the table and the paschal candle, facing the congregation, and sing the following ancient Easter hymn. The indented verses may be omitted to shorten the hymn.

CANTOR OR READER
**Rejoice, heavenly powers!
Sing, choirs of angels!
Jesus Christ, our light, is risen!
Sound the trumpet of salvation!**

**Rejoice, O earth, in shining splendor,
Radiant in the brightness of your Sovereign!
Christ has conquered! Glory fills you!
Night vanishes for ever!**

**Rejoice, O servant church! Exult in glory!
The risen Savior shines upon you!
Let this place resound with joy,
Echoing the mighty song of all God's people!**

> **My dearest friends,
> Standing with me in this holy light,
> Join me in asking God's mercy,
> That God may give an unworthy minister
> Grace to sing these Easter praises.**

CANTOR OR READER
God be with you.

PEOPLE
And also with you.

CANTOR OR READER
Lift up your hearts.

PEOPLE
We lift them to God.

CANTOR OR READER
Let us give thanks to God Most High.

PEOPLE
It is right to give God thanks and praise.

CANTOR OR READER
**It is truly right
That with full hearts and minds and voices
We should praise you, the unseen God,
The eternal Creator,
And your only begotten one,
Our Savior Jesus Christ.**

For Christ has ransomed us
With the blood
And for our salvation
Has paid you the cost
Of Adam and Eve's sin!

This is our Passover feast,
When Christ, the true lamb, is slain,
Whose blood consecrates the homes
Of all believers.

This is the night
When first you saved our ancestors:
You freed the people of Israel
From their slavery
And led them dry-shod through the sea.

This is the night when the pillar of fire
Destroyed the shadows of sin!

This is the night when Christians everywhere,
Washed clean of sin
And freed from all defilement,
Are restored to grace
And grow together in holiness.

This is the night when Jesus Christ
Broke the chains of death
And rose triumphant from the grave.

> O God, how wonderful your care for us!
> How boundless your merciful love!
> To ransom a slave
> You gave your only child.
>
> O happy fault,
> O necessary sin of Eve and Adam,
> That gained for us so great a redeemer!
>
> Most blessed of all nights, chosen by God
> To see Christ rising from the dead!
>
> Of this night scripture says:
> "The night will be as clear as day;
> It will become my light, my joy."

**The power of this holy night
Dispels all evil,
Washes guilt away,
Restores lost innocence,
Brings mourners joy;
It casts out hatred, brings peace,
And humbles earthly pride.**

**Night truly blessed
When heaven is wedded to earth
And humanity is reconciled with God!**

**Therefore, gracious Creator,
In the joy of this night,
Receive our evening sacrifice of praise,
Your church's solemn offering.**

**Accept this Easter candle,
A flame divided but undimmed,
A pillar of fire that glows to your honor, O God.**

**Let it mingle with the lights of heaven
And continue bravely burning
To dispel the shadows of this night!**

**May the Morning Star which never sets
Find this flame still burning:
Christ, that Morning Star,
Who came back from the dead,
And shed your peaceful light
On all creation,
Your only begotten one
Who lives and reigns for ever.**

PEOPLE
Amen.

*At the conclusion of the Easter proclamation, if individual
candles have been provided for the congregation, it may
be wise for safety reasons to ask the people to extinguish
their candles and be seated. As this is done, only those
electric lights necessary for reasonable vision should be
turned on.*

SERVICE OF THE WORD

*The number of Old Testament lessons traditionally read
for the vigil varies from two to twelve. The reading of
Exodus 14 is always included. Four Old Testament lessons
with accompanying prayers are suggested here.*

*Other lessons traditionally used are: Genesis 7:1-5, 11-18;
8:6-18; 9:8-13 (Noah and the flood); Ezekiel 36:16-17a,
18-28 (a new heart and a new spirit); Ezekiel 37:1-14 (the
valley of the dry bones); Jonah 3:1-10 (our missionary
calling); Zephaniah 3:14-20 (the gathering of God's people); Isaiah 54:5-14 (love calls us back); Isaiah 4:2-6 (hope
for Israel); and Daniel 3:1-29 (song of three men).*

*It is customary for certain psalms or canticles to be sung
following particular readings. These have been noted.*

*The people serving as readers may stand, if they are able,
around the paschal candle and move after each reading so
that the one reading stands between the table and the
paschal candle, facing the congregation and flanked by the
other readers. It they are able, they may hold their candles
during the readings.*

GREETING

*A leader may introduce the Service of the Word in these
or similar words.*

LEADER
Dear brothers and sisters in Christ:
We have begun our solemn vigil.
As we watch and wait,
let us listen to the word of God,
recalling God's saving acts throughout history
and how, in the fullness of time,
God's Word became flesh and dwelt among us:
Jesus Christ, our Redeemer!

PEOPLE
We do not live by bread alone,
but by every word that proceeds from the mouth of God.

OLD TESTAMENT READINGS

FIRST LESSON
The Creation   Genesis 1:1-2:3 or Genesis 1:1, 26-31
Anthem   Psalm 33:1-11 or Psalm 46:5-10
Collect

LEADER
Let us pray.

ALL
Almighty God, who wonderfully created,
yet more wonderfully restored,
the dignity of human nature,
grant that we may share the divine life
of the one who came to share our humanity:
Jesus Christ, our Redeemer.
Amen.

SECOND LESSON
Abraham's and Sarah's Faithfulness   Genesis 22:1-18
Anthem   Psalm 33:12-22 or Psalm 16
Collect

LEADER
Let us pray.

ALL
Gracious God of all believers,
through Sarah's and Abraham's trustful obedience
you made known your covenant love
to our ancestors and to us.
By the grace of Christ's trustful obedience,
even unto death,
fulfill in your church and in all creation
your promise of a new covenant,
written not on tablets of stone
but on the tablets of human hearts;
through Jesus Christ our Savior.
Amen.

THIRD LESSON
Israel's Deliverance at the Red Sea   Exodus 14:15-15:1 or
Exodus 14:21-29

Anthem   The Song of Moses   Exodus 15:1-19
Collect

LEADER
Let us pray.

ALL
God our Savior,
even today we see the wonders of miracles
you worked long ago.
You once saved a single nation from slavery,
and now you offer that salvation to all
through the grace of baptism.
May all the peoples of the world become true
daughters and sons of Abraham and Sarah
and be made worthy of the heritage of Israel;
through Jesus Christ,
our only mediator and advocate.
Amen.

FOURTH LESSON
Salvation Offered Freely to All   Isaiah 55:1-11
Anthem   The First Song of Isaiah   Isaiah 12:2-6
Collect

LEADER
Let us pray.

ALL
Eternal God, you created all things
by the power of your Word,
and you renew the earth by your Spirit.
Give now the water of life
to all who thirst for you,
and nourish with the spiritual food of bread and wine
all who hunger for you,
that our lives on earth may bear the abundant fruit
of your heavenly reign;
through Jesus Christ,
the firstborn from the dead,
who, with you and the Holy Spirit,
lives and reigns for ever.
Amen.

ACT OF PRAISE

The readers may return to their places, and all who are able may stand to sing the gloria or another hymn of praise. Musical settings of a gloria are on pages 451 and 460.

During the singing of this hymn, the candles on or near the table may be lighted, additional electric lights may be turned on, and the church bell may be pealed joyfully. In some congregations it is the custom not to use the organ until this hymn.

NEW TESTAMENT READINGS

The people may be seated. A collect may be said prior to the Epistle.

EPISTLE LESSON
Our Death and Resurrection
in Jesus Christ   Romans 6:3-11
Anthem   Psalm 114, Psalm 118, or another hymn

All who are able may stand for the reading of the Gospel suggested in the ecumenical lectionary. The reading may be introduced by singing or saying an alleluia and/or "Glory to You, O Christ." It may be followed by "Praise to You, O Christ" and/or an alleluia.

GOSPEL LESSON
Christ's Resurrection   Year A: Matthew 28:1-10
                                         Year B: Mark 16:1-8
                                         Year C: Luke 24:1-12

SERMON

HYMN

All who are able may stand for a hymn introducing the baptism theme.

SERVICE OF WATER

If there are candidates for baptism, the Order for Baptism, beginning on page 129, may be used. When this occurs, the affirmation of faith in the Order for Baptism is addressed to all and replaces the renewal of baptismal vows in the vigil.

If any of the newly baptized are to be received into the local church, the Order for Reception of Members, beginning on page 157, may be used.

Following the benediction that concludes the Order for Baptism, the vigil continues with the blessing of the people on page 242.

GREETING

A pitcher of water and one or more basins may be placed where they may be seen by all. Sprigs of pine or another native tree may be placed near the pitcher and basins.

The one presiding, near the pitcher of water, may lead the people in a responsive greeting, using the following or other suitable words. The people may be seated.

LEADER
Dear friends,
on this night of prayerful vigil
as we come to this font of living water,
let us recall the meaning of baptism.

For just as the body is one
and has many members,
and all the members of the body,
though many,
are one body,
so it is with Christ.

PEOPLE
For by one Spirit
we were all baptized into one body—

Jews or Greeks, slaves or free—
and all were made to drink of one Spirit.

LEADER
**Now you are the body of Christ
and individually members of it.**[19]

BLESSING OF WATER

One of the following prayers or a similar one may be said.

Ⓐ

LEADER
Let us pray.

**We thank you, God,
for the gift of creation
called forth
by your saving Word.
Before the world had shape
and form, your Spirit
moved over the waters.
Out of the waters of the deep,
you formed the
firmament and brought
forth the earth
to sustain all life.**

**In the time of Noah
you washed the earth
with the waters of the flood,
and your ark of salvation
bore a new beginning.**

**In the time of Moses
your people Israel
passed through the
Red Sea waters
from slavery to freedom
and crossed the flowing
Jordan to enter
the promised land.**

Ⓑ

LEADER
**Eternal God,
on this night of watching
and waiting,
we offer our prayers to you.**

PEOPLE
Be with us
as we recall the wonder
of our creation
and the greater wonder
of our redemption.

*As the following words are
spoken, the water may be
poured into the basins.*

LEADER
**Bless this water.
It makes the seeds to grow.
It refreshes us
and makes us clean.**

PEOPLE
You have made of it
a servant of your
loving-kindness:
Through water you set your
people free and quenched
their thirst in the desert.

In the fullness of time,
you sent Jesus Christ
who was nurtured in the
water of Mary's womb.

Jesus was baptized by John
in the water of the Jordan,
became living water to a
woman at the Samaritan
well, washed the feet
of the disciples,
and sent them forth to
baptize all the nations by
water and the Holy Spirit.

*As the following words are
spoken, the water may be
poured into the basins.*

Bless by your Holy Spirit,
gracious God, this water
that by it we may be
reminded of our baptism
into Jesus Christ and
that by the power of your
Holy Spirit we may be kept
faithful until you receive us
at last in your eternal home.

ALL
Glory to you,
eternal God, the one
who was, and is,
and shall always be,
world without end.
Amen.

LEADER
With water
the prophets announced
a new covenant that you
would make with all
humanity.

PEOPLE
By water, made holy
by Christ in the Jordan,
you made our sinful nature
new in the bath
that gives rebirth.

LEADER
Let this water remind us
of our baptism.

PEOPLE
Let us share the joy
of our brothers and sisters
throughout the world who
are baptized this Easter;
through Jesus Christ
our risen Savior.
Amen.

RENEWAL OF BAPTISMAL VOWS

All who are able may stand. The following creed in question form; a full creed, statement of faith, or covenant; or

*another form prepared for the occasion may be used. The
questions are addressed to the congregation as individuals
for affirmation of each person's baptism.*

LEADER
**Do you reaffirm your renunciation of evil
and renew your commitment to Jesus Christ?**

PEOPLE
I do.

LEADER
Do you believe in God?

PEOPLE
I believe in God,
the creator of heaven and earth.

LEADER
Do you believe in Jesus Christ?

PEOPLE
I believe in Jesus Christ,
the only one begotten of God before all worlds.

LEADER
Do you believe in the Holy Spirit?

PEOPLE
I believe in God, the Holy Spirit.

LEADER
**Will you continue
in the apostles' teaching and community,
in the breaking of bread,
and in prayer?**

PEOPLE
I will, with God's help.

LEADER
**Will you strive for justice and peace among all people,
respecting the dignity of every human being?**

PEOPLE
I will, with God's help.

BLESSING OF THE PEOPLE

All who are able may stand. In these or similar words, a leader may invoke God's blessing upon all who have renewed their vows.

LEADER
Let us pray.

Eternal God,
you have come to us in Jesus Christ,
given us a new birth by water
and the Holy Spirit,
and forgiven all our sins.
Bless us now with the grace we need
to fulfill what we have promised.

PEOPLE
Keep us faithful to our Savior Jesus Christ,
for ever and ever.
Amen.

While the choir sings an anthem (such as one based on Ephesians 4:4-6) or as the congregation sings a hymn, leaders may move among the congregation and sprinkle the people with water from the basins using the sprigs from a tree. The mood appropriate for the occasion is joy.

At the conclusion of the sprinkling, the leaders may return to the baptismal font and pour the remaining water from the basins into the font in full view of the people.

If an anthem, rather than a congregational hymn, is sung during the sprinkling, a hymn may be sung by all as an introduction to the service of bread and wine.

SERVICE OF BREAD AND WINE

GREETING

All who are able may stand. The one presiding may lead the following, or another, greeting from the table.

LEADER
Alleluia!
Christ is risen.

PEOPLE
Christ is risen indeed!
Alleluia!

PASSING THE PEACE

All who are able may stand. These or other words may
introduce the passing of the peace.

LEADER
So if you are about to offer your gift
to God at the altar
and there remember that your sister or brother
has something against you,
leave your gift in front of the altar,
go at once and make peace with your brother or sister,
and then come back and offer your gift.[20]

PEOPLE
In response to Christ's command,
we reach out to each other in love.

Leaders of the service may move among the congregation
to shake hands, embrace, or make another sign of peace.
A verse of a hymn may be sung as this is done. When the
people have exchanged greetings of peace, all may return
to their seats.

The order continues with a Service of Word and Sacra-
ment, beginning with the offertory. A special preface for
Easter may be included within the communion prayer. A
preface for Easter is on page 497.

Order for Thanksgiving for the Birth or Adoption of a Child

INTRODUCTION

This order may be used before a child's baptism. It provides a ritual acknowledgement of the important event of birth or adoption. It may be used when baptismal counseling or the assignment of baptism to particular days in the church year, such as Easter or Pentecost, causes a delay. It may be used when parents wish their children to make their own decisions of faith. Options are indicated in the order for use when children have been baptized previously.

It is appropriate that this order be held within a Sunday service of the church. This order may be incorporated within a Service of Word and Sacrament or a Service of the Word. During that service one or more of the following scripture passages may be used:

Deuteronomy 6:4-7: Diligently teach your children.
Deuteronomy 31:12-13: Do this that your children may hear and learn.
1 Samuel 1:9-11, 20-28; 2:26: Birth and presentation of Samuel.
Psalm 8: God's graciousness.
Psalm 78: God's glorious deeds.
Matthew 18:1-4: Those who humble themselves like children will be the greatest.
Mark 10:13-16: Blessing of the children.
Luke 2:22-32,52: Jesus' presentation in the temple.

This order is based on one developed by the Commission on Worship of the Consultation on Church Union (COCU) and is used by permission. There are minor variations in the order offered here. The order from the Consultation on Church Union begins with the presentation on page

247. Helpful commentary is included in the COCU publication, "An Order of Thanksgiving for the Birth or Adoption of a Child."[21]

OUTLINE

This order may be incorporated into a Service of Word and Sacrament or a Service of the Word following the sermon. An affirmation of faith and a hymn may precede this order.

> **Greeting and Introduction**
> **Presentation**
> **Act of Praise**
> **Prayer of Thanksgiving and Intercession**
> **Naming the Child**
> **Covenant**
> **Congregational Assent**
> **Blessing**
> **Prayer**
> **Benediction**

A hymn may be sung. A Service of Word and Sacrament or a Service of the Word continues, omitting the affirmation of faith.

Following the sermon, all who are able may stand and unite in an affirmation of faith and a hymn.

A leader may invite those who wish to give thanks for their child to come forward with the child.

GREETING AND INTRODUCTION

LEADER
**Hear the promise of God to Sarah and Abraham:
I will indeed bless you,
and I will multiply your descendants
as the stars of heaven
and as the sand which is on the seashore.[22]**

**With the people of Israel,
we give thanks to God
for the coming of a child,
a sign of God's blessing,
a gift of hope.**

**God creates all things;
all life is a gift from God.
For this we give thanks.
We give special thanks for children
who remind us powerfully and personally
of the reality of God's creating and creative powers.
Children are a sign of God's creation.**

**They are also a sign of God's salvation.
The trust of a child before all risk
leads us in the way of God.
The prophet Isaiah writes:
The wolf shall dwell with the lamb,
and the leopard shall lie down with the kid,
and the calf and the lion and the fatling together,
and a little child shall lead them.[23]
Jesus came into our midst as a child,
and we are to come to Jesus
with the openness of children.
Only then may we have hope
of entering the realm of God.**

Jesus said,
"Who is my mother,
and who are my brothers?"
And stretching out his hand toward the disciples,
Jesus said, "Here are my mother and brothers!
For whoever does the will of my Father in heaven
is my brother, and sister, and mother."[24]

This service offers thanks for God's creation
in the hope of God's salvation.
We give thanks to our creating God
for the gift of a child.

PRESENTATION

A leader may address the congregation in the following or similar words.

LEADER
**Members of Christ's family,
I present to you _____ *and/or* _____**
                      mother   father
together with _____
                     child
whose coming into *her/his/their* **home**
she/he/they **now acknowledge(s)
with gratitude and faith.**

ACT OF PRAISE

LEADER
**Within the family of Christ,
the** *birth/adoption* **of a child is an occasion for thanksgiving.
Life is God's gift,
and children are a heritage from God.
Therefore we who are entrusted with their care
are given both great responsibility and opportunity.
Because God has favored us
through the coming of this child,
let us offer our praise.**

A hymn of praise, a psalm, or a canticle may be sung.

PRAYER OF
THANKSGIVING AND INTERCESSION

Ⓐ *for the birth of a child*

LEADER

**O God, like a mother who
comforts her children,
you strengthen us
in our solitude;
you sustain us
and provide for us.
We come before you with
gratitude for the gift of this
child, for the joy which has
come into this family, and
for the grace with which you
surround them and all of us.
As a father cares for his
children, so continually
look on us with
compassion and goodness.
Pour out your Spirit.
Enable your servants
to abound in love,
and establish our homes
in holiness;
through Jesus Christ.
Amen.**

Ⓑ *for the adoption of
a child*

LEADER

**O God,
you have adopted all of us
as your children.
We give thanks to you
for the child who has come
to bless this family
and for the parent(s) who
have welcomed this child
as** *her/his/their* **own.
By the power
of your Holy Spirit,
fill their home
with love, trust, and
understanding;
through Jesus Christ.
Amen.**

NAMING THE CHILD

Ⓐ *for a child already named*

LEADER

**What name have you given
this child?**

*The parent(s) presenting
the child respond(s) with
the child's full name.*

Ⓑ *for conferring the name*

LEADER

**What name do you now
give this child?**

*Each parent may place
a hand on the child.*

PARENT(S)

I/We **name you** _____.

full name

COVENANT

LEADER
addressing the parent(s)
In accepting _____ **as a gift from God,**
_{name}
**you also acknowledge your faith in Jesus Christ
and the responsibility that God places upon you.**

*The parent(s) respond with the following or similar words,
saying them or repeating them after the leader.*

PARENT(S)
I/We receive _____
_{name}
from the hand of a loving Creator.
With humility and hope,
I/we accept the obligation which is *mine/ours*
to love and nurture *him/her*
and to lead *him/her* to Christian faith
by teaching and example.
I/We ask for the power of the Holy Spirit
and the support of the church
that *I/we* may be *a good steward/good stewards*
of this gift of life.

CONGREGATIONAL ASSENT

All who are able may stand.

LEADER
addressing the congregation
**The church is the family of Christ,
the community in which we grow
in faith and commitment.**

PEOPLE
We rejoice to take _____ under our care.
_{name}
We seek God's grace to be a community
in which the gospel is truly proclaimed to all.
We will support you and minister with you
as workers together in Christ Jesus
and heirs of Christ's promise.

BLESSING

A leader may take the child and say the following or other words of blessing.

A *for an unbaptized child*

LEADER

—————————,
    name

**may the eternal God bless
you and watch over you.
May Jesus Christ
incorporate you into his
death and resurrection
through baptism.
May the Holy Spirit
sanctify you and bring you
to life everlasting.
Amen.**

B *for a baptized child*

LEADER

—————————,
    name

**may the eternal God bless
you and watch over you.
May Jesus Christ
incorporate you into his
death and resurrection.
May the Holy Spirit
sanctify you and bring you
to life everlasting.
Amen.**

The leader may return the child to the family.

PRAYER

A leader may offer this or other prayers.

LEADER
**Gracious God,
from whom every family in heaven and on earth is named:
Out of the treasures of your glory strengthen us
through your Spirit.
Help us joyfully to nurture ——————
within your church.**   *name*
Bring *her/him* **by grace to** *baptism/Christian maturity*
that Christ may dwell in *her/his* **heart through faith.
Give power to** —————— **and to us**
    name
**that with all your people we may grasp
the breadth and length,
the height and depth of Christ's love.
Enable us to know this love,
though it is beyond knowledge,**

**and to be filled with your own fullness;
through Jesus Christ our Lord.
Amen.**

*If the Lord's Prayer is not used at another point in the
service, it may now be prayed by all.*

BENEDICTION

LEADER
**Glory to God,
who, by the power at work among us,
is able to do far more than we can ask or imagine.
Glory be given to this God from generation to generation
in the church and in Christ Jesus for ever!**

ALL
Amen.

Family members return to their places in the congregation.

*At the conclusion of this order, a hymn may be sung and
a Service of Word and Sacrament or a Service of the
Word continues, omitting the affirmation of faith.*

Order for
Times of Passage: Farewell

People experience periods in their lives which shape the future. The church celebrates and acknowledges the most familiar of those passage times: birth, marriage, death.

There are other passage times in each of our lives. People leave the local church to move to another community. Couples become engaged. A person secures a new job. One "returns" from a personal or family crisis. These moments in the life of the individual can be deep and important spiritual and educational experiences. Though these passages are not those for which major religious rites are celebrated, the faith community can celebrate with individuals in such moments of significance and meaning.

There is not a singular way in which times of passage should be observed. One example is this service of farewell. It is important that worship leaders seek to be intentional in designing ways appropriate to the person and the setting for the observance. The service may include words and symbols which link it to the stories and images of the faith community. People who are experiencing the particular time of passage being celebrated should be involved in the planning and, where appropriate, in the leadership of the liturgy.

The service may include an opportunity to name the event being observed, a time for people to witness to their experiences and feelings, and a reading and exposition of the word which gives perspective to that being experienced. There may also be a sense of sending forth those leaving to new ministry. There may be an offering of thanksgiving for the journey of faith and for the sharing in the midst of this community of God's people.

A Service of Word and Sacrament or a Service of the Word may provide the context in which the special celebration is held. In those services, it is suggested that it follow the sermon and be associated with the prayers of the people.

Scripture and the proclamation of the word should be used freely. The Bible is the story of God's saving acts in history and of the response of the people of God to those acts. The events described in the Bible cover a panorama of human experiences. Search the scriptures to find the verses and stories and challenges that relate most deeply to the time of passage which is being acknowledged. Music is also an important vehicle for expressing feelings for which words may not provide adequate expression, depending on the setting of the celebration.

Celebration of passages provides an opportunity for people to remember stories of the experience being observed and to draw new insights from them. Such stories may be shared in different ways, both verbally and visually, using drawings, slides, movies, skits, interpretive dance, mime, and other media. Full consideration should be given to ethnic and local customs of the church and of the individual.

On rare occasions, services may recall periods of separation, but not farewell: when children are missing; when people slip into a hopeless life on the street; when family members, friends, and community residents are held hostage; when families must endure endless waiting for loved ones in prison. All these are times of passage, and all will require special prayers and special services.

As one example of the kind of service that may be held at a time of passage, this order is for those moving away. This may be used for people moving permanently from the community for new jobs or into care facilities or retirement communities. It may also be used for those leaving for a particular time period, such as those who leave for college or military service.

A portion of this order is for use when a pastor or another authorized minister is leaving a local church that she or he has served. In these cases, it is appropriate to have a representative of the association and/or conference participate in the service. If the authorized minister has served in another organization on behalf of the local church, it is also appropriate to have a representative of that organization participate in the service.

OUTLINE

This order may be used alone. When it is incorporated into a Service of Word and Sacrament or a Service of the Word, it may follow the sermon.

Greeting
Remembrance and Recognition
Giving and Sharing Symbols

> **Ending an Authorized Ministry**
>   **Recognition of the End**
>   **Vows of Release**
>   **Witness of the Association/Conference**

Prayer
Hymn of Thanksgiving
Benediction

A Service of Word and Sacrament or a Service of the Word may continue.

GREETING

LEADER
Our church family is constantly changing.
People come and go.
Babies are born.
Children grow up.
People commit themselves to one another.
Loved ones and friends among us
come to the end of their lives.
Individuals move into our community and church life.
Others leave us, moving away to new places,
new experiences, and new opportunities.

It is important and right
that we recognize these times of passage,
of endings and beginnings.
Today we share the time of farewell
with *a friend/friends* **who** *is/are* **leaving.**

REMEMBRANCE AND RECOGNITION

An opportunity may be given for the recognition that it is in the midst of the congregation of God's people that Christians gather at significant times of passage in their lives. The member(s) of the local church leaving the community are invited to come forward. Others who have been closely involved may be invited to join them.

The pastor or another representative of the local church and one or two friends may speak of the occasion being observed and share brief stories reminding the congregation of the gifts and contributions of the person(s) leaving. The person(s) being recognized may speak of the significance of the church for their faith and life.

GIVING AND SHARING SYMBOLS

Symbols may be given to those leaving and to the church, with appropriate words of appreciation and thanks.

*If an authorized minister is leaving, family and friends
may return to their places in the congregation, and other
representatives who will participate in the ending of the
authorized ministry may come forward.*

**If the person leaving is not an authorized minister who has
been serving in or on behalf of the church, the service continues with the prayer on page 258.**

ENDING AN AUTHORIZED MINISTRY

RECOGNITION OF THE END

*A representative of the covenantal partners—the local
church, association, or conference—may lead in these
or other appropriate words.*

LEADER
On _____, this local church called
<u>date</u>
_____ to serve as _____.
name   position

AUTHORIZED MINISTER
I thank _____ , its members and friends,
church name
for the love, kindness, and support shown me these last
_____ years.
number of years
I ask forgiveness for the mistakes I have made.
I am grateful for the ways my leadership
has been accepted.
As I leave, I carry with me all that I have learned here.

PEOPLE
We receive your thankfulness, offer forgiveness,
and accept that you now leave to minister elsewhere.
We express our gratitude for your time among us.
We ask your forgiveness for our mistakes.
Your influence on our faith and faithfulness will not
leave us at your departure.

AUTHORIZED MINISTER
I forgive you and accept your gratitude,
trusting that our time together and our parting
are pleasing to God.

VOWS OF RELEASE

All who are able may stand for these or similar words.

LEADER
addressing the congregation
Do you, the members and friends of _____
local church
release _____
name
from the duties of _____**?**
position

PEOPLE
We do, with the help of God.

A *for use when called to another position*

LEADER
Do you offer your encouragement for *her/his* **ministry soon to begin as** _____
position
of _____**?**
location of ministry

PEOPLE
We do,
with the help of God.

B *for use when retiring or not yet called to another position*

LEADER
Do you offer your encouragement for *her/his* **ministry as it unfolds in new ways?**

PEOPLE
We do,
with the help of God.

LEADER
addressing the authorized minister
Do you, _____**,**
name
release this local church from turning to you and depending on you?

AUTHORIZED MINISTER
I do, with the help of God.

LEADER
Do you offer your encouragement for the continued ministry here and on the relationship with another who will come to serve?

AUTHORIZED MINISTER
I do, with the help of God.

WITNESS OF THE ASSOCIATION/CONFERENCE
*Church officers may come forward. A representative
of the association or conference addresses them, using
these or similar words.*

REPRESENTATIVE
On behalf of the _____
association/conference
and the United Church of Christ,
I witness to the words spoken:
words of thankfulness, forgiveness, and release.
The member churches of our association and
conference hold each of you in prayer.
We pledge our support in the transitions signified
in this service.

OFFICERS
Thanks be to God.

PRAYER

All who are able may stand.

LEADER
Let us pray.

A

LEADER
**O God,
we give thanks
for remembered times
when we, together,
have shared the life of faith.
We thank you for the
moments we have shared
with** *this person/these people*
**in worship, in learning,
in service.
We pray that**

_____
name(s)

**will be aware of your
Spirit's guidance**

B

ALL
**God, whose everlasting love
for all is trustworthy,
help each of us
to trust the future
which rests in your care.
The time we were together
in your name saw our
laughter and tears,
our hopes and
disappointments.
Guide us as we hold these
cherished memories but
move in new directions,
until that time to come**

as *he/she/they* **move(s)**
to *a new and unknown place/*
new and unknown places,
in the name of Jesus
the Savior.

PEOPLE
Amen.

when we are completely
one with you
and with each other,
in the name of Jesus Christ
we pray.
Amen.

HYMN OF THANKSGIVING

BENEDICTION

LEADER
Go now,
surrounded by our love
and led by the promises of God,
the presence of Jesus Christ,
and the guidance of the Holy Spirit.
Amen.

When the Order for Times of Passage is incorporated into
a Service of Word and Sacrament or a Service of the Word,
those who have gone forward to participate in this order
may return to their places in the congregation and the ser-
vice continues.

Order for Special Occasions in a Church's Life

INTRODUCTION

It is important to observe special occasions in the life of a local church that mark points of passage and growth. These occasions include the anniversary of the founding of a local church, the burning of a mortgage, the dedication and consecration of buildings or newly designed space, the dedication of gifts, reunions of members and of specific groups within the local church, and times of recovenanting of the people or between pastor and people.

Each of these times can be deep and important spiritual and educational moments for the members of the local church. The uniqueness of these times and of the faith experiences out of which they grow makes it impossible for one service to cover all occasions. It is important for members of the church, particularly those people who have some direct relationship to the event that is to be celebrated, to share in the planning and leading of the service.

A Service of Word and Sacrament or a Service of the Word may provide the context within which the special celebration is held. It is suggested that the special observance follow the sermon and be associated with the prayers of the people. In the case of dedications, items related to the liturgical life of the church may be dedicated at those points in the service and at those places in the room where they will normally function. Items not related to one part of the liturgical order of service may be dedicated at the time of the prayers of the people or at the offertory.

The resources in this order require further development by the planners of each specific service.

Symbols are important means of communication which help people to relate the past to the present and to connect the item being dedicated to the life and mission of the

church. Wherever possible, it is helpful to include symbols
as well as words in a service such as this. Mortgages held up
and symbolically burned visibly bring home the reality of
the moment. Charters or other items from the past help to
focus on the journey that has been made to this point of
anniversary observance. When a new or renovated building
is dedicated, beginning the ceremony outdoors and entering
the new or renovated space is an effective and dramatic way
of centering on the nature of the occasion. Use of a specific
gift can enhance the service, such as dedication of a baptismal font followed by a baptism.

Music may play a role in harmonies and in words expressed
in choral texts and hymns. Feelings for which words may
not provide adequate expression may be celebrated through
song and instrumental music. Music may provide an opportunity for moving through the church building in a festive
manner. It may also be incorporated with dance or other
movement to celebrate special occasions and gifts. Music
may be commissioned for the occasion.

OUTLINE

This order may be incorporated into a Service of Word and Sacrament or a Service of the Word following the sermon, or its elements may be incorporated into a service at various points.

> **Hymn, Anthem, or Other Music**
> **Address**
> **Reading of Scripture**
> **Litany**
> **Proclamation**
> **Prayer**

A Service of Word and Sacrament or a Service of the Word may continue, or a hymn and a benediction may close the order.

This order may follow the sermon in a Service of Word and Sacrament or a Service of the Word, or its elements may be incorporated into a service at various points.

HYMN, ANTHEM, OR OTHER MUSIC

A hymn or anthem may be sung, or instrumental music may be played. Many hymns are appropriate, but a special one may be written for the occasion. Dance by a small group or movement through the building by the congregation may be included.

ADDRESS

A leader may introduce the reason for the celebration, using words, pictures, or other symbols.

READING OF SCRIPTURE

Choose scripture stories and challenges that reflect most deeply the event the church is celebrating. Possible scripture lessons include the following.

OLD TESTAMENT	NEW TESTAMENT
1 Chronicles 29:10-18	Matthew 7:24-27
2 Chronicles 6:18-31	John 2:13-17
Psalms 24, 84, 122	1 Corinthians 3:9-17
Isaiah 6:1-8	Ephesians 2:19-22
	Revelation 21:2-5

Representatives of the church who have a special relationship to the event being celebrated may read the lessons.

LITANY

A litany of thanksgiving, affirmation, and hope may be written for the occasion by people in the church family. A litany of memories written by those who have been in the church the longest time or a litany of dreams and hopes written by children are two possibilities among many.

The following litanies are based on a traditional one used for the dedication of a church building. They will need to be adapted to the specific situation.

Ⓐ *for a building dedication*

LEADER

**For the worship of God
in prayer and praise,
for the preaching
of the Word,
for the celebration
of the holy sacraments,**

PEOPLE

We dedicate this building.

LEADER

**For the comfort
of those who mourn,
for the help of those
who are perplexed,
for the guidance of those
who seek strength,**

PEOPLE

We dedicate this building.

LEADER

**For the support
and nurture of families,
for the guidance
of children,
for the calling of youth
to a life of service,**

PEOPLE

We dedicate this building.

LEADER

**For guarding against evil,
for fostering faithfulness,
for promoting peace and
justice in all the earth,**

PEOPLE

We dedicate this building.

Ⓑ *for an anniversary or
other special occasion*

LEADER

**For the worship of God
in prayer and praise,
for the preaching
of the Word,
for the celebration
of the holy sacraments,**

PEOPLE

Offered by this church,
we give thanks.

LEADER

**For the comfort
of those who mourn,
for the help of those
who are perplexed,
for the guidance of those
who seek strength,**

PEOPLE

Offered by this church,
we give thanks.

LEADER

**For the support
and nurture of families,
for the guidance
of children,
for the calling of youth
to a life of service,**

PEOPLE

Offered by this church,
we give thanks.

LEADER

**For guarding against evil,
for fostering faithfulness,**

LEADER
**For the opening of minds
to your truth,
for the care of the needy,
for the giving of hope
and courage,**

PEOPLE
We dedicate this building.

LEADER
**For the unity
of all believers in Christ,
for the carrying of the
gospel into all the world,
for the furtherance
of the unity of all people,**

PEOPLE
We dedicate this building.

LEADER
**For the consecration
of life and service,
in grateful remembrance
of those who have gone
before us,
and in gratitude for our life
together in this church,**

PEOPLE
We dedicate this building
to the glory of God,
to the honor of Jesus Christ,
and to the praise
of the Holy Spirit.

ALL
Thanks be to God!

**for promoting peace and
justice in all the earth,**

PEOPLE
Offered by this church,
we give thanks.

LEADER
**For the opening of minds
to your truth, for the care
of the needy, for the giving
of hope and courage,**

PEOPLE
Offered by this church,
we give thanks.

LEADER
**For the unity
of all believers in Christ,
for the carrying of the
gospel into all the world,
for the furtherance
of the unity of all people,**

PEOPLE
Offered by this church,
we give thanks.

LEADER
**For the consecration
of life and service,
in grateful remembrance
of those who have gone
before us, and in gratitude
for our life together
in this church,**

ALL
**We give thanks to you
for this church's past and
pray for your continued
blessing and guidance.
Amen.**

PROCLAMATION

*A time of celebration is a time to remember. Stories of
history, heritage, planning, and effort enable people to
stay in touch with the faith experience of those who have
gone before them. Stories may be shared verbally and
visually, using such means as drawings, slides, movies,
skits, interpretive dance, mime, and other media. Full
consideration needs to be given to ethnic and local customs of the church and its members as sources of material.*

*Anniversaries and special occasions are also times to look
to the future. People may be invited to write down their
hopes and plans for what they want the church to be and
do in five or ten or twenty-five years. These may be shared
in the service.*

PRAYER

*Prayers may be offered at specific places that focus on the
theme or themes of the observance. At the anniversary of
a church building, prayers of blessing and hope may be
offered at each of the four corners of the building. Specific
themes may be associated with the corners, as is sometimes
done in African religious rituals. These themes could be:
worship and celebration, learning and growth, service and
action, and community and relationship. If prayers do not
focus on such themes, one of these general prayers or a
prayer prepared for the occasion may be used.*

A *for a dedication*

ALL
**O God of all creation,
we give thanks for the
calling to be your church
and for the power you give
us to fulfill our calling.
We are a people
with a past full of assurance
and a future full of hope.**

B *for a special occasion*

ALL
**Eternal God,
we offer thanksgiving
and praise to you
on this festive day.
We give you thanks
for those who responded
to your call to establish
this church.**

Today we dedicate
this _____ to you.
May the meaning we see
in this _____
live on in us so that each
time we see it or use it,
we may be reminded
of your holy presence.
May we pass on to our
children and our children's
children the significance
of this _____
so that their journey
of faith may be enhanced.
To you be the power
and the glory for ever.
Amen.

We acknowledge our
gratitude for the continuing
ministry and mission
of our church through
_____ years.
We thank you for all that
our church has meant to its
members, to those its
ministry has touched,
and to the United Church
of Christ.
In tender memory,
we rejoice at the inspiration
which has been found here,
through the preaching
of your word,
through the singing
of hymns to your praise,
and through the sharing of
life-sustaining sacraments.

Look upon us this day
with mercy.
Bless us as we reconsecrate
ourselves to you.
Sanctify our lives and our
work through this church.
Help us to preserve the best
of our past and to be open
to new vision.
May this local church long
continue to be a sign
of your Spirit and a witness
to Jesus Christ,
in whose name we pray.
Amen.

*This order may conclude with a hymn and a benediction,
or a Service of Word and Sacrament or a Service of the
Word may continue.*

Order for Reconciliation of a Penitent Person

INTRODUCTION

Services of reconciliation are one means by which the church expresses the universal priesthood of all believers (1 Peter 2:5,9; Revelation 5:10). Christians are called to "bear one another's burdens and so fulfill the law of Christ" (Galatians 6:2). Priesthood, by definition, is a ministry exercised in behalf of others. It is the privilege and responsibility of Christians to intercede for one another, share mutual concerns, forgive one another's sins with God's help, and assure one another of God's forgiveness when Christians are alienated from God and neighbors. This order offers the freeing power of confession and absolution.

This order may be adapted to the particular circumstance in which it is to be used. It is absolutely essential that great care be taken to protect the confidentiality of the conversation with the penitent person. A pastor or another representative of the church may lead the service. It is recommended that this order be used only after the one leading it has had adequate opportunity to establish a relationship with the person seeking reconciliation.

For full participation, the person seeking reconciliation must have a copy of the order. A careful review of the order may provide a way of interpreting the meaning and purpose of personal confession.

OUTLINE

Greeting
Words of Comfort from Scripture
Confession
Pastoral Conversation
Prayer of the Penitent Person
Assurance of Pardon
Thanksgiving
Passing the Peace

GREETING

When the person seeking reconciliation arrives, the pastor or another representative of the church may greet the person informally and establish an atmosphere of openness.

LEADER

——————,
name
**the grace of our Savior Jesus Christ
be with you.**

PENITENT PERSON
And also with you.

A

LEADER
**Hear the words
of the psalmist:
Have mercy on me, O God,
according to your
loving-kindness;
in your great compassion
blot out my offenses.
Wash me through
and through
from my wickedness,
and cleanse me
from my sin.
For I know my
transgressions,
and my sin is ever
before me.**[25]

B

LEADER
**Let us say together these
words of the psalmist:**

ALL
**Have mercy on me, O God,
according to your
loving-kindness;
in your great compassion
blot out my offenses.
Wash me through
and through
from my wickedness
and cleanse me
from my sin.
For I know my
transgressions,
and my sin is ever
before me.**[26]

WORDS OF COMFORT FROM SCRIPTURE

Scripture may be read as a reminder of God's promise of love and forgiveness. The reading may be shared by those present. One or more of the following or other passages may be read.

Isaiah 53:4-6
Ezekiel 11:19-20
Matthew 6:14-15, 9:12-13, 11:28-30
Luke 6:31-38, 11:9-10, 15:1-7
John 3:16
Colossians 1:3-14, 3:1-17
1 Timothy 1:5
1 John 1:1-2, 5-10

CONFESSION

A confession may be said by all. After a period of silence, the person seeking reconciliation may be encouraged to make a confession in his or her own words.

GENERAL CONFESSION

LEADER
Let us pray.

A

ALL
**Most merciful God,
we confess that we have
sinned against you
in thought, word, and deed,
by what we have done,
and by what we have
left undone.
We have not loved you
with our whole heart.
We have not loved our
neighbors as ourselves.
We are truly sorry,
and we humbly repent.
For the sake of our Savior
Jesus Christ, have mercy
on us and forgive us that
we may delight in your will
and follow in your ways,
to the glory of your name.
Amen.**[27]

B

ALL
**Gracious God,
our sins are too heavy
to carry, too real to hide,
and too deep to undo.
Forgive what our lips
tremble to name,
what our hearts can no
longer bear, and what has
become for us a consuming
fire of judgment.
Set us free from a past
that we cannot change;
open to us a future in which
we can be changed;
and grant us grace to grow
more and more
in your likeness and image;
through Jesus Christ
our Savior.
Amen.**

INDIVIDUAL CONFESSION
The person seeking reconciliation may confess silently and/or aloud.

PASTORAL CONVERSATION

The pastor or another representative of the church may encourage dialogue with the person and offer understanding, comfort, counsel, and support.

PRAYER OF THE PENITENT PERSON

Ⓐ	Ⓑ	Ⓒ
PENITENT PERSON	PENITENT PERSON	PENITENT PERSON
Almighty God, God of strength and mercy, who sent Jesus to save and forgive, I trust you. Forgive my sins. Refresh my spirit. Free me to love myself, my neighbor, and you. Amen.	Lord Jesus, have mercy on me, a sinner. Amen. *The petition may be repeated several times.*	God, be merciful to me, a sinner. Amen.

ASSURANCE OF PARDON

The person seeking reconciliation is assured of God's forgiveness with the following or similar words. Agreement about questions to be asked should be reached in advance.

Ⓐ	Ⓑ	Ⓒ
LEADER	LEADER	LEADER
This is a true saying, and worthy of all to be received,	**If we confess our sins, God is faithful and just,**	**I acknowledged my sin to you, and I did not hide my iniquity;**

that Christ Jesus came into the world to save sinners.[28]

This is God's gift to us and to the world, so we can know abundant life.

and will forgive our sins and cleanse us from all unrighteousness.[29]

**I said, "I will confess my transgressions to God";
then you forgave the guilt of my sin.**[30]

AND

A pastor or another representative of the church may ask the following or a similar question, and the person may respond in this or some other way.

LEADER

_____,
name

do you believe the promise of God's forgiveness?

PENITENT PERSON
I believe.

When it seems appropriate, the following question may also be asked.

LEADER
Do you forgive those who have sinned against you?

Time may be given for the one seeking reconciliation to reflect and to respond in this or some other way.

PENITENT PERSON
I do, with God's help.

The leader may give the declaration of pardon in these or similar words.

LEADER
**In Christ's name,
and as one with you in the church,
I declare to you:
Your sins are forgiven.
Go in peace,
in the knowledge of God's mercy.**

THANKSGIVING

*A pastor or another representative of the church may offer
a prayer in her or his own words or may use the brief
prayer and/or the acclamation.*

A

LEADER
**Creator and Savior,
giver and forgiver of life,
we give you thanks for _____,**
name
your *son/daughter* **in faith,
who, feeling your presence
and trusting your grace,
has thrown off the anxiety of sin
to receive the hope of your love.
We offer our thanks to you,
our good and gracious God,
in the name of Jesus Christ
by whom all sins are forgiven.**

PENITENT PERSON
Amen.

B

LEADER
**Now there is rejoicing in heaven;
for you were lost,
and are found;
you were dead,
and now you are alive in Jesus Christ.
God has put away all your sins.**[31]

PASSING THE PEACE

*A pastor or another representative of the church and the
one reconciled may greet each other, hold hands, or
embrace, and conclude their time together.*

LEADER
The peace of God be with you always.

PENITENT PERSON
And also with you.

Order for
Corporate Reconciliation

INTRODUCTION

Services of reconciliation are one means by which the church expresses the universal priesthood of all believers (1 Peter 2:5, 9; Revelation 5:10). Christians are called to "bear one another's burdens and so fulfill the law of Christ" (Galatians 6:2). Priesthood, by definition, is a ministry exercised in behalf of others. It is the privilege and responsibility of Christians to intercede for one another, share mutual concerns, forgive one another's sins with God's help, and assure one another of God's forgiveness when Christians are alienated from God and neighbors. This order offers the freeing power of confession and absolution.

This order may be adapted to the particular circumstance in which it is to be used. It is intended for any occasion when a local church assembles for the confession of sin and the assurance of God's pardon. The occasion may be one related to communal, national, or global strife; or to one of the penitential days or seasons of the church year; or in preparation for Holy Communion. When it is used in relation to Holy Communion but on a separate occasion, this service and a Service of Word and Sacrament may be used in full. When it is used on the same occasion as Holy Communion, this order may be used in full and a Service of Word and Sacrament may begin at the offertory.

The Order for Corporate Reconciliation may require considerable preparation if it is to be used in relation to some specific strife or difficulty. When this occurs, the relevance of the order may be enhanced significantly by the use of prayers, litanies, and exhortations specifically prepared for the occasion.

The theme of this service is not human sinfulness but divine grace which makes reconciliation possible. Joy, expressed through music and in other ways, is appropriate. The placement of hymns and other music in the service is left to the discretion of those planning the service. The order may be led by a pastor or other representatives of the church.

Each worshiper needs a copy of the order. A careful review of the order may provide a way of interpreting the meaning and purpose of confession.

OUTLINE

This order may be used alone or incorporated into a Service of Word and Sacrament.

Greeting
Sentences
Collect
Examination of Conscience
Prayer
Reading of Scripture
Sermon
Affirmation of Faith
Call to Confession
Confession of Sin
Silence
Assurance of Pardon
Affirmation of Pardon

Order for Word and Sacrament, beginning with the offertory

Prayers
Collect
Passing the Peace
Lord's Prayer
Act of Praise
Benediction

When this order is used in relation to Holy Communion but on a separate occasion, this order and a Service of Word and Sacrament may be used in full. When it is used on the same occasion as Holy Communion, this order may be used through the affirmation of pardon and a Service of Word and Sacrament may then begin at the offertory.

GREETING

All who are able may stand. A leader may greet the people with one of these or with other words and then explain briefly the specific purpose of the service.

A

LEADER
**The grace of our Lord
Jesus Christ
and the love of God
and the communion
of the Holy Spirit
be with you all.**[32]

PEOPLE
And also with you.

B

LEADER
**In the name
of the triune God:
Creator, Liberator,
and Healer.**

PEOPLE
Amen.

SENTENCES

All who are able may stand. One of the following or other appropriate sentences from scripture may be read.

A

LEADER
**Bless the Holy One,
O my soul;
and all that is within me,
bless God's holy name!**

PEOPLE
Bless the Holy One,
O my soul,
and forget not
all God's benefits,

B

LEADER
**Jesus said:
Ask, and it will be given;
seek, and you will find;
knock, and it will be
opened to you.**

PEOPLE
For everyone
who asks receives,
and those who seek find,

LEADER
**Who forgives
all your iniquity,
who heals all your diseases,**

PEOPLE
Who redeems your life
from the grave,
who crowns you
with steadfast love
and mercy,

LEADER
**Who satisfies you with
good as long as you live,**

PEOPLE
So that your youth is
renewed like the eagle's.[33]

and to each who knocks
it will be opened.[34]

COLLECT

*All who are able may stand. One of the following prayers
or a similar one may be offered.*

LEADER
Let us pray.

A

ALL
**God of ancient wisdom
and emerging truth, your
love makes all things new.
Fill us with the hope,
not of those who think
they are without sin,
but of those who know
they have sinned,
who trust in your mercy,
and who long
for your heavenly reign
to come on the earth;
through Jesus Christ,**

B

ALL
**God of all mercy
and consolation,
come to the aid
of your people,
turning us from our sin
to live for you alone.
Give us the power
of your Holy Spirit,
that we may attend to your
word, confess our sins,
receive your forgiveness,
and grow into the fullness
of Jesus Christ,**

| who lived and died and rose again for us and for our salvation. Amen. | the one begotten by you before all worlds, our Savior and Redeemer. Amen.[35] |

EXAMINATION OF CONSCIENCE

The people may be seated. One or more of the following may be used. Silent reflection may follow each response.

A

LEADER
Hear the commandments of God:
I am the Holy One, your God,
who brought you out of bondage.
You shall have no other gods but me.

PEOPLE
God, have mercy on us
and guide us in your way.

LEADER
You shall not make for yourself any idol.

PEOPLE
God, have mercy on us
and guide us in your way.

LEADER
You shall not invoke with malice
the name of the Holy One, your God.

PEOPLE
God, have mercy on us
and guide us in your way.

LEADER
Remember the Sabbath day and keep it holy.

PEOPLE
God, have mercy on us
and guide us in your way.

LEADER
Honor your father and your mother.

PEOPLE
God, have mercy on us
and guide us in your way.

LEADER
You shall not commit murder.

PEOPLE
God, have mercy on us
and guide us in your way.

LEADER
You shall not commit adultery.

PEOPLE
God, have mercy on us
and guide us in your way.

LEADER
You shall not steal.

PEOPLE
God, have mercy on us
and guide us in your way.

LEADER
You shall not be a false witness.

PEOPLE
God, have mercy on us
and guide us in your way.

LEADER
**You shall not covet anything
that belongs to your neighbor.**

PEOPLE
God, have mercy on us
and guide us in your way.[36]

B
LEADER
**Jesus said the first commandment is:
The Holy One, our God, is the only Holy One;
and you shall love the Holy One, your God,
with all your heart, and with all your soul,
and with all your mind,
and with all your strength.
The second commandment is this:
You shall love your neighbor
as you love yourself.
No other commandment is greater than these.**[37]

©

LEADER
Let us call to mind the words of Jesus Christ:
Blessed are the poor in spirit;

PEOPLE
Theirs is the reign of God.

LEADER
Blessed are those who mourn;

PEOPLE
They shall be comforted.

LEADER
Blessed are the meek;

PEOPLE
They shall inherit the earth.

LEADER
Blessed are those who hunger and thirst for righteousness;

PEOPLE
They shall be satisfied.

LEADER
Blessed are the merciful;

PEOPLE
They shall obtain mercy.

LEADER
Blessed are the pure in heart;

PEOPLE
They shall see God.

LEADER
Blessed are the peacemakers;

PEOPLE
They shall be called children of God.

LEADER
Blessed are those persecuted for righteousness' sake;

PEOPLE
Theirs is the reign of God.

LEADER
Blessed are you when people revile you and persecute you
and utter all kinds of evil against you falsely on my account.

PEOPLE
Rejoice and be glad, for your reward is great in heaven.[38]

PRAYER

The following prayer or a similar one may be offered.

LEADER
Let us pray.

PEOPLE
Merciful God,
from whom come all holy desires and just works,
breathe into our hearts by your Holy Spirit
the gift of obedient faith,
that we, knowing your will,
may treasure these words in our minds and hearts
and may in all things love and serve you.
Amen.[39]

READING OF SCRIPTURE

*The lectionary lessons for the day, one of these suggested
sets of lessons, or other appropriate lessons may be read.
One or more of these penitential psalms may be said or
sung: Psalm 6, 32, 38, 51, 102, 130, and 143. Appropriate
lessons include the following.*

Ⓐ
Ezekiel 11:19-20
Ephesians 5:1-14
Matthew 22:34-40

Ⓑ
Isaiah 1:10-18
Ephesians 4:17-32
John 15:12-17

SERMON

*A sermon may be offered. A less formal address may be
used in which the people are invited to share in dialogue
and all present are given an opportunity to offer mutual
consolation. There may be silence for reflection.*

AFFIRMATION OF FAITH

*All who are able may stand for a form of the Statement of
Faith of the United Church of Christ, a creed, or a church*

*covenant. Forms of the United Church of Christ State-
ment of Faith, historic creeds, and other affirmations are
in the Resource Section, beginning on page 509.*

CALL TO CONFESSION

*All who are able may stand. One of the following or other
sentences from scripture may be said in preparation for
the prayers of confession.*

A

LEADER
**When I declared
not my sin,
my body wasted
away through
my groaning all
day long.**

PEOPLE
For day and
night your hand
was heavy
upon me;
my strength
was dried up
as by the heat
of the summer.

LEADER
**I acknowledged
my sin to you,
and I did not
hide my iniquity;**

PEOPLE
I said:
"I will confess my
transgressions
to God";
then you forgave
the guilt of
my sin.[40]

B

LEADER
**If we say
we have no sin,
we deceive
ourselves, and
the truth is not
in us.**

PEOPLE
If we confess
our sins,
God is faithful
and just
and will forgive
our sins
and cleanse us
from all
unrighteousness.[41]

C

LEADER
**Since we have a
great high priest
who has passed
through the
heavens, Jesus,
the only one
begotten by God,**

PEOPLE
Let us then
with confidence
draw near to the
throne of grace,
that we may
receive mercy
and find grace
to help in time
of need.[42]

CONFESSION OF SIN

The people may sit or those who are able may kneel. All may join in one of these prayers or a general confession prepared for the occasion. A special litany may be used responsively or antiphonally. A litany may be read twice, giving each half of the congregation opportunity to make confession and receive the promise of forgiveness.

LEADER
Let us confess our sins.

A

ALL
Gracious God, our sins are too heavy to carry, too real to hide, and too deep to undo. Forgive what our lips tremble to name, what our hearts can no longer bear, and what has become for us a consuming fire of judgment. Set us free from a past that we cannot change; open to us a future in which we can be changed; and grant us grace to grow more and more in your likeness and image;

B

ALL
Most merciful God, we confess that we have sinned against you in thought, word, and deed, by what we have done, and by what we have left undone. We have not loved you with our whole heart. We have not loved our neighbors as ourselves. We are truly sorry, and we humbly repent. For the sake of our Savior Jesus Christ, have mercy on us and forgive us that we may delight in your will

C

ALL
Have mercy on us, O God, according to your steadfast love; according to your abundant mercy blot out our transgressions. Wash us thoroughly from our iniquity, and cleanse us from our sin. Create in us a clean heart, O God, and put a new and right spirit within us. Cast us not away from your presence, and take not your Holy Spirit from us. Restore to us the joy of your salvation,

| through Jesus Christ our Savior. Amen. | and follow in your ways, to the glory of your name. Amen.[43] | and uphold us with a willing spirit.[44] Amen. |

SILENCE

Time may be given for individuals to confess specific sin silently.

ASSURANCE OF PARDON

In these or similar words, a leader and all present assure each other of God's mercy and pardon.

A

LEADER
While we were yet helpless, at the right time Christ died for the ungodly.

PEOPLE
God's love for us is shown in this: While we were yet sinners, Christ died for us.[45]

B

LEADER
Jesus said: Come to me, all of you who are tired from carrying heavy loads,

PEOPLE
And I will give you rest.

LEADER
Take my yoke and put it on you, and learn from me,

PEOPLE
Because I am gentle and humble in spirit; and you will find rest.

C

LEADER
Jesus said to a sinner: Where are your accusers? Has no one condemned you?

PEOPLE
Neither do I condemn you; go, and do not sin again.[47]

> LEADER
> **For the yoke
> I will give you
> is easy,**
>
> PEOPLE
> And the load I
> will put on you
> is light.[46]

AFFIRMATION OF PARDON

All who are able may stand as a leader asks these or similar questions to the congregation as individuals.

LEADER
**Do you believe that God is willing,
for Christ's sake, to forgive all your sins?**

PEOPLE
I believe.

LEADER
Do you forgive those who have sinned against you?

PEOPLE
I do, with the help of God.

LEADER
**Do you resolve to offer yourself
to the guidance of the Holy Spirit
that you may have the power to resist evil
and to do what is good?**

PEOPLE
I do.

LEADER
**In Christ's name, and as one with you in the church,
I declare to you: Your sins are forgiven.**

PEOPLE
In Christ's name,
and as sisters and brothers in the church,
we declare to you: Your sins are forgiven.

ALL
Thanks be to God.

If Holy Communion is to be celebrated, a Service of Word and Sacrament follows, beginning with the offertory. If Holy Communion is not to be celebrated on this occasion, this order continues.

PRAYERS

Prayers of thanksgiving and intercession may be offered by leaders and the people.

COLLECT

LEADER
Let us pray.

ALL
O God,
from whom come all holy desires,
all good counsels,
and all just works;
give to us, your servants,
that peace which the world cannot give
that our hearts may be set
to obey your commandments;
and that we,
being defended from the fear of our enemies,
may live in peace and quietness;
through the intercession
of Jesus Christ our Savior,
who lives and reigns
with you and the Holy Spirit,
one God for ever.
Amen.[48]

PASSING THE PEACE

As a sign of their reconciliation with God and each other, all may greet those around them with an embrace or handshake, accompanied by such words as: "The peace of God be with you," and the response:

"And also with you." Leaders may move among the congregation to share the signs of peace.

LORD'S PRAYER

If this prayer is not incorporated elsewhere in the service, it may be said here.

ACT OF PRAISE

A gloria, doxology, or hymn of praise may be sung.

BENEDICTION

A

LEADER
**Go forth into the world in peace;
be of good courage;
hold fast to that which is good;
render to no one evil for evil;
strengthen the fainthearted;
support the weak;
help the afflicted;
honor all people;
love and serve God, rejoicing in the power of the Holy Spirit.**

PEOPLE
Thanks be to God.[49]

B

LEADER
**Hear the promise of Jesus Christ:
Peace I leave with you;
my peace I give to you;
not as the world gives do I give to you.
Let not your hearts be troubled,
neither let them be afraid.**[50]

The grace of Jesus Christ be with you all.

PEOPLE
Amen.

Order for Recognition of the End of a Marriage

INTRODUCTION

This order is intended for those occasions when a man and a woman who have experienced a divorce wish to acknowledge responsibility for their separation, affirm the good that continues from the previous relationship, and promise in the presence of God, family, and supportive friends to begin a new relationship. Great sensitivity to the particular circumstances of the couple will be needed on the part of those who assist them in planning the service. Considerable advance preparation may be necessary. The promises indicated within the order should be developed by the woman and man themselves, with whatever counsel they request.

The service is penitential in nature and cannot be construed to be an encouragement of divorce or a deprecation of marriage. It does not celebrate the failure of a relationship, but acknowledges that a divorce has occurred and that two human beings are seeking in earnest to reorder their lives in a wholesome, redemptive way. The service is a reminder that nothing can separate people from the love of God in Jesus Christ.

Elements of the service may be used during pastoral counseling when a public service seems inappropriate.

Hope and joy are appropriate in this service as a man and woman pledge goodwill to each other and responsibly arrange for continuing obligations they may share.

If there are children of mature age in the family of the divorced woman and man, they may wish to share in this service in a supportive way. With great care, the one presiding may include them.

OUTLINE

Greeting
Introduction
Prayers
Reading of Scripture
Statements of Commitment
Affirmation
Benediction

*A divorced woman and man may invite the pastor or
another representative of the church to lead the service in
a supportive informal gathering of members and friends.*

GREETING

*All may stand for one or more of the following or for other
words of scripture.*

A

LEADER
**Let us remember these words from Jesus:
Where two or three are gathered in my name,**

PEOPLE
There am I in the midst of them.[51]

B

LEADER
**God is our shelter and strength,
always ready to help in times of trouble.**

PEOPLE
So we will not be afraid,
even if the earth is shaken
and mountains fall into the ocean depths;

LEADER
**Even if the seas roar and rage,
and the hills are shaken by the violence.[52]**

PEOPLE
God is our shelter and strength.

C

LEADER
God be with you.

PEOPLE
And also with you.

LEADER
Let us with confidence draw near to the throne of grace;

PEOPLE
That we may receive mercy
and find grace to help in time of need.[53]

INTRODUCTION

In these or similar words, a leader may explain the nature and purpose of the service. There are optional words for use if the man and woman are parents.

LEADER
**We are here
to witness an end and a beginning
and to share the making of new commitments.
_____ and _____ have decided,**
_{woman}   _{man}
**after much effort, pain, and anger,
that they will no longer be wife and husband,
but they wish to respect and be concerned for each other.**

---

for parents

LEADER
**They are now, and will continue to be,
parents to their child(ren),
and they wish to be responsible for** *him/her/each of them*.

LEADER
_____ and _____ are grateful to you,
_{man}   _{woman}
**who are family and friends,
for your love and support, your efforts of healing,
and your presence here.**

Those gathered may say in unison or repeat after the leader the following or other words of support.

PEOPLE
_____ and _____,
_{woman}   _{man}
in this difficult time,
we join with you as your friends.
We have been with you
in your joys, in your struggles, and in your tears.
We have not always known how to be helpful.
Although we may not fully understand,
we accept your decision.
We care, and we give you our love.

PRAYERS

*One or both of the following prayers or other prayers may
be offered. The second prayer is a prayer of confession
and is followed by words of assurance concerning God's
mercy and grace.*

Ⓐ

LEADER
Let us pray.

**O God, make us aware of your presence.
You have blessed us in all our moments:
of joining, of relating, of intending, and of beginning.
Be with us in our times of separating and of ending,
releasing us from those vows we can no longer keep;
we ask in Christ's name.**

PEOPLE
Amen.

Ⓑ

LEADER
Let us ask God for the forgiveness we need.

ALL
**God of all mercy,
we know that you love us even when we are not sure
that we love ourselves.
Embrace us when frustration and failure
leave us hollow and empty.
Forgive our sins,
and grant us forgiving hearts toward others.
In the confession of our lips,
show us now the promise of a new day,
the springtime of the forgiven;
through Jesus Christ,
who is able to make all things new.
Amen.**

LEADER
**God's love for us is shown in this:
While we were yet sinners,
Christ died for us.**[54]

READING OF SCRIPTURE

One or more lessons may be read. The man and woman, other family members, or friends may assist with the scripture reading.

PSALMS

Psalms 13; 31:1-2, 9-10, 14, 16; 91:1-6, 9-12; 130:1-7

NEW TESTAMENT

Mark 4:35-41
Mark 9:33-37, *if children are involved*
Romans 8:35, 37-39
1 John 4:1-12, 19-21

STATEMENTS OF COMMITMENT

In these or similar words, the leader may invite the woman and man to speak words leading to hope about the future.

LEADER

_____ **and** _____ ,
man woman

some of us/your family and friends **were present
when you made your commitment to marriage.
Before God, and all of us,
we invite you to share the new commitments
you are prepared to make.**

Here may follow personal words spoken by the woman and man. The words may express some of the agreements they have made with each other after much work, anguish, and counseling. Areas that may be included are:

- *regret, apology, and confession related to unfulfilled intentions;*
- *mutual care and respect;*
- *support and care for their children;*
- *the need for supportive friends;*
- *affirmation of good continuing from their life together.*

The leader may invite words of support and love from those present or from a representative among them.

AFFIRMATION

The leader or the entire gathering may say these or similar words of affirmation. There are optional words that recognize the presence of children from the relationship.

LEADER/ALL
**We affirm you in the new commitments you have made:
commitments which find you separated
but still concerned about each other
and wishing each other goodwill,**

> **commitments which enable you
> to support and to love your child(ren),**

**and commitments which help
to heal the pain you may feel.
Count on God's presence;
trust our support;
begin anew.**

BENEDICTION

A
LEADER
Go in peace.

PEOPLE
Amen.

B
LEADER
**Go forth into the world
in peace;
be of good courage;
hold fast to that
which is good;
render to no one evil for evil;
strengthen the fainthearted;
support the weak;
help the afflicted;
honor all people;
love and serve God,
rejoicing in the power
of the Holy Spirit.**

PEOPLE
Amen.[55]

Order for Healing
for Use with an Individual

INTRODUCTION

Services of healing have a biblical heritage appropriate for the full life of a local church. Anointing and the laying on of hands are acts closely related to the covenant of faithful love between God and Israel and between God and the church. In scripture, monarchs are anointed, prophets commissioned, the Holy Spirit conferred, the sick healed, and the dead raised in acts of faith accompanied by anointing with oil, the laying on of hands, or touch in another form. The symbolism of touch has survived almost universally among churches in the laying on of hands at confirmation and ordination. The power of touch in healing is finding renewed acceptance as is the unity of the total person.

In the New Testament, faith, forgiveness of sins, and healing are frequently inseparable but distinct aspects of one experience. Out of mercy and compassion, God works to bring about reconciliation that restores peace between God and humanity, among individuals and communities, within each person, and between humankind and the creation. Guilt, anxiety, fear, broken relationships, and the loneliness of alienation all contribute to human sickness. Healing, in the Christian sense, is the reintegration of body, mind, emotions, and spirit that permits people, in community, to live life fully in a creation honored by prudent and respectful use.

In this healing service, four themes are intertwined: God's word, growth in faith, forgiveness of sin, human touch.

In scripture, God's word reassures us of the Creator's love and compassion. Jesus' acts of healing, the healing ministry of the New Testament church, and contemporary experiences of healing all testify to the health and fullness God makes possible in human life.

Faith in the inclusive sense of trust and belief in God's unmerited goodness is an integral cornerstone of the New Testament understanding of healing. Individuals and communities of believers nurture each other in their mutual growth in faith. God does not promise that we will be spared suffering, but does promise to be with us in our suffering. Trusting that promise, we are enabled to bear the unbearable and recognize God's sustaining nearness in pain, in sickness, and in injury.

Forgiveness of sin is often closely associated with healing in the New Testament. The connection of forgiveness and healing affirms the psychosomatic unity of individuals recognized by modern health sciences. It admits the importance of openness and honesty to every relationship of love. It sets health in the context of relationships restored by confession and forgiveness.

In the New Testament, touch plays a central role in the healing ministry. The power of touch is recognized, whether in the anointing with oil, the laying on of hands, or the less formal gesture of holding someone's hand or touching a wound. Jesus frequently touched others: blessing children, washing feet, healing injuries or disease, and raising people from death. Jesus also allowed himself to be touched, washed, embraced, anointed. To allow oneself to be touched is an act of openness. To touch another is an act of acceptance in which a person transfers something of oneself to another: love, affection, protection, strength, power, acceptance. Touch in the healing ministry embodies the embrace of God for the redeemed creation when in the mystery of last things God will make all things new.

In James (5:13-16), prayer, anointing, confession, and forgiveness are shown to have a place in healing. This passage may be included in the scripture read during the service.

This order is a brief service for use in the privacy of a sickroom or home or in some other place when time or circumstances prohibit the sick person from sharing in a corporate service of healing. When this service is to be used, it is recommended that the pastor or another representative of the church visit privately with the sick person to review the meaning and purpose of this service and its compatibility with modern medicine. A preliminary visit will also open the way for trust and affection. At that time, the person requesting the service may determine which elements of the service best meet his or her needs.

The service may be led by more than one person. It is often helpful to allow time for personal reflection and prayer following the service.

Holy Communion may be celebrated in the same visit as the Order for Healing for Use with an Individual. If so, following the prayers of intercession in this order, begin with the communion prayer in the Brief Order for One Who Is Sick on page 91, and continue with that order.

This service requires careful preparation. Private counsel and prayer allow for a deeper exploration of the problems and the resources available for healing, including medical, emotional, and spiritual aid. It is especially important that this service bring personal affirmation to the sick person, no matter how formally or informally it is led.

Directions for standing and sitting or kneeling have been omitted from the instructions for this service. Those planning the service need to be sensitive to physical and other limitations of those who participate and give helpful directions accordingly.

Olive oil is traditionally used in anointing. For use in sickrooms and homes, it may be placed in a pen-like vial that is easily carried from place to place.

OUTLINE

Sections of this order that fit the particular needs of the sick person may be used, or the entire order may be used.

Greeting and Preparation
Reading of Scripture
Confession of Sin
Reaffirmation of Faith
Assurance of Pardon

> **Order for Anointing, with the laying on of hands as an option**

> **Order for the Laying on of Hands, without anointing**

Prayers of Intercession

> **Brief Order for the Service of Word and Sacrament for One Who Is Sick, beginning with the communion prayer**

> **Prayer of Our Savior**
> **Benediction**

A pastor or another representative of the church may use the sections of this order that fit the particular needs of the sick person who has requested this ministry and is unable to participate in a corporate service of healing.

GREETING AND PREPARATION

A pastor or another representative of the church, in the name of Jesus Christ and the church, may greet the sick person and others who are present, explain briefly the meaning and nature of the service, and invite all to participate fully. The following words may be used in greeting.

LEADER
**Grace and peace to you from Jesus Christ.
Your brothers and sisters of** _____
send you their love.   _{local church}

READING OF SCRIPTURE

One or more of the following lessons may be read, depending on the circumstances of the sick person. Others present may assist with the readings. If anointing with oil is to follow, it is recommended that the lesson from James conclude the readings. Lessons may be interpreted briefly.

PSALMS
Psalms 20, 23, 91, 103, 145:13-21

EPISTLES
Acts 3:1-10
Hebrews 12:1-2
James 5:13-16
1 John 1:5-2:2, 5:13-15

GOSPELS
Matthew 8:1-4, 8:5-13, 8:14-17, 9:2-8
Mark 6:7, 12-13; 10:46-52
Luke 17:11-19
John 9:1-12

CONFESSION OF SIN

If it seems appropriate, the leader may invite the sick person to share any trouble or difficulty that hinders her or his relationship with God. The words below may be used.

Ⓐ

LEADER

——————————,
      name
**the scriptures tell us
to bear one another's
burdens and so fulfill
the law of Christ.**[56]
As your *sister/brother*
**in Christ,
I ask you now,
are you at peace with God,
or is there anything in your
life that causes you to feel
separated from God
and less than the full person
God calls you to be?**

Ⓑ

LEADER

——————————,
      name
**the scriptures tell us
not to be anxious
about our lives
or about tomorrow.
Are there anxieties
that cause you to feel
separated from the peace
which God promises?**

Time for silence, reflection, and personal sharing may be given. Counsel, within the competency of the pastor or the other representative, may be offered. If the person desires it, a prayer of confession may be said, such as the following, one from a Service of Word and Sacrament, an extemporaneous one, or one from another source. The Order for Reconciliation of a Penitent Person, which begins on page 268, may be used.

LEADER
Let us ask God for the forgiveness we need.

ALL
**Have mercy on us, O God,
according to your steadfast love;
according to your abundant mercy
blot out our transgressions.
Wash us thoroughly from our iniquity,
and cleanse us from our sin.**

Create in us a clean heart, O God,
and put a new and right spirit within us.
Cast us not away from your presence,
and take not your Holy Spirit from us.
Restore to us the joy of your salvation,
and uphold us with a willing spirit.[57]
Amen.

REAFFIRMATION OF FAITH

If it seems appropriate, the sick person may be given an
opportunity to reaffirm a personal commitment to Jesus
Christ in these or similar words.

LEADER

————————,
    name

do you reaffirm your faith in Jesus Christ?

INDIVIDUAL
I do.

ASSURANCE OF PARDON

God's pardon is declared in these or similar words.

Ⓐ
LEADER

————————,
    name

take comfort
in the assurance
that even those things
that are hidden from
memory, or are too deep
for our words,
are not beyond God's
forgiving love.
God, who knows us
completely, bestows
pardon and peace.

INDIVIDUAL
Amen.

Ⓑ
LEADER
God's love for us
is shown in this:
While we were yet sinners,
Christ died for us.[58]

INDIVIDUAL
Amen.

If anointing and the laying on of hands are not part of the service, continue with the prayers of intercession on page 305. If anointing is omitted, but the laying on of hands is part of the service, continue with that order on page 304.

ORDER FOR ANOINTING

THANKSGIVING OVER OIL

If the sick person is to be anointed with oil, one of the following prayers or a similar one may be said.

A

LEADER

O God, our Redeemer, giver of health and salvation, we give you thanks for the gift of oil. As the apostles anointed many who were sick, and you healed them, so may your Holy Spirit come on us and on this oil that the one who receives this anointing in repentance and faith may be made well in accordance with your will; through Jesus Christ our Savior.

INDIVIDUAL

Amen.[59]

B

LEADER

Eternal God, you are the Sun of Righteousness who rises with healing in your wings to put to flight all enemies that assault us. We thank you for oil, used by prophets and apostles as a sign of your grace and favor. Send your Holy Spirit on us and on this medicine of mercy that through this anointing your servant may again know the health that comes from you; through Jesus Christ our Savior.

INDIVIDUAL

Amen.

ACT OF ANOINTING AND THE LAYING ON OF HANDS

Touching the thumb to the oil and then to the sick person's forehead, the pastor or another representative of the church may make the sign of the cross and say the following or similar words of anointing.

LEADER

————————,
name

**on your confession of repentance and faith,
you are now anointed with oil
in the name of Jesus Christ,
for the forgiveness of sins,
for the strengthening of your faith,
and for healing and peace,
according to God's grace and wisdom.**

INDIVIDUAL
Amen.[60]

*If both anointing and the laying on of hands are
desired, the following or similar words may be said.
All people present may be invited to participate in the
laying on of hands.*

LEADER

————————,
name

I/we **lay** *my/our* **hands upon you
in the name of our Sovereign and Savior
Jesus Christ,
calling upon Christ
to uphold and fill you with grace
that you may know the healing power
of God's love.**

INDIVIDUAL
Amen.[61]

**If the laying on of hands has occurred or will not occur,
continue with the prayers of intercession on the next page.**

ORDER FOR THE LAYING ON OF HANDS

*All people present may be invited to lay on hands as
the following or similar words are said.*

A

LEADER

———————,
name

on your confession
of repentance and faith,
I lay my hands upon you
in the name
of Jesus Christ,
for the forgiveness of sins,
for the strengthening
of your faith, and for
your healing and peace,
according to God's grace
and wisdom.

INDIVIDUAL
Amen.[62]

B

LEADER

———————,
name

I lay my hands upon you
in the name of our
Sovereign and Savior
Jesus Christ,
calling upon Christ
to uphold and fill you
with grace
that you may know
the healing power
of God's love.

INDIVIDUAL
Amen.[63]

PRAYERS OF INTERCESSION

*All present may be invited to join the leader in offering
prayers for the sick person and for physicians, nurses, and
others who minister to that person's needs.*

**If Holy Communion is desired, begin with the commu-
nion prayer in a Brief Order of Word and Sacrament for One
Who Is Sick on page 91, and continue with that order.**

PRAYER OF OUR SAVIOR

BENEDICTION

LEADER
May God bless you and keep you.
May God's face shine upon you
and be gracious to you.
May God look upon you with kindness
and give you peace.[64]

PEOPLE
Amen.

Order for Healing for Congregational Use

INTRODUCTION

Services of healing have a biblical heritage appropriate for the full life of a local church. Anointing and the laying on of hands are acts closely related to the covenant of faithful love between God and Israel and between God and the church. In scripture, monarchs are anointed, prophets commissioned, the Holy Spirit conferred, the sick healed, and the dead raised in acts of faith accompanied by anointing with oil, the laying on of hands, or touch in another form. The symbolism of touch has survived almost universally among churches in the laying on of hands at confirmation and ordination. The power of touch in healing is finding renewed acceptance as is the unity of the total person.

In the New Testament, faith, forgiveness of sins, and healing are frequently inseparable but distinct aspects of one experience. Out of mercy and compassion, God works to bring about reconciliation that restores peace between God and humanity, among individuals and communities, within each person, and between humankind and the creation. Guilt, anxiety, fear, broken relationships, and the loneliness of alienation all contribute to human sickness. Healing, in the Christian sense, is the reintegration of body, mind, emotions, and spirit that permits people, in community, to live life fully in a creation honored by prudent and respectful use.

In this healing service, four themes are intertwined: God's word, growth in faith, forgiveness of sin, human touch.

In scripture, God's word reassures us of the Creator's love and compassion. Jesus' acts of healing, the healing ministry of the New Testament church, and contemporary experiences of healing all testify to the health and fullness God makes possible in human life.

Faith in the inclusive sense of trust and belief in God's unmerited goodness is an integral cornerstone of the New Testament understanding of healing. Individuals and communities of believers nurture each other in their mutual growth in faith. God does not promise that we will be spared suffering, but does promise to be with us in our suffering. Trusting that promise, we are enabled to bear the unbearable and recognize God's sustaining nearness in pain, in sickness, and in injury.

Forgiveness of sin is often closely associated with healing in the New Testament. The connection of forgiveness and healing affirms the psychosomatic unity of individuals recognized by modern health sciences. It admits the importance of openness and honesty to every relationship of love. It sets health in the context of relationships restored by confession and forgiveness.

In the New Testament, touch plays a central role in the healing ministry. The power of touch is recognized, whether in the anointing with oil, the laying on of hands, or the less formal gesture of holding someone's hand or touching a wound. Jesus frequently touched others: blessing children, washing feet, healing injuries or disease, and raising people from death. Jesus also allowed himself to be touched, washed, embraced, anointed. To allow oneself to be touched is an act of openness. To touch another is an act of acceptance in which a person transfers something of oneself to another: love, affection, protection, strength, power, acceptance. Touch in the healing ministry embodies the embrace of God for the redeemed creation when in the mystery of last things God will make all things new.

In James (5:13-16), prayer, anointing, confession, and forgiveness are shown to have a place in healing. This passage may be included in the scripture read during the service.

Use of this order requires careful preparation. Private counsel and prayer allow for a deeper exploration of the problems and the resources available for healing, including medical, emotional, and spiritual aid. It is recommended that the public service of healing be supported by intercessory prayer groups that meet on a regular basis.

Directions for standing and sitting or kneeling have been omitted from the instructions for this service. Those planning the service will need to be especially sensitive to physical and other limitations of those who participate and give helpful directions accordingly.

Olive oil is traditionally used in anointing. It may be placed in a small bowl or other vessel.

OUTLINE

If this order is used alone, music is to be incorporated into the service. When used within another service, this order may begin with the prayers of intercession and conclude with the prayer of thanksgiving and with a dismissal if people have come forward.

Greeting
Sentences
Hymn
Reading of Scripture
Sermon
Call to Confession
Silence
Corporate Confession
Assurance of Pardon
Prayers of Intercession

| Order for Anointing, with the laying on of hands as an option | Order for the Laying on of Hands, without anointing |

Prayer of Thanksgiving
Lord's Prayer

Dismissal

Hymn of Parting
Benediction

At the conclusion of the prayer of thanksgiving and a dismissal, if necessary, a Service of Word and Sacrament or a or a Service of the Word may continue.

When used within another service, this order may begin with the prayers of intercession and conclude with the prayer of thanksgiving.

When used within a Service of Word and Sacrament or a Service of the Word, it may be incorporated within the prayers of the people.

When used within Service of Word and Sacrament II, it may be appropriate to begin the abbreviated order for healing following the assurance of pardon and prior to the passing of the peace.

When this order for healing is used by itself, a prelude and postlude, anthems, and other music or use of other arts may be incorporated within it in accordance with local custom and in recognition of the role of music and non-verbal expression in healing.

GREETING

LEADER
**The grace of our Lord Jesus Christ
and the love of God
and the communion of the Holy Spirit
be with you all.**[65]

PEOPLE
And also with you.

SENTENCES

One or more of these may be said.

[A]
LEADER
**Jesus said:
Heal the sick and tell them,
"God's heavenly reign is near you."**[66]

[B]
LEADER
**Hear these words of Jesus:
I tell you,**

whatever you ask in prayer,
believe that you receive it,
and you will.[67]

ⓒ
LEADER
The apostle Paul said:
Do not conform yourselves
to the standards of this world,
but let God transform you inwardly
by a complete change of your mind.[68]

HYMN

The congregation may sing a hymn about God's love for the human family.

READING OF SCRIPTURE

One or more psalms may be read or sung and lessons read. Members of the local church may be invited to assist with the reading. If anointing with oil is to follow, it is recommended that the reading from James be included among the lessons.

OLD TESTAMENT
Genesis 1:26-31
2 Kings 5:1,9-15
Psalms 20, 23, 91, 103, 145:13-21

EPISTLES
Acts 3:1-10
Hebrews 12:1-2
James 5:13-16
1 John 1:5-2:2, 5:13-15

GOSPELS
Matthew 8:1-4, 8:5-13, 8:14-17, 9:2-8
Mark 6:7, 12-13; 10:46-52
Luke 17:11-19
John 9:1-12

SERMON

CALL TO CONFESSION

A leader may use her or his own words; appropriate sections from the Order for Corporate Reconciliation, which begins on page 275; or one of the following to invite all present to seek the forgiveness of God and neighbor.

A

LEADER
**To bear one another's
burdens in prayer
is a holy privilege.
It also demands a
willingness to be a channel
for God's power.
Therefore, in silence,
let us offer our confessions
to God that we may be
cleansed of anything that
might hinder our efforts
as intercessors.**[69]

**In confessing,
let us name those sins
which separate and distort:
sins of pride, self-love,
and resentment;
sins of hatred, bitterness,
and jealousy.
Let us name also our
connection with humanity's
sins: sins of poverty, war,
hunger, injustice, neglect,
and discrimination.**

B

LEADER
**Jesus said: Ask,
and it will be given;
seek, and you will find;
knock, and it will be
opened to you.**

PEOPLE
For everyone who asks
receives, and those
who seek find,
and to each who knocks
it will be opened.[70]

LEADER
**Friends in Christ,
God knows our needs
before we ask and
in our asking prepares us
to receive the gift of grace.
God ministers to us
not as one who is absent
but as one who is present
in human hands, voices,
and lives full
of the Holy Spirit.**

**Let us open our lives
to God's healing presence
and forsake all that
separates us from God
and neighbor.**

**Let us be mindful
not only of personal evil
but also of our communal
sins of family, class, race,
and nation.**

**Let us confess to God
in silence whatever has
wounded us or brought
injury to others
in body, mind, or spirit
that we may receive mercy
and become for each other
ministers of God's grace.**

SILENCE

Silence may be offered for personal examination of conscience and for prayers for forgiveness.

CORPORATE CONFESSION

If it seems appropriate to summarize the prayers of all corporately, one of the following prayers or one in a leader's own words may be used.

LEADER
Let us confess our sins together.

A
ALL
**Have mercy on us, O God, according to your steadfast love; according to your abundant mercy blot out our transgressions.
Wash us thoroughly from our iniquity,
and cleanse us from our sin.
Create in us a clean heart,**

B
ALL
**Eternal God,
in whom we live and move
and have our being,
whose face is hidden
from us by our sins,
and whose mercy we forget
in the hardness
of our hearts,
cleanse us, we pray,**

O God,
and put a new and right
spirit within us.
Cast us not away
from your presence,
and take not your
Holy Spirit from us.
Restore to us the joy
of your salvation,
and uphold us
with a willing spirit.[71]
Amen.

from all our offenses,
and deliver us from proud
thoughts and vain desires,
that with lowliness and
meekness we may draw
near to you,
trusting in your grace,
and finding in you
our refuge and strength;
through Jesus Christ
our Savior.
Amen.[72]

ASSURANCE OF PARDON

*In these or similar words, the people are assured of God's
mercy and pardon.*

LEADER
**If we confess our sins,
God is faithful and just
and will forgive our sins
and cleanse us from all unrighteousness.[73]**

**Brothers and sisters,
I announce with joy that we are forgiven.**
PEOPLE
Thanks be to God.

PRAYERS OF INTERCESSION

*Requests for intercessory prayers may be gathered on
cards provided before the service or may be invited orally.
The names and needs of the persons desiring prayers may
be read or repeated briefly and time given after each name
for the congregation to pray in silence. Others present may
be invited to join a leader in offering prayers for those who
are sick and for physicians, nurses, and others who minister to individuals' needs. The following prayer may be
used as a model of a prayer for those who are sick.*

LEADER
**O God of all comfort,
our help in time of need,
we humbly ask you
in the power of your Holy Spirit
to enter and heal your servant**

————————.
name

Look upon *her/him* **with your mercy;
comfort** *him/her* **with the assurance
of your care and goodness;
save** *her/him* **from temptation and despair;
give** *him/her* **patience under affliction;
and enable** *her/him*
**to live the remainder of life in peace;
through Jesus Christ,
who came that we may have life
and have it more abundantly.
Amen.**[74]

*If the laying on of hands is to take place without anoint-
ing, continue with the Order for the Laying on of Hands
on page 318. If neither anointing nor the laying on of
hands is to take place, continue with the prayer of thanksgiving on page 319.*

ORDER FOR ANOINTING

THANKSGIVING OVER OIL
*If oil is to be used, one of the following prayers or a
similar one may be said.*

A
LEADER
**O God, our Redeemer,
giver of health
and salvation,
we give you thanks
for the gift of oil.
As the apostles anointed
many who were sick,**

B
LEADER
**Eternal God, you are
the Sun of Righteousness
who rises with healing
in your wings to put
to flight all enemies
that assault us.
We thank you for oil,**

and you healed them,
so may your Holy Spirit
come on us and on this oil,
that *the one/those* who
receive(s) this anointing
in repentance and faith
may be made well
in accordance
with your will;
through Jesus Christ
our Savior.

PEOPLE
Amen.[75]

used by prophets
and apostles as a sign
of your grace and favor.
Send your Holy Spirit
on us and on this
medicine of mercy that
through this anointing
your servants may again
know the health
that comes from you;
through Jesus Christ
our Savior.

PEOPLE
Amen.

INVITATION TO ANOINTING
AND THE LAYING ON OF HANDS

*In these or similar words, the people may be invited to
receive anointing. The indented words may be included
if those to be anointed also will have hands laid on them.
Instructions may be included to indicate the designated
place for people to gather.*

LEADER
Those who desire to be anointed

    and to have hands laid on them

for spiritual healing may come forward.
If you wish us to come to you, raise your hand
or ask your neighbor to identify you for us.
You may come for yourself,
or you may come as a channel of God's healing power
for someone else.
During the anointing,

    and the laying on of hands,

we invite all present to make silent prayers
for each one who is seeking God's healing.

ACT OF ANOINTING

Touching the thumb to the oil and then to each person's forehead, a leader may make the sign of the cross and say these or similar words.

Ⓐ

LEADER

——————————,
name
**on your confession
of repentance and faith,
you are now anointed
with oil in the name
of Jesus Christ,
for the forgiveness
of sins,
for the strengthening
of your faith,
and for healing
and peace,
according to God's grace
and wisdom.**

PEOPLE
Amen.[76]

Ⓑ

LEADER

——————————,
name
**as I anoint you,
so may God grant you
the powerful presence
of the Holy Spirit.
With infinite mercy,
may God forgive your sins,
release you from suffering,
and restore you to health
and strength. May God
deliver you from all evil,
preserve you in all
goodness, and bring you
to everlasting life;
through Jesus Christ
our Savior.**

PEOPLE
Amen.[77]

ACT OF THE LAYING ON OF HANDS

The pastor and/or other representatives of the church may say these or similar words as they lay hands on each individual who desires it.

LEADER

——————————, *I/we* **lay** *my/our* **hands upon you**
name
**in the name of our Sovereign and Savior
Jesus Christ, calling upon Christ
to uphold and fill you with grace,
that you may know the healing power of God's love.**

PEOPLE
Amen.[78]

If the laying on of hands has occurred or will not occur, continue with the prayer of thanksgiving on the next page.

ORDER FOR THE LAYING ON OF HANDS

INVITATION TO THE LAYING ON OF HANDS

Those who wish to receive the laying on of hands may be invited to come forward with these or other words. Instructions may be included to indicate the designated place for people to gather.

LEADER
**Those who desire to have hands laid on them
for spiritual healing may come forward.
If you wish us to come to you, raise your hand
or ask your neighbor to identify you for us.
You may come for yourself
or you may come as a channel of God's healing power
for someone else.
During the laying on of hands,
we invite all present to make silent prayers
for each one who is seeking God's healing.**

ACT OF THE LAYING ON OF HANDS WITHOUT ANOINTING

The pastor and/or other representatives of the church may say these or similar words as they lay hands on each individual who desires it.

A LEADER	**B** LEADER	**C** LEADER
————, name	————, name	————, name
on your confession of repentance and faith, *I/we* **lay** *my/our* **hands upon you**	*I/we* **lay** *my/our* **hands upon you in the name of our Sovereign and Savior Jesus Christ,**	**as** *I/we* **lay** *my/our* **hands upon you, so may God grant you the powerful presence**

in the name
of Jesus Christ,
for the
forgiveness
of sins,
for the
strengthening
of your faith,
and for healing
and peace,
according
to God's grace
and wisdom.

PEOPLE
Amen.[79]

calling on Christ
to uphold
and fill you
with grace,
that you may
know the
healing power
of God's love.

PEOPLE
Amen.[80]

of the
Holy Spirit.
With infinite
mercy, may
God forgive
your sins,
release you
from suffering,
and restore you
to health
and strength.
May God
deliver you
from all evil,
preserve you
in all goodness,
and bring you
to everlasting
life; through
Jesus Christ
our Savior.

PEOPLE
Amen.[81]

PRAYER OF THANKSGIVING

*If people have come forward for anointing or for the lay-
ing on of hands, they may remain for this prayer and the
Lord's Prayer and be dismissed to their places in the
congregation prior to the hymn. This prayer or another,
written or extemporaneous, may be offered.*

LEADER
Let us pray.

ALL
We give praise and thanks to you, O God!
In Jesus Christ, you have given us life;
brought ministry, forgiveness, healing, and peace;
commanded the disciples to heal the sick;
and continued the healing ministry among us to this day.

Keep us mindful of your love and mercy
that we may be faithful
throughout all our days,
in the name of Jesus Christ.
Amen.

LORD'S PRAYER

DISMISSAL

If people have come forward for anointing or the lay-
ing on of hands, they may be dismissed in these or
similar words.

LEADER
Go in peace to love and serve God.

HYMN OF PARTING

BENEDICTION

LEADER
May God bless you and keep you.
May God's face shine upon you
and be gracious to you.
May God look upon you with kindness
and give you peace.[82]

PEOPLE
Amen.

Services
of Marriage

Order for Marriage

INTRODUCTION

The essence of marriage is a covenanted commitment that has its foundation in the faithfulness of God's love. The marriage ceremony is the glad occasion on which two people unite as husband and wife in the mutual exchange of covenant promises. The one presiding acts as an official representative of the church and gives the marriage the church's blessing. The congregation joins in affirming the marriage and in offering support and thanksgiving for the new family.

It is the responsibility of the one who presides to meet with the couple prior to the marriage ceremony in order to counsel them concerning the Christian understanding of the marriage relationship.

Congregational participation, ethnic traditions, and local customs may be taken into consideration when planning the Order for Marriage. Hymns and other music of joy, praise, and thanksgiving may be included in the service after consultation with the congregation's music leaders and in keeping with a sense of the appropriateness of their use in a religious service. Psalms may be sung or said responsively, and other readings or statements may be used.

The one presiding may invite the couple to share in the writing and planning of their service. A Christian marriage ceremony is a service of worship offered to God. Family and friends of the couple may be invited to share the leadership of the service by reading scripture or by offering prayers or in other ways.

If the couple desires to be married within the regular Sunday service of the congregation, the Order for Marriage may be celebrated following the sermon.

If a couple requests Holy Communion on the occasion of their wedding, a Service of Word and Sacrament may be used as indicated in this order. The one presiding needs to use informed judgment as to circumstances in which Holy Communion can be celebrated meaningfully and with theological and biblical integrity. The religious affiliations of those to be assembled for the wedding will affect the decision. When a Service of Word and Sacrament is used, the prayers and other elements of the service printed here may be substituted in the proper places in that service.

All present may more easily participate in the service if a copy of this order is available to them in a bulletin.

It is the responsibility of the one presiding at the marriage to understand and conform to the marriage laws in the place where the ceremony is to be held.

OUTLINE

Prelude
Entrance
Greeting
Introduction
Prayer
Reading of Scripture
Sermon
Declaration of Intention
Pledge of Support
Vows of the Marriage Covenant
Exchange of Symbols
Announcement of Marriage
Blessing
Passing the Peace

Prayer of Thanksgiving
Prayer of Our Savior

Order for Holy Communion

Benediction
Hymn or Postlude

PRELUDE

ENTRANCE

Banners, ribbons, flowers, candles, white carpeting, or other items may be used in the procession in accordance with local custom. A hymn, psalm, canticle, or anthem may be sung, or instrumental music may be played.

The couple to be married may enter the sanctuary together or separately. They may be accompanied by their parents, other members of the family, and friends. People in the congregation who are able may stand for the processional.

GREETING

The couple to be married and the wedding party may stand, if they are able, facing the one presiding. Usually the groom is at the right of the bride as they face forward.

The one presiding may use one of the following greetings or another one based on scripture.

A

PASTOR
The grace of our Lord Jesus Christ and the love of God and the communion of the Holy Spirit be with you all.[1]

PEOPLE
And also with you.

B

PASTOR
Love comes from God. Everyone who truly loves is a child of God.[2] **Let us worship God.**

INTRODUCTION

The one presiding may state the Christian understanding of marriage, using one of the following or other words.

A

PASTOR

**Dearly beloved,
we are gathered here
as the people of God
to witness the marriage
of** _____
<small>bride</small>
and _____.
<small>groom</small>
**We come to share
in their joy and
to ask God to bless them.**

**Marriage is a gift of God,
sealed by a sacred covenant.
God gives human love.
Through that love,
husband and wife come
to know each other
with mutual care
and companionship.
God gives joy.
Through that joy,
wife and husband
may share their new life
with others as Jesus
shared new wine at the
wedding in Cana.**

**With our love and our
prayers, we support**
_____ **and**
<small>groom</small>
_____
<small>bride</small>
**as they now freely give
themselves to each other.**

B

PASTOR

**Dear friends,
we have come together
in the presence of God
to witness the marriage
of** _____
<small>bride</small>
and _____,
<small>groom</small>
**to surround them
with our prayers,
and to share
in their joy.**

**The scriptures teach us
that the bond and covenant
of marriage is a gift of God,
a holy mystery
in which man and woman
become one flesh,
an image of the union
of Christ and the church.**

**As this woman and this
man give themselves
to each other today,
we remember that
at Cana in Galilee
our Savior Jesus Christ
made the wedding feast
a sign of God's reign
of love.**

**Let us enter into this
celebration confident that
through the Holy Spirit,
Christ is present
with us now.
We pray that this couple
may fulfill God's purpose
for the whole of their lives.**

PRAYER

One of these, a prayer of confession with an assurance of pardon, or a prayer for illumination may be offered.

PASTOR
Let us pray.

Ⓐ

ALL
**O God,
we gather to celebrate
your gift of love
and its presence among us.
We rejoice that two people
have chosen to commit
themselves to a life
of loving faithfulness
to one another.
We praise you, O God,
for the ways you have
touched our lives
with a variety
of loving relationships.
We give thanks that we
have experienced your love
through the life-giving love
of Jesus Christ
and through the care and
affection of other people.**

**At the same time,
we remember and confess
to you, O God,
that we often have failed
to be loving,
that we often have taken
for granted the people
for whom we care most.
We selfishly neglect
and strain the bonds
that unite us with others.**

Ⓑ

ALL
**Gracious God,
always faithful
in your love for us,
we rejoice in your presence.
You create love.
You unite us
in one human family.
You offer your word
and lead us in light.
You open your loving arms
and embrace us
with strength.
May the presence of Christ
fill our hearts with new joy
and make new the lives
of your servants whose
marriage we celebrate.
Bless all creation through
this sign of your love
shown in the love**

of _____
                 groom

and _____
                 bride

**for each other.
May the power of your
Holy Spirit sustain them
and all of us in love
that knows no end.
Amen.**

We hurt those who love us
and withdraw from the
community that encircles us.
Forgive us, O God.
Renew within us
an affectionate spirit.
Enrich our lives
with the gracious gift
of your love
so that we may embrace
others with the same love.
May our participation
in this celebration
of love and commitment
give to us a new joy and
responsiveness to the
relationships we cherish;
through Jesus Christ
we pray.
Amen.

PASTOR
Through the great depth
and strength of God's love
for us, God reaches out to us
to forgive our sins
and to restore us to life.
Be assured, children of God,
that God's love enfolds us
and upbuilds us
so that we may continue
to love one another
as God has loved us.[3]

READING OF SCRIPTURE

The congregation may be seated. One or more scripture
lessons may be read by the one presiding, by members of
the family, or by members of the wedding party. If Holy
Communion is to be celebrated, it is appropriate that the

readings include a Gospel lesson. A hymn, psalm, or other music may be offered between readings or before or after the sermon. Passages for consideration for use include the following ecumenical suggestions.

OLD TESTAMENT

Genesis 1:26-28, 31; 2:18-24
Psalms 23, 33, 34, 37:3-7, 67, 100, 103, 112, 117, 121, 127,
        128, 136, 145, 148, 150
Song of Solomon 2:8-13, 8:6-7
Jeremiah 31:31-34
Isaiah 54:5-8
Hosea 2:16-23

EPISTLES

Romans 8:31-39; 12:1-2, 9-18
1 Corinthians 6:15-20, 13:1-13
Ephesians 3:14-21; 5:2, 21-33
Colossians 3:12-17
1 Peter 3:1-9
1 John 3:18-24, 4:7-16
Revelation 19:1, 5-9

GOSPELS

Matthew 5:1-12; 5:13-16; 7:21, 24-29; 19:3-6; 22:35-40
Mark 10:6-9, 13-16
John 2:1-11, 15:9-17

SERMON

A brief sermon, charge, or other response to scripture may be given.

Depending on the religious affiliations of those gathered for the marriage service, it may be appropriate for all who are able to stand and say a creed or affirmation of faith. Forms of the United Church of Christ Statement of Faith, historic creeds, and other affirmations are in the Resource Section, beginning on page 509.

DECLARATION OF INTENTION

PASTOR
addressing the couple
**Before God and this congregation,
I ask you to affirm your willingness
to enter this covenant of marriage
and to share all the joys and sorrows
of this new relationship,
whatever the future may hold.**

PASTOR
addressing the groom

—————————,
         groom
will you have —————————— **to be your wife,**
                 bride
**and will you love her faithfully
as long as you both shall live?**

GROOM
I will, with the help of God.

PASTOR
addressing the bride

—————————,
         bride
will you have —————————— **to be your husband,**
                 groom
**and will you love him faithfully
as long as you both shall live?**

BRIDE
I will, with the help of God.

PLEDGE OF SUPPORT

This pledge of support should be used at the discretion of the pastor and in consultation with the people involved. It allows the family and congregation to pledge their support and encouragement to the couple. It is important to consider use of the pledge when there are children from previous relationships.

Children who will share in the new family may be addressed in these or similar words. They may stand, if able, at their places or may move near the couple.

PASTOR
addressing each child by name

_____,
    name(s)

**you are entering a new family.
Will you give to this new family
your trust, love, and affection?**

EACH CHILD
I will, with the help of God.

PASTOR
addressing the bride and groom

_____ **and** _____,
   bride   groom

**will you be faithful and loving parents
to _____?**
    name(s) of child(ren)

COUPLE
We will, with the help of God.

The pastor may invite the immediate families of the groom and bride, including adults or younger children from previous relationships, to stand in place, if they are able, and to offer their support in these or similar words.

PASTOR
addressing the families
Will the families of _____ **and** _____
                             groom   bride
please stand/please answer **in support of this couple.
Do you offer your prayerful blessing
and loving support to this marriage?
If so, please say, "I do."**

FAMILY MEMBERS
I do.

All family members may be seated. The person(s) who escorted the bride may be seated with her family.

The pastor may address the congregation in these or similar words.

PASTOR
addressing the congregation
**Do you, as people of God,
pledge your support and encouragement
to the covenant commitment that**

_____ and _____ are making together?
       bride   groom
If so, please say, "We do."

PEOPLE
We do.

An intercessory prayer, using the following or other words, may be offered.

PASTOR
**God of our mothers and of our fathers,
hear our pledges encouraging and supporting this union**

of _____ and _____ .
          groom   bride
**Bless us as we offer our prayerful
and loving support to their marriage.
Bless them as they pledge their lives
to each other.
With faith in you and in each other,
may this couple always bear witness
to the reality of the love
to which we witness this day.
May their love continue to grow,
and may it be a true reflection
of your love for us all;
through Jesus Christ.
Amen.**

VOWS OF THE MARRIAGE COVENANT

The pastor may introduce the covenant promises in the following or similar words.

A

PASTOR

_____ **and**
  bride

_____,
  groom
**by your covenant promises
shared with us,
unite yourselves in marriage
and be subject to one
another out of reverence
for Christ.**

B

PASTOR

_____ **and**
  bride

_____,
  groom
**speak your covenant
promises that you have
come to offer before God.**

If able, the couple may face each other and join hands, the woman first giving her bouquet, if any, to an attendant. The groom and bride may say these or other words of covenant.

BRIDE

_____,
  groom
I give myself to you
to be your wife.
I promise to love and sustain you
in the covenant of marriage,
from this day forward,
in sickness and in health,
in plenty and in want,
in joy and in sorrow,
as long as we both shall live.

GROOM

_____,
  bride
I give myself to you
to be your husband.
I promise to love and sustain you
in the covenant of marriage,
from this day forward,
in sickness and in health,
in plenty and in want,
in joy and in sorrow,
as long as we both shall live.

EXCHANGE OF SYMBOLS

It is recommended that the giving and receiving of rings or other symbols be shared equally by both bride and groom.

PASTOR

_____ **and** _____,
   groom   bride
what will you share to symbolize your love?

The groom and bride may name the symbol(s) and present them/it to the pastor, who may hold or place a hand on the symbol(s) and offer one of these or another prayer.

A

PASTOR
By *these symbols/this symbol*
of covenant promise,
Gracious God,
remind _____ **and**
                 bride
_____ **of your**
   groom
encircling love and
unending faithfulness that
in all their life together
they may know joy and
peace in one another.

PEOPLE
Amen.

B

PASTOR
Eternal God,
who in the time of Noah
gave us the rainbow
as a sign of promise,
bless *these symbols/this symbol*
that *they/it* **also may be**
signs/a sign **of promises**
fulfilled in lives
of faithful loving;
through Jesus Christ
our Savior.

PEOPLE
Amen.

If both husband and wife receive symbols, options A and B are used.

A

GROOM

_____,
   bride

I give you *this/these* _____
                    symbol(s)
as a sign of my love and faithfulness.

BRIDE
I receive *this/these* _____
                    symbol(s)
as a sign of our love and faithfulness.

B

BRIDE

_____,
  groom

I give you *this/these* _____
                         symbol(s)
as a sign of my love and faithfulness.

GROOM
I receive *this/these* _____
                        symbol(s)
as a sign of our love and faithfulness.

ANNOUNCEMENT OF MARRIAGE

*If able, the couple may stand or kneel and join hands, and
the pastor may place a hand on their joined hands while
announcing the marriage, using one of these or other words.*

A

PASTOR
addressing the couple

_____ and
     bride

_____,
    groom

**you have committed
yourselves to each other
in this joyous
and sacred covenant.
Become one.
Fulfill your promises.
Love and serve God,
honor Christ
and each other,
and rejoice in the power
of the Holy Spirit.**

addressing the congregation

**By their promises
made before us this day,**

_____ and
     groom

_____
     bride

B

PASTOR
addressing the congregation

**Those whom God has
joined together
let no one separate.**[5]

addressing the couple

_____ and
     bride

_____,
    groom

**you are wife and husband
with the blessing
of Christ's church.
Be merciful
in all your ways,
kind in heart,
and humble in mind.
Accept life,
and be most patient and
tolerant with one another.
Forgive as freely
as God has forgiven you.
And, above everything else,**

have united themselves
as husband and wife
in sacred covenant.
Those whom God has
joined together
let no one separate.[4]

be truly loving.
Let the peace of Christ
rule in your hearts,
remembering that
as members of one body
you are called to live
in harmony,
and never forget to be
thankful for what God
has done for you.[6]

BLESSING

*If they are able, the couple may stand or kneel, with
children from previous relationships who will share their
household, if any, standing nearby. A blessing may be
given for the couple or the family.*

🅐 *blessing for the couple*

PASTOR
**The grace of Christ attend you;
the love of God surround you;
the Holy Spirit keep you
that you may grow
in holy love,
find delight in each other
always, and remain faithful
until your life's end.**

PEOPLE
Amen.

🅑 *blessing for the family*

PASTOR
**May the God
of Sarah and Abraham,
who watches over all the
families of the earth,
bless your new family
and establish your home
in peace and steadfast love.**

PEOPLE
Amen.

PASSING THE PEACE

*The one presiding may invite those who are able to stand
and exchange gestures of peace.*

PASTOR
The peace of God be with you always.

PEOPLE
And also with you.

The bride and groom may embrace. Using the same words as the pastor or similar ones, the groom and bride may move among the congregation exchanging the peace. After passing the peace, the people may be seated, and the couple may return to their places.

If Holy Communion is to be celebrated, the service continues on page 341; if it is not celebrated, the prayer begins.

PRAYER OF THANKSGIVING

The people may be seated. One of these or a similar prayer of thanksgiving and intercession may be offered.

PASTOR
Let us pray.

Ⓐ
PASTOR
**Most gracious God,
we give you thanks
for your tender love.
You sent Jesus Christ
to come among us,
to be born of a human
mother, and to make the
way of the cross
into the way of life.
We thank you, too,
for consecrating the
union of a man and a
woman in Christ's name.**

**By the power of your
Holy Spirit, pour out
the abundance
of your blessing**

on _____
groom

and _____**.**
bride

Ⓑ
PASTOR
**Merciful God,
we thank you
for your love that lives
within us and calls us
from loneliness
to companionship.
We thank you for all who
have gone before us:
for Adam and Eve,
for Sarah and Abraham,
for Joseph and Mary,
and for countless parents
whose names we do
not know.**

**We thank you for our
own parents, and for all,
whether married or
single, who are mother
or father to us,
as we grow to the fullness
of the stature of Christ.**

Defend them
from every enemy.
Lead them into all peace.
Let their love for each
other be a seal
on their hearts,
a mantle
about their shoulders,
and a crown
on their heads.
Bless them in their work
and in their
companionship,
in their sleeping
and in their waking,
in their joys
and in their sorrows,
in their lives
and in their deaths.
Nurture them
in a community
of the faithful
gathered about you.

Bless _____
<small>groom</small>
and _____,
<small>bride</small>
that they may have the
grace to live the promises
they have made.
Defend them from all
enemies of their love.
Teach them the patience
of undeserved
forgiveness.
Bring them to old age,
rejoicing in love's winter
more fully than
in its springtime.

The following words of the prayer may be used if children are present who will share in the couple's household. If these words are not used, continue with option A or B of the prayer.

PASTOR
Bless *this child/these children*,

_____,
<small>name(s) of child(ren)</small>
that *he/she/they* may find in this new home
a haven of love and joy
where Jesus Christ is honored
in kind words and tender deeds.

PASTOR
**Finally, in your mercy,
bring** _____
bride

and _____
groom

**to that table where your
saints feast for ever in
your heavenly home;
through Jesus Christ
our sovereign Savior
who, with you and
the Holy Spirit,
lives and reigns,
one God,
for ever and ever.**

PEOPLE
Amen.[7]

PASTOR
**At the last,
receive them and all of us
at the love feast
prepared for all
the faithful
in your eternal home,
where Jesus Christ,
with you
and the Holy Spirit,
one God,
reigns in love for ever.**

PEOPLE
Amen.

PRAYER OF OUR SAVIOR

*Standing, sitting, or kneeling, all may sing or say the
prayer received from Jesus Christ.*

A
ALL
**Our Father
in heaven,
hallowed be
your name,
your kingdom
come, your will
be done,
on earth
as in heaven.
Give us today
our daily bread.
Forgive us
our sins as we
forgive those
who sin**

B
ALL
**Our Father,
who art
in heaven,
hallowed be
thy name. Thy
kingdom come.
Thy will be
done on earth
as it is
in heaven.
Give us this day
our daily bread.
And forgive us
our trespasses,
as we forgive**

C
ALL
**Our Father,
who art
in heaven,
hallowed be
thy name. Thy
kingdom come.
Thy will be
done on earth
as it is
in heaven.
Give us this day
our daily bread.
And forgive us
our debts,
as we forgive**

against us.
Save us
from the time
of trial
and deliver us
from evil.
For the
kingdom,
the power,
and the glory
are yours now
and for ever.
Amen.[8]

those who
trespass against
us. And lead us
not into
temptation,
but deliver us
from evil.
For thine
is the kingdom,
and the power,
and the glory,
for ever and ever.
Amen.

our debtors.
And lead us
not into
temptation,
but deliver us
from evil.
For thine
is the kingdom,
and the power,
and the glory,
for ever.
Amen.

If Holy Communion is not to be celebrated, continue with the benediction on page 345.

ORDER FOR HOLY COMMUNION

If the sacrament of Holy Communion is to be celebrated, a Service of Word and Sacrament may be used, beginning with the offering of the communion elements. The groom and bride, others in the wedding party, or members of the family may bring the communion elements to the table. The invitation and prayers below may be substituted for ones in a Service of Word and Sacrament. Holy Communion is properly the supper of Jesus Christ, and all Christians present may receive. Practical arrangements for the wedding party will be necessary, such as chairs for them during parts of the service.

INVITATION

The pastor may go to the table and give this or another invitation.

PASTOR
**This table is open to all
who wish to receive Jesus Christ**

**in company with all believers
in all time and beyond time.**

**This is the joyful feast of the people of God.
Christ is present with gifts of new life,
as once Christ was present at Cana in Galilee
with the gift of new wine.**

**We come to know Christ
in the breaking of bread and the pouring of wine.**

COMMUNION PRAYER

*All who are able may stand. This prayer may replace
the communion prayer in a Service of Word and
Sacrament.*

PASTOR
God be with you.

PEOPLE
And also with you.

PASTOR
Lift up your hearts.

PEOPLE
We lift them to God.

PASTOR
Let us give thanks to God Most High.

PEOPLE
It is right to give God thanks and praise.

PASTOR
**Blessed are you,
O God our Creator.
From the womb of your being
you brought forth worlds.
Into mere dust you blew the breath of life,
creating women and men
to bear your likeness in the world.
You create, love, and care for all that is.
We praise and thank you,
nurturing God, that in Jesus
you bring joy and hope to loving hearts,
and offer health and power to human relationships.**

**Even the powers of sorrow and death
could not contain Christ's joy.
From the tomb our risen Savior came
to share bread again among the beloved.
In the glory of your banquet hall,
Christ prepares a wedding feast
for all the faithful who even now praise you.**

PEOPLE
Holy, holy, holy God of love and majesty,
the whole universe speaks of your glory,
O God Most High.
Blessed is the one who comes
in the name of our God!
Hosanna in the highest!

*The people may be seated or those who are able may
kneel. At the words concerning the bread and wine,
the one presiding may indicate the elements.*

PASTOR
**Merciful God,
we remember that on the night
of betrayal and desertion,
Jesus took bread, gave thanks to you,
broke the bread,
and gave it to the disciples, saying:
"Take and eat, this is my body broken for you."**

**Likewise, Jesus took the cup of blessing and said:
"Drink of this cup.
It is the new covenant in my blood,
poured out for you and for many
for the forgiveness of sins.
Do this in memory of me."[9]**

**With joy we thank you,
God of gladness and warmth,
that at Pentecost you sent your Holy Spirit
to dance about the heads of your people,
enabling your word to be heard afresh.
Now send your Holy Spirit on these gifts
of bread and wine and on us**

**that we may be set afire with your love
and leap with joy at your presence.
Pour out your blessing on**

_____ **and** _____.
    bride   groom

**May they sing a new song of your great love
in communion with you and all your saints
in heaven and on earth.
May their love for each other
proclaim the love of Christ for all of us.
May the faithful service of all your people
bring peace, justice, joy, and love to all the world;
through Christ, with Christ, and in Christ,
in the unity of the Holy Spirit,
all glory and honor are yours, Holy God,
now and for ever.**

PEOPLE
Amen.

*If the Prayer of Our Savior has not been said earlier in
the service, it may be said before the sharing of the
communion elements.*

*For the sharing of the communion elements, the peo-
ple may come forward or receive where they are. If
they come forward, the pastor may give each person
the bread, and the bride and groom may offer the
chalice(s) or individual cups. If trays of individual
cups are used, the groom and bride may be located at
the sides of the pastor, next to attendants with empty
trays for the used cups. Hymns of joy and thanksgiving
may be sung by the congregation while the elements
are being shared.*

PRAYER OF THANKSGIVING

*When all have been served and the table is in order,
the wedding party may return to its place and all who
are able may stand for the prayer of thanksgiving.*

PASTOR
Let us pray.

ALL
Thank you, O God,
for refreshing us at your table.
By your grace you have nourished us
with the living presence of Christ,
the bread of life,
that we may share life together.
Send us forth in the power of your Holy Spirit
to give ourselves in love
until your entire human family is gathered
at your table,
glorifying and praising you
in the name of Jesus Christ.
Amen.

BENEDICTION

All who are able may stand. One of these or another bless-
ing may be given for all present.

A

PASTOR
Go forth in the love of God;
go forth in hope and joy,
knowing that God
is with you always.

And the peace of God,
which passes all
understanding,
keep your hearts and minds
in the knowledge
and love of God
and of Christ Jesus;[10]
and the blessing of God,
Creator, Redeemer, and
Sanctifier, be with you,
and remain with you always.

PEOPLE
Amen.

B

PASTOR
May God bless you
and keep you.
May God's face shine
upon you
and be gracious to you.
May God look upon you
with kindness
and give you peace.[11]

PEOPLE
Amen.

HYMN OR POSTLUDE

A hymn may be sung or other suitable music offered as the wedding party and congregation depart.

Order for the
Blessing of a Civil Marriage

INTRODUCTION

This order is provided for couples who have entered marriage in a civil ceremony. If the blessing takes place within a regular Sunday service of the congregation, it may follow the sermon. The couple may be invited to come forward and stand before the pastor, if they are able. At the conclusion of the blessing, the couple may return to the congregation, and the service may continue according to the customary order. This order may be used on an occasion set aside for the blessing of a marriage alone.

The couple may wish to use the Order for Marriage as the basis for the blessing of their civil marriage. If so, it will be necessary to reword that text.

The pledge of support from the Order for Marriage on page 331 may be used totally or in part. It includes statements by children from previous relationships, other family members, and the congregation.

It is the responsibility of the one presiding to confirm that a civil ceremony already has taken place and that the marriage laws of the place in which the blessing of the marriage is to be held are fully respected.

OUTLINE

This order may be used alone or as part of a Service of Word and Sacrament or a Service of the Word following the sermon. If this order is not incorporated into another service, add the starred (*) items and music.

> **Greeting**
> **Introduction**
> **Prayer***
> **Reading of Scripture***
> **Sermon***
> **Promises**
> **Blessing of Symbols**
> **Announcement of Marriage**
> **Blessing and Thanksgiving**
> **Benediction***

A Service of Word and Sacrament or a Service of the Word may continue.

GREETING

*The married couple, with special guests invited to join
them, may stand facing the one presiding, if they are able.
The greeting may be omitted if the blessing takes place
within another service.*

PASTOR
**The grace of our Lord Jesus Christ
and the love of God
and the communion of the Holy Spirit
be with you all.**[12]

PEOPLE
And also with you.

INTRODUCTION

*The one presiding may state the reason for gathering,
using one of the following or other words.*

A
PASTOR

_____ **and**
  husband

_____ **have given**
  wife
**themselves to each other
as husband and wife
according to the laws
of the state.
They are here to declare
their love for each other
and to receive on their
marriage the blessing
of God and the church.**

B
PASTOR

_____ **and**
  husband

_____ **have been**
  wife
**married according to
the laws of the state;
they have made a solemn
contract with each other.
Now, in faith, they come
before the church to declare
their marriage covenant
and to acknowledge God's
good news for their lives.**[13]

*The service may continue with the prayer, recommenda-
tions for scripture readings, and a sermon from the Order
for Marriage. The prayer begins on page 328. If this blessing
takes place within another service, the reading of scripture
and sermon will have occurred earlier in the service.*

PROMISES

*The couple reaffirms the promises made in the civil
ceremony. It may be necessary to adjust the wording here
to conform to promises made earlier. The wife and husband, if they are able, may face each other and join hands.*

PASTOR

—————————,
    wife

you have given yourself to ———————————
to be his wife.   husband
Do you reaffirm your promise
to love and sustain him in the covenant of marriage,
in sickness and in health,
in plenty and in want,
in joy and in sorrow,
as long as you both shall live?

WIFE
I do.

PASTOR

—————————,
    husband

you have given yourself to ———————————
to be her husband.   wife
Do you reaffirm your promise
to love and sustain her in the covenant of marriage,
in sickness and in health,
in plenty and in want,
in joy and in sorrow,
as long as you both shall live?

HUSBAND
I do.

BLESSING OF SYMBOLS

*The pastor may hold or place a hand on the ring(s) or
other symbol(s) and say one of the following.*

Ⓐ *for ring(s) or other symbol(s)*

PASTOR
**Eternal God,
who in the time of Noah
gave us the rainbow
as a sign of promise,
bless** *these symbols/this symbol*
that *they/it* **also may be**
signs/a sign **of promises
fulfilled in lives
of faithful loving;
through Jesus Christ
our Savior.**

PEOPLE
Amen.

Ⓑ *for ring(s)*

PASTOR
**Bless, O God, the wearing
of** *these rings/this ring*
to be *symbols/a symbol*
**of the covenant promises
by which these children
of yours have given
themselves to each other;
through Jesus Christ.**

PEOPLE
Amen.[14]

ANNOUNCEMENT OF MARRIAGE

If they are able, the couple may stand or kneel and join hands, and the pastor may place a hand on their joined hands while addressing the couple with these or other words.

PASTOR
Those whom God has joined together let no one separate.[15]

_____ **and** _____,
   wife   husband

**you are wife and husband
with the blessing of Christ's church.
Help each other; be united; live in peace.
The God of love and peace be with you always.**

BLESSING AND THANKSGIVING

The blessing on page 337 and the prayer of thanksgiving on page 338 from the Order for Marriage may be used.

If Holy Communion is to be celebrated, consult the instructions on page 341. This order may be concluded with a benediction from the Order for Marriage on page 345 or another benediction, or a Service of the Word may continue.

Order for Renewal of the Marriage Covenant

INTRODUCTION

This order is for couples who are celebrating an anniversary of their marriage or for couples who are celebrating reconciliation in their marriage.

If the renewal takes place within a Sunday service of the congregation, it may follow the sermon. The couple may be invited to come forward and stand before the pastor, if they are able. At the conclusion of the renewal, the couple may return to the congregation, and the service may continue according to the customary order. This order also may be used on an occasion set aside for the renewal of the marriage covenant alone.

The couple may wish to use the Order for Marriage as the basis for the renewal of their covenant. If so, it will be necessary to reword the text to indicate reaffirmation.

It is the responsibility of the one presiding to confirm that a valid marriage has previously taken place.

The couple, their family, or friends may share memories and special symbols during the service.

OUTLINE

This order may be used alone or as part of a Service of Word and Sacrament or a Service of the Word following the sermon. If this order is not incorporated into another service, add the starred (*) items and music.

Greeting
Introduction
Prayer*
Reading of Scripture*
Sermon*
Renewal of Covenant Promises
Recognition of Renewal
Blessing and Thanksgiving
Benediction*

A Service of Word and Sacrament or a Service of the Word may continue.

GREETING

The married couple, with special guests invited to join them, may stand facing the pastor, if they are able. The greeting may be omitted if the renewal of the marriage covenant takes place within another service.

PASTOR
Dear friends,
let us love one another,
because love comes from God.
Whoever loves is a child of God and knows God.

PEOPLE
Whoever does not love
does not know God,
for God is love.[16]

INTRODUCTION

A *at an anniversary*

PASTOR

_____ **and**
        wife

_____ **,**
    husband
we rejoice to celebrate
with you the renewal
of your marriage covenant,
on your _____ anniversary.
We celebrate the delight
you have found
in each other
and thank you
for being a sign of God's
love among us.

B *at a time of*
reconciliation

PASTOR

_____ **and**
        wife

_____ **,**
    husband
we rejoice to celebrate
with you the renewal
of your marriage covenant,
as you recommit yourselves
as wife and husband.
We celebrate the delight
you have found
in each other
and thank you
for being a sign of God's
love among us.

The couple may describe one or two memories, or other family members or friends may bring greetings or reminisce as a way of celebrating the years of marriage.

The service may continue with the prayer, recommendations for scripture reading, and sermon from the Order for Marriage. The prayer begins on page 328. If the renewal of the marriage covenant takes place within another service, the reading of scripture and sermon will have occurred earlier in the service.

RENEWAL OF COVENANT PROMISES

The husband and wife, if they are able, may face each other and join hands. The following promises may be made, or the couple may write their own. It is recommended that those who have experienced reconciliation write promises which clearly express their newly reestablished relationship to say to each other now.

A   *at an anniversary*

PASTOR

_____ **and**
<small>husband</small>

_____ **,**
<small>wife</small>

**on this _____ anniversary
of your marriage,
I invite you to renew
your covenant promises.**

B   *at a time of
reconciliation*

PASTOR

_____ **and**
<small>husband</small>

_____ **,**
<small>wife</small>

**as you recommit yourselves
to each other in marriage,
I invite you to renew
your covenant promises.**

WIFE

_____ **,**
<small>husband</small>

I am blessed to be your wife,
and I promise anew
to love and sustain you
in the covenant of marriage,
in sickness and in health,
in plenty and in want,
in joy and in sorrow,
as long as we both shall live.

HUSBAND

———————,
<u>wife</u>

I am blessed to be your husband,
and I promise anew
to love and sustain you
in the covenant of marriage,
in sickness and in health,
in plenty and in want,
in joy and in sorrow,
as long as we both shall live.

RECOGNITION OF RENEWAL

*If they are able, the couple may stand or kneel and join
hands, and the pastor may place a hand on their joined
hands while addressing the couple with these or similar words.*

PASTOR
Those whom God has joined together let no one separate.[17]

——————— and ———————,
    husband   wife

you have spoken again your covenant of love.
God grant you grace
to fulfill in your life together
the solemn promises you made
in the springtime of your love
and renewed today
in the presence of the church.

BLESSING AND THANKSGIVING

*The blessing on page 337 and the prayer of thanksgiving
on page 338 from the Order for Marriage may be used.*

***If Holy Communion is to be celebrated, consult the instruc-
tions on page 341. This order may be concluded with a
benediction from the Order for Marriage on page 345 or
another benediction, or a Service of the Word may continue.***

Services of Memorial and Thanksgiving

Order for
the Time of Dying

INTRODUCTION

When the church is notified that a person is near death, the pastor, perhaps with another representative, may go as soon as possible to minister to the dying person and to others who are present, using all or part of this service. In this ministry, sensitivity to local and ethnic customs is of great importance and may require that the prayers be memorized or that the themes of the prayers be expressed freely in the representative's own words.

It is wise to assume that the dying person is able to hear the spoken prayers and psalms even when vital life signs are visibly failing. The use of silence is also appropriate, as human presence itself is a ministry.

Human touch, both with the one dying and with others who are present, is a sign of comfort and solidarity. The representative may hold the hand of the dying person or touch the head or shoulder while offering the prayers and psalms. Others present may be invited to reach out to each other, the representative, and the dying person.

If death has occurred before the representative arrives, the order may begin with the commendation, continue with psalms for the comfort of the living followed by the Lord's Prayer, and end with a benediction.

OUTLINE

If the person has died before the representative arrives, the order may be: commendation, psalms, Lord's Prayer, and benediction.

> **Greeting**
> **Prayers for the Person near Death**
> **Psalms**
> **Lord's Prayer**
> **Prayer for Those Who Care for the Sick**
> **Prayer for the Grieving**

> **Commendation, for use if death has occurred**

> **Benediction**

GREETING

When the pastor or another representative arrives, this greeting or some other may be used informally.

REPRESENTATIVE
**The love of God,
and the peace of Christ,
and the comfort of the Holy Spirit
be with all of you.**

PEOPLE
And also with you.

PRAYERS FOR THE PERSON NEAR DEATH

One or both of the following may be used or the representative may offer similar prayers in her or his own words while touching the person. Others present may share in the laying on of hands.

Ⓐ
REPRESENTATIVE
**Almighty God,
by your gentle power
you raised Jesus Christ from death.
Watch over this child of yours,
our** *brother/sister,* **_____.**
name

Fill *his/her* **eyes with light
that** *he/she* **may see, beyond human sight,
a home within your love,
where pain is gone and physical frailty becomes glory.
Banish fear.
Brush away tears.
Let death be gentle as nightfall,
promising a new day
when sighs of grief turn to songs of joy,
and we are joined again
in the presence of Jesus Christ in our heavenly reunion.**

PEOPLE
Amen.[1]

🅱

REPRESENTATIVE
Eternal God,
you know our needs before we ask,
and you hear our cries
through lips unable to speak.
Hear with compassion
the yearnings of your servant _____,
and the prayers _{name}
that we would pray had we the words.
Grant *her/him* **the assurance**
of your embrace,
the ears of faith
to hear your voice,
and the eyes of hope
to see your light.
Release *him/her* **from all fear**
and from the constraints of life's faults
that *he/she* **may breathe** *his/her* **last**
in the peace of your words:
Well done,
good and faithful servant;
enter into the joy of your God.[2]
We ask this through Jesus Christ our Savior.

PEOPLE
Amen.

PSALMS

A representative may read one or more Psalms: 23; 46:1-3, 10-11; or others. Selected passages begin on page 518.

LORD'S PRAYER

Near the dying person, all present may hold hands, if able, and say in full voice the prayer received from Jesus Christ.

REPRESENTATIVE
Let us pray as Christ our Savior has taught us.

A

ALL
**Our Father
in heaven,
hallowed be
your name,
your kingdom
come, your will
be done, on earth
as in heaven.
Give us today
our daily bread.
Forgive us our sins
as we forgive those
who sin against us.
Save us from the
time of trial
and deliver us
from evil.
For the kingdom,
the power,
and the glory
are yours now
and for ever.
Amen.**[3]

B

ALL
**Our Father,
who art in heaven,
hallowed be
thy name.
Thy kingdom
come. Thy will
be done on earth
as it is in heaven.
Give us this day
our daily bread.
And forgive us
our trespasses,
as we forgive those
who trespass
against us.
And lead us not
into temptation,
but deliver us
from evil.
For thine
is the kingdom,
and the power,
and the glory,
for ever and ever.
Amen.**

C

ALL
**Our Father,
who art in heaven,
hallowed be
thy name.
Thy kingdom
come. Thy will
be done on earth
as it is in heaven.
Give us this day
our daily bread.
And forgive us
our debts,
as we forgive
our debtors.
And lead us not
into temptation,
but deliver us
from evil.
For thine
is the kingdom,
and the power,
and the glory,
for ever.
Amen.**

PRAYER FOR THOSE
WHO CARE FOR THE SICK

In these or similar words, the representative may pray for family, physicians, nurses, and others who minister to the dying person.

REPRESENTATIVE
**Merciful God,
we thank you for all who minister to** _____
in this time of *her/his* **great need.**

name

Give them compassion and tenderness
and the fullest use of their gifts
that they may have the blessed peace
of knowing they honor you
in their acts of healing and comfort.
As death draws near
and there is no more they can do,
let them hear again the words of Jesus Christ:
As often as you did it to one of the least of these,
you did it to me;[4]
and fill them with the joy of your Holy Spirit.

PEOPLE
Amen.

PRAYER FOR THE GRIEVING

In these or similar words, the representative may pray for all who bear the burden of grief.

REPRESENTATIVE
Great God of all mystery,
if in the presence of death our thoughts are startled
and our words flutter about like frightened birds,
bring us stillness
that we may cover the sorrow of our hearts
with folded hands.
Give us grace to wait on you silently and with patience.
You are nearer to us than we know,
closer than we can imagine.
If we cannot find you,
it is because we search in far places.
Before we felt the pain,
you suffered it;
before the burden came upon us,
your strength lifted it;
before the sorrow darkened our hearts,
you were grieved.
As you walk in the valley of every shadow,
be our good shepherd
and sustain us while we walk with you,

lest in weakness we falter.
Though the pain deepens,
keep us in your way
and guide us past every danger;
through Jesus Christ our Savior.

PEOPLE
Amen.[5]

If death has not occurred, omit the commendation.

COMMENDATION

*If death has already occurred, the representative may
say the following or other words while touching the
deceased person.*

REPRESENTATIVE
Depart, O Christian *sister/brother*,
**out of this world:
in the name of God Most Holy,
who created you;
in the name of Jesus Christ,
who redeemed you;
in the name of the Holy Spirit,
who sanctifies you.
May you rest this** *day/night*
in the peace of God's eternal home.

PEOPLE
Amen.[6]

AND

Ⓐ
REPRESENTATIVE
**Into your hands,
O merciful Savior,
we commend
our** *brother/sister*,

—————————.
name
Accept, we pray,

Ⓑ
REPRESENTATIVE
**Into your hands,
O merciful Savior,
we commend your**

servant —————————.
name
**Acknowledge,
we humbly pray,**

this *son/daughter* **of yours, whose name you know. Receive** *her/him* **into your merciful arms, into the shelter of your care, and into the glorious company of your saints in light. May** *he/she* **and all the departed rest in your peace.**

PEOPLE
Amen.

a sheep of your own fold, a lamb of your own flock, and a *daughter/son* **of your own redeeming. Receive** *him/her* **into the arms of your mercy, into the blessed rest of everlasting peace, and into the company of the saints in light.**

PEOPLE
Amen.[7]

BENEDICTION

This or another benediction may conclude the service.

REPRESENTATIVE
May God bless you and keep you. May God's face shine upon you and be gracious to you. May God look upon you with kindness and give you peace.

PEOPLE
Amen.[8]

Order for Thanksgiving for One Who Has Died

INTRODUCTION

In the Christian community, death is a corporate experience that touches the life of the entire family of faith. When a death occurs, the immediate family is encouraged to notify the church as soon as possible and to share fully in planning a service. They may also assist in leading the service. Sensitive consideration is to be given to ethnic traditions, local customs, and the particular circumstances of the bereaved.

The service recognizes both the pain and sorrow of the separation that accompanies death and the hope and joy of the promises of God to those who die and are raised in Jesus Christ. The service celebrates the life of the deceased, gives thanks for that person's life, and commends that life to God. It offers consolation to the bereaved by acknowledging their grief and anger or guilt. It provides the Christian community and others an opportunity to support the bereaved with their presence. Its purpose is to affirm once more the powerful, steadfast love of God from which people cannot be separated, even by death.

The service is an act of corporate worship: God's word is read and proclaimed, hymns may be sung, prayers offered, and the sacrament of Holy Communion shared by those who desire it. The service should be at an hour convenient for the immediate family and the community of faith. If possible, the service most appropriately is held in the place where the congregation regularly gathers for worship. If it is held in another place, it is important that it remain a corporate act of the church's worship. This order, or some other, in the hands of the congregation will enable full participation in the service.

The presence of the coffin may help the bereaved and the congregation to confront and deal with the reality of death. The coffin is closed for the service. A white pall or another appropriate covering may be placed over the coffin symbolizing the resurrection, de-emphasizing the relative expense of coffins, and showing the equality of all people in the services of the church.

The service may also be used when the body of the deceased is not present. Then the committal service may be held prior to this service, within it, or following it. Consult the Order for Committal, beginning on page 384, for directions.

If it is the custom of the congregation to use a large paschal candle, it is lighted as a symbol of resurrection faith. If the coffin is present, the candle is placed near the coffin.

Christians often hold membership in praiseworthy organizations other than the church. It is most appropriate for memorial rituals of those groups to be held apart from the Order for Thanksgiving for One Who Has Died to avoid compromising this service's integrity.

Customs surrounding death vary, especially those related to racial and ethnic traditions. Local churches may observe special anniversaries of a death or hold a service once a year to remember all who have died during the year. Prayers, readings, and ritual observances from various traditions may be incorporated at all remembrance times.

OUTLINE

Prelude
Procession and Sentences
Hymn of Adoration
Greeting
Prayer
Reading of Scripture
Sermon
Words of Remembrance
Affirmation of Faith
Hymn, Anthem, or Other Music
Prayers of Thanksgiving and Intercession

Order for Holy
Communion from
Brief Order for the
Service of Word and
Sacrament, beginning
with the communion
prayer

Silence
Prayer of Our Savior

Commendation
Song of Simeon
Benediction
Hymn
Postlude

PRELUDE

The service may begin with music for a service of the resurrection. If the coffin is set in place before the people arrive or is not present at all, the service may continue with the opening hymn or the greeting.

PROCESSION AND SENTENCES

If the coffin is brought into the church in a procession, a leader may meet it at the entrance and say any of the following sentences as she or he precedes the coffin and family up the aisle to the chancel. If there is no procession, the sentences may be used following the greeting. Those who are able may stand for the procession. The one presiding may say one or more sentences.

LEADER
Hear the promises of God.

Ⓐ
LEADER
**God is near to all who call,
who call from their hearts.
The desires of those who fear God are fulfilled;
their cries are heard;
they are saved.**[9]

Ⓑ
LEADER
**I am the resurrection and the life;
all who believe in me,
though they die,
yet shall they live,
and whoever lives and believes in me shall never die.**[10]

Ⓒ
LEADER
**Fear not,
I am the first and the last,
and the living one;
I died, and behold I am alive for evermore.**[11]

☐

LEADER
**Fear not,
for I am with you,
be not dismayed,
for I am your God;
I will strengthen you,
I will help you,
I will uphold you with my victorious hand.**[12]

☐

LEADER
**When we were baptized into Christ Jesus,
we were baptized into Christ's death.
By our baptism, then,
we were buried with Christ
and shared Christ's death,
in order that,
just as Christ was raised from death
by the glorious power of God,
so too we might live a new life.**[13]
**For if we have been united with Christ
in a death like Christ's,
we shall certainly be united with Christ
in a resurrection like Christ's.**[14]

☐

LEADER
**Blessed are the dead
who die in Christ.
"Blessed indeed," says the Spirit,
"that they may rest from their labors,
for their deeds follow them!"**[15]

HYMN OF ADORATION

*As the procession nears the chancel, a hymn may be sung.
If there is no procession, the people who are able may rise
for the opening hymn as a leader enters; or a leader may
enter during the prelude and open with the greeting and/or
the sentences. Then the service may continue with the hymn.*

GREETING

All who are able may stand. A leader may greet the people informally, name the person for whom they gather in thanksgiving, and interpret briefly the meaning of the service. One or more of the following greetings may be used.

Ⓐ

LEADER

**The grace of our Lord Jesus Christ
and the love of God
and the communion of the Holy Spirit
be with you all.**[16]

PEOPLE

And also with you.

Ⓑ

LEADER

**Friends,
we gather here in the protective shelter
of God's healing love.
We are free to pour out our grief,
release our anger,
face our emptiness,
and know that God cares.
We gather here as God's people,
conscious of others who have died
and of the frailty
of our own existence on earth.
We come to comfort and to support one another
in our common loss.
We gather to hear God's word of hope
that can drive away our despair
and move us to offer God our praise.
We gather to commend to God with thanksgiving
the life of** _____
                      name
**as we celebrate the good news of Christ's resurrection.
For whether we live or whether we die,
we belong to Christ who is Lord
both of the dead and of the living.**[17]

C

LEADER
**Gracious is our God and righteous;
our God is full of compassion.**

PEOPLE
I will walk in the presence of God
in the land of the living.

LEADER
**I will fulfill my vows to God
in the presence of all God's people.**

PEOPLE
Precious in the sight of God
is the death of those who die in faithfulness.[18]

PRAYER

---

*The people may be seated. The service may continue with
a confession of sin and an assurance of pardon or a collect
or a prayer of thanksgiving for the communion of saints.*

A

LEADER
**The peace of Christ
be with you.**

PEOPLE
And also with you.

LEADER
Let us pray.

ALL
**Almighty God,
whose will is sovereign and
whose mercy is boundless,
look upon us in our sorrow
and enable us to hear
your word.
Help us hear so that,
through patience
and the encouragement
of the scriptures,**

B

ALL
**Holy God,
whose ways are not our
ways and whose thoughts
are not our thoughts,
grant that your Holy Spirit
may intercede for us
with sighs too deep
for human words.
Heal our wounded hearts
made heavy by our sorrow.
Through the veil of our
tears and the silence
of our emptiness,
assure us again
that ear has not heard,
nor eye seen,
nor human imagination
envisioned,**

we may hold fast to the
assurance of your favor
and the hope of life eternal;
through Jesus Christ
our risen Savior.
Amen.

what you have prepared
for those who love you;
through Jesus Christ,
the firstborn from the dead.
Amen.

READING OF SCRIPTURE

The psalms, read responsively or antiphonally or sung, may be used before and/or after the lessons. It is appropriate to include at least one Gospel lesson. Where it is the custom, all who are able may stand for the Gospel reading. Members of the family of the deceased and other lay persons may be readers. A gloria may be said or sung at the conclusion of the final psalm. Suggested readings include the following.

PSALMS
Psalms 23; 27:7-14; 42:1-5; 46; 90:1-4, 12-17; 121; 130; 139:1-18, 23-24

OLD TESTAMENT
Job 19:25-27
Isaiah 25:6-9, 61:1-3
Lamentations 3:22-26, 31-33

EPISTLES
Acts 10:34-43
Romans 8:9-11, 31-39
1 Corinthians 13, 15:12-20, 15:35-50
2 Corinthians 4:7-11, 16; 5:1-5
Ephesians 3:14-21
1 Thessalonians 4:13-18
2 Timothy 1:8-13
Revelation 21:1-6

GOSPELS
Matthew 5:3-10, 11:28-30
Luke 23:33, 39-43
John 6:37-40; 11:17-27; 12:24-26; 14:1-3, 18-19, 25-27

SERMON

The people may be seated for a sermon.

WORDS OF REMEMBRANCE

A leader or a friend or member of the family of the deceased may offer thanksgiving for the one who has died and recall the individual's uniqueness if this is desired and has not been done during the sermon.

AFFIRMATION OF FAITH

All who are able may stand and affirm the resurrection faith by saying a creed, statement of faith, or other affirmation, such as the following from Romans. Other affirmations of faith are in the Resource Section, beginning on page 509.

LEADER
Let us say again what we believe.

ALL
**We believe there is no condemnation
for those who are in Christ Jesus,
and we know that in everything
God works for good with those who love God,
who are called according to God's purpose.
We are sure that neither death, nor life,
nor angels, nor principalities,
nor things present, nor things to come,
nor powers, nor height, nor depth,
nor anything else in all creation,
will be able to separate us
from the love of God in Christ Jesus our Lord.[19]
Amen.**

HYMN, ANTHEM, OR OTHER MUSIC

Music may be offered in God's praise.

Prayers of
Thanksgiving and Intercession

_These or other similar prayers may be offered. A litany may
be used. The prayers may be used individually or together,
with or without each "Amen" said by the pastor or people.
Prayers to be offered at the death of a child follow the
general prayers._

LEADER
Let us pray.

A

LEADER
**Merciful God, we thank you for your word;
it is a lamp for our feet, a light for our path.
We thank you especially that in the night of our grief
and in the shadows of our sorrow,
we are not left to ourselves.
We have the light of your promises
to sustain and comfort us.
Through our tears,
give us vision to see in faith
the consolation you intend for us.
In your mercy,
grant us the unfailing guidance of your saving Word,
both in life and in death;
through Jesus Christ our risen Savior.**

PEOPLE
Amen.

B

LEADER
**O God, our strength and our redeemer,
giver of life and conqueror of death,
we praise you with humble hearts.
With faith in your great mercy and wisdom,
we entrust _____ to your eternal care.**
name

We praise you for your steadfast love for _her/him_
all the days of _her/his_ **earthly life.**

We thank you for all that *he/she* **was**
to those who loved *him/her*

> **and for** *his/her* **faithfulness**
> **to the church of Jesus Christ.**
> *Mention may be made of the person's Christian life*
> *and service.*

We thank you that for _____
                                    name

> **all sickness and sorrow are ended, and**

death itself is past
and that *she/he* **has entered the home**
where all your people gather in peace.
Keep us all in communion with your faithful people
in every time and place,
that at last we may rejoice together in the heavenly family
where Jesus Christ reigns
with you and the Holy Spirit,
one God, for ever.

PEOPLE
Amen.

Ⓒ
LEADER
God of all mercies and all comfort,
in tender love and compassion,
embrace your sorrowing servants.
Be their refuge and strength,
an ever present help in trouble.
Show them again the love of Christ
that passes all human understanding;
for by death Christ has conquered death,
and by rising Christ has opened to all of us
the gates of everlasting life.
Thanks be to you, O God.

PEOPLE
Amen.

D

LEADER
Let us pray for ourselves.

PEOPLE
O God, whose days are without end
and whose mercies cannot be counted,
awaken us to the shortness and uncertainty of human life.
By your Holy Spirit,
lead us in faithfulness all our days.
When we have served you in our generation,
may we be gathered with those who have gone before,
having the testimony of a good conscience,
in the communion of your holy church,
in the confidence of a certain faith,
in the comfort of a saving hope,
in favor with you, our God,
and at perfect peace with the world;
through Jesus Christ our Redeemer.
Amen.

*At the death of a child, the following prayers or others
in the leader's own words may be offered.*

E

LEADER
**Gentle God,
born an infant in Jesus Christ
in the family of Joseph and Mary,
we give you thanks for ——————— born among us
full of hope and promise.** name
**We remember that Jesus Christ lifted children
into loving arms to embrace and bless them.
We ask you to embrace and bless ———————
as part of your heavenly family where,** name
**by your grace, our lives are brought to fullness
in the peace of your eternal home.
We ask this through Jesus Christ,
your beloved child, and our risen Savior.**

PEOPLE
Amen.

F *for parents*

LEADER
**God of all mercies,
whose heart aches with our human hurting,
we commend to your love the parent(s) of this child,**

_____,
name(s) of parent(s)

and all *his/her/their* **children who mourn.**

**Sustain the family
in this loss and in their loneliness.
Kindle anew the ashes of joy.
Grant the peace of knowing
that this child is with you,
the Mother and Father of us all,
both in this life
and in the life that is to come;
through Jesus Christ our Savior.**

PEOPLE
Amen.

If Holy Communion is not to be celebrated, the service may be concluded with silence, the Prayer of Our Savior, the commendation, and the closing acts that follow.

If Holy Communion is to be celebrated, the service continues with the offertory of the bread and wine in the Brief Order for the Service of Word and Sacrament on page 83. Members of the family or friends of the deceased may bring the bread and wine to the table. All Christians present may be invited to receive. After the post-communion prayer of thanksgiving from the Brief Order for the Service of Word and Sacrament, the Order for Thanksgiving for One Who Has Died may continue with the commendation on page 381 and the closing acts which follow it.

SILENCE

Silence may be observed for reflection and prayer.

PRAYER OF OUR SAVIOR

Standing, sitting, or kneeling, all may sing or say the prayer received from Jesus Christ.

LEADER
Let us pray as Christ our Savior has taught us.

Ⓐ

ALL
**Our Father
in heaven,
hallowed be
your name,
your kingdom
come, your will
be done,
on earth
as in heaven.
Give us today
our daily bread.
Forgive us
our sins as we
forgive those
who sin
against us.
Save us
from the time
of trial
and deliver us
from evil.
For the
kingdom,
the power,
and the glory
are yours now
and for ever.
Amen.**[20]

Ⓑ

ALL
**Our Father,
who art
in heaven,
hallowed be
thy name. Thy
kingdom come.
Thy will be
done on earth
as it is
in heaven.
Give us this day
our daily bread.
And forgive us
our trespasses,
as we forgive
those who
trespass against
us. And lead us
not into
temptation,
but deliver us
from evil.
For thine
is the kingdom,
and the power,
and the glory,
for ever and ever.
Amen.**

Ⓒ

ALL
**Our Father,
who art
in heaven,
hallowed be
thy name. Thy
kingdom come.
Thy will be
done on earth
as it is
in heaven.
Give us this day
our daily bread.
And forgive us
our debts,
as we forgive
our debtors.
And lead us
not into
temptation,
but deliver us
from evil.
For thine
is the kingdom,
and the power,
and the glory,
for ever.
Amen.**

COMMENDATION

All who are able may stand. The leader may go to the coffin for one of the following or another commendation. The words are also appropriate if no coffin is present.

Ⓐ

LEADER
**Holy God,
by your mighty power
you gave us life,
and in your love
you have given us new life
in Jesus Christ.
We now entrust**

_____
name

**to your merciful care.
We do this in the faith
of Christ Jesus,
who died and rose again
to save us and is now alive
and reigns with you
and the Holy Spirit
in glory for ever.**

PEOPLE
Amen.

Ⓑ

LEADER
**Into your hands,
O merciful Savior,
we commend your servant**

_____
name

**Acknowledge,
we humbly pray,
a sheep of your own fold,
a lamb of your own flock,
and a** *daughter/son*
**of your own redeeming.
Receive** *her/him* **into the
arms of your mercy,
into the blessed rest
of everlasting peace,
and into the company
of the saints in light.**

PEOPLE
Amen.[21]

SONG OF SIMEON

All who are able may stand and sing or say the ancient Nunc Dimittis. *Musical settings are on pages 458 and 466.*

ALL
**Holy One,
now let your servant go in peace;
your word has been fulfilled:
my own eyes have seen the salvation
which you have prepared in the sight of every people:
a light to reveal you to the nations
and the glory of your people Israel.**[22]

At the request of the family of the deceased or in the case of cremation, the Order for Committal may take place, following instructions in that order on page 384.

BENEDICTION

While all who are able stand, a leader may give the benediction. According to local custom, the hymn may precede the benediction.

Ⓐ

LEADER
Now may the God of peace who brought again from the dead our Savior Jesus, the great shepherd of the sheep, by the blood of the eternal covenant, equip you with everything good that you may do God's will, working in you that which is pleasing in God's sight, through Jesus Christ; to whom be glory for ever and ever.

PEOPLE
Amen.[23]

Ⓑ

LEADER
May God bless you and keep you.

PEOPLE
Amen.

LEADER
May God's face shine upon you and be gracious to you.

PEOPLE
Amen.

LEADER
May God look upon you with kindness and give you peace.[24]

PEOPLE
Amen.

for use, except during Lent

LEADER
Alleluia. Christ is risen.

PEOPLE
Christ is risen indeed. Alleluia.

LEADER
Let us go forth in the name of Christ.

PEOPLE
Thanks be to God.

HYMN

All who are able may stand for a hymn. If there is to be a recessional, the leader(s) may precede the coffin and the family to the door.

POSTLUDE

Order for Committal

INTRODUCTION

The Order for Committal is a summary of the Easter faith.
It may be used in its full form before or following the Order
for Thanksgiving for One Who Has Died, or apart from
that service. If, for pastoral and practical reasons, the committal is incorporated within the Order for Thanksgiving for
One Who Has Died, it may follow the commendation and
Song of Simeon and precede the benediction and closing
hymn. When this occurs, the greeting and opening sentences
of the Order for Committal may be omitted. The committal
proper may be said by the leader who is near the coffin, if
it is present. The Lord's Prayer may be omitted. The service
may be closed with the benediction from either order,
followed by a hymn.

If the Order for Committal is used alone, the leader may
wish to incorporate within it appropriate parts of the Order
for Thanksgiving for One Who Has Died.

Customs concerning interment, entombment, scattering of
ashes, burial at sea, and giving of the body to research
institutions are diverse. The Order for Committal may be
adapted to respect these customs, but it remains a summary
of the Easter faith.

OUTLINE

This order may be used alone. When it is incorporated into the Order for Thanksgiving for One Who Has Died, the greeting, sentences, and Lord's Prayer may be omitted and a benediction from either order may be used.

Greeting
Sentences
Committal
Lord's Prayer
Prayers
Benediction

When this order is incorporated into the Order for Thanksgiving for One Who Has Died, the greeting and sentences may be omitted.

A leader may precede the coffin and the congregation to the site of burial.

GREETING

LEADER
The peace of Christ be with you.

PEOPLE
And also with you.

SENTENCES

A leader may read one or more of the following opening sentences or any not used in the Order for Thanksgiving for One Who Has Died.

A

LEADER
**We would not have you ignorant,
brothers and sisters,
concerning those who are asleep,
that you may not grieve
as others do who have no hope.
For since we believe
that Jesus died and rose again,
even so, through Jesus,
God will bring with Jesus
those who have fallen asleep.**[25]

B

LEADER
**"Death is swallowed up in victory.
O death, where is your victory?
O death, where is your sting?"
Thanks be to God,
who gives us the victory
through our Lord Jesus Christ.**[26]

Ⓒ
LEADER
Jesus said:
So you have sorrow now,
but I will see you again
and your hearts will rejoice,
and no one will take your joy from you.[27]

Ⓓ
LEADER
Behold, I am coming soon.
I am the Alpha and the Omega,
the first, and the last,
the beginning and the end.[28]

COMMITTAL

At the head of the coffin or near the urn of ashes and facing
the people, a leader may say the following or similar words.

Ⓐ
LEADER
Almighty God,
in whose eternal care
are all your people,
we commit *this body/ these ashes*
of _____ **to**
            name
the earth/ the sea/ the elements/
this resting place
in confident and certain
hope of the resurrection
to eternal life;
through Jesus Christ,
the firstborn from the dead.
PEOPLE
Amen.

Ⓑ
LEADER
Eternal God, who breathed
into lifeless dust
and brought forth Adam
and Eve in your image,
we return to *the earth/*
the sea/ the elements/
this resting place
the *breathless body/*
lifeless ashes
of your servant

_____ ,
     name
believing that as you raised
Jesus Christ from death,
you will breathe life
into us again
so that we may live
with you for ever.
PEOPLE
Amen.

According to local custom, the leader(s) and members of the family may cast earth upon the coffin during or following the committal.

LORD'S PRAYER

If this prayer was said in a service immediately prior to the committal or will follow shortly in a service after the committal, it may be omitted here.

LEADER
Let us pray as Christ our Savior has taught us.

A	**B**	**C**
ALL	ALL	ALL
Our Father in heaven, hallowed be your name, your kingdom come, your will be done, on earth as in heaven. Give us today our daily bread. Forgive us our sins as we forgive those who sin against us. Save us from the time of trial and deliver us from evil. For the kingdom, the power, and the glory are yours now and for ever. Amen.[29]	**Our Father, who art in heaven, hallowed be thy name. Thy kingdom come. Thy will be done on earth as it is in heaven. Give us this day our daily bread. And forgive us our trespasses, as we forgive those who trespass against us. And lead us not into temptation, but deliver us from evil. For thine is the kingdom, and the power, and the glory, for ever and ever. Amen.**	**Our Father, who art in heaven, hallowed be thy name. Thy kingdom come. Thy will be done on earth as it is in heaven. Give us this day our daily bread. And forgive us our debts, as we forgive our debtors. And lead us not into temptation, but deliver us from evil. For thine is the kingdom, and the power, and the glory, for ever. Amen.**

PRAYERS

A leader may use one of these or her or his own words.

A

LEADER
**Almighty God,
by the death
of Jesus Christ
you have taken
away the sting
of death,
by Christ's time
in the tomb you
have sanctified
the graves
of the saints,
and by Christ's
glorious
resurrection
you have
brought life
and immortality
to light.
We thank you
for the victory
of life over death
which you have
won for us
and for all who
sleep in Christ.
Keep us
in everlasting
communion with
all who wait
for you on earth
and all who are
with you in
heaven, where
Christ reigns**

B

LEADER
**Almighty God,
fountain of all
mercy and giver
of all comfort,
deal graciously,
we pray, with all
who mourn,
that casting all
their care on you,
they may know
the consolation
of your love;
through Jesus
Christ our
Savior.**

PEOPLE
Amen.[31]

C

LEADER
**Let us pray for
our own needs.**

ALL
**Merciful God,
support us all the
day long of this
life full of trouble,
until the shadows
lengthen and the
evening comes,
and the busy
world is hushed,
and the fever
of life is over,
and our work
is done.
Then in your
tender mercy
grant us a safe
lodging, and
a holy rest,
and peace
at the last;
through Jesus
Christ our
Redeemer.
Amen.**[32]

**with you and the
Holy Spirit,
ever one God,
for ever
and ever.**

PEOPLE
Amen.[30]

BENEDICTION

*When used within the Order for Thanksgiving for One
Who Has Died, one of the following benedictions or one
from that order may be used, followed by a hymn.*

A

LEADER
**May the God of hope
fill you with all joy
and peace in believing,
so that by the power
of the Holy Spirit
you may abound in hope.**[33]
Go in the peace of Christ.

PEOPLE
Amen.

B

LEADER
**The peace of God,
which passes all
understanding,
keep your hearts and minds
in the knowledge
and love of God,
and of Christ Jesus
our risen Savior.**[34]
**And the blessing
of God Almighty,
Creator,
Redeemer,
and Comforter,
be among you and
remain with you always.
Amen.**

Services of
Recognition and
Authorization of Ministries

Order for Recognition of a Student in Care of Association

INTRODUCTION

In this order the people of God celebrate the initial response of a Christian to the call of God to serve in the ordained ministry of the church. It is an occasion for entering a covenant of support with the candidate. In this service the association offers its nurture as the candidate seeks to understand more fully God's purpose for her or his life and pursues the study and other preparation necessary for ordination to Christian ministry.

More than one student may be recognized in one service. Representatives of the association committee on the ministry, in consultation with the candidates, plan the service of recognition.

The service may be held at any meeting or service of worship at which the association is assembled. This may be an association meeting, a special occasion such as a banquet, or a Service of Word and Sacrament or a Service of the Word.

The candidate(s) may sit with the congregation until requested to come forward at the presentation.

OUTLINE

This order is to be held during a gathering of the association. It may be incorporated into a Service of Word and Sacrament or a Service of the Word following the sermon or may be used during a meeting or other event.

> **Greeting**
> **Presentation**
> **Recognition**
> **Vows**
> **Prayer of Recognition**
> **Declaration**

A Service of Word and Sacrament or a Service of the Word may continue, or a hymn and a benediction may close the order.

When this order is part of a Service of Word and Sacrament or a Service of the Word, it may follow the sermon. A hymn may be sung. After the hymn, all may be seated except the representative(s) of the association, the representative(s) of the local church(es) where the candidate(s) are members, the advisor(s) of the student(s), and the candidate(s) for recognition.

The greeting may be used at the opening of the service rather than at the opening of this order.

GREETING

The moderator or another representative of the association may greet the people, and they may respond in these or similar words.

ASSOCIATION REPRESENTATIVE
**Greetings in the name of Jesus Christ,
the head of the church,
who is not without witnesses in any age.**

**Hear these words to Timothy:
As for you,
be strong through the grace that is ours
in union with Christ Jesus.**

PEOPLE
Take the teachings that you heard me proclaim
in the presence of many witnesses,
and entrust them to reliable people,
who will be able to teach others also.

ASSOCIATION REPRESENTATIVE
Do your best to win full approval in God's sight;

PEOPLE
Be a worker who is not ashamed of your work,
one who correctly teaches the message of God's truth. [1]

PRESENTATION

A representative of each local church that is recommending a student to be received in care of the association may address a representative of the association in these or similar words. The candidate's full name may be used in the first reference. Thereafter, the first name only may be used.

EACH LOCAL CHURCH REPRESENTATIVE
addressing the association representative

———————————— United Church of Christ,
local church

after carefully considering the call to ordained ministry
of ————————————,
full name of candidate

respectfully requests that the ———————————— Association
association

receive ———————————— as a student in care of this association,
name

according to the faith and order
of the United Church of Christ.

RECOGNITION

The candidate(s) may stand, if able, before the association and be addressed in these or similar words by representative(s) of the association.

ASSOCIATION REPRESENTATIVE
**The recognition of a student in care
is the way an association of the United Church of Christ
affirms a person's call from God
to prepare for ordained ministry in Christ's church.
We celebrate the action of your local church(es)
to recommend you.
We affirm the action of the committee on the ministry
to receive you into care.**

**An ordained minister of the United Church of Christ
is one of its members who has been called by God
and ordained to preach and teach the gospel,
to administer the sacraments and rites of the church,
and to exercise pastoral care and leadership.**[2]
**Your intention to prepare yourself for this ministry
will require diligent and prayerful work.
The association, through its committee on the ministry,
promises to assist you in your pilgrimage of learning**

**so that when you request ordination,
you will have been nurtured
by Christ's church in our midst.
With you, we seek the guidance of the Holy Spirit
as the future opens before you,
and we invite you to call on the association
wherever we may be helpful to you
in your preparation for ordained ministry.**

VOWS

ASSOCIATION REPRESENTATIVE
addressing the candidate(s)

**As you enter into this covenant
with this association,
do you promise to seek its guidance,
to receive its support,
and to communicate with it regularly
through your advisor?**

CANDIDATE
I do, with God's help.

ASSOCIATION REPRESENTATIVE
addressing the local church representative(s)

**As a representative of the local church
of a newly recognized student in care of this association,
do you join in this covenant,
on behalf of the local church,
vowing to encourage** *him/her*
**in the preparation for ordained ministry,
and undergirding** *him/her*
with prayer, support, and nurture?

LOCAL CHURCH REPRESENTATIVE
I do, with God's help.

ASSOCIATION REPRESENTATIVE
addressing the advisor(s)

**As advisor(s) of a newly recognized
student in care of association,
do you join in this covenant,**

pledging to support *her/him*
in ways mutually agreeable to you
as *she/he* **continues the pilgrimage of learning,**
to maintain regular contact with *her/him* ,
and to report regularly on the relationship
to the association,
through the committee on the ministry?

ADVISOR
I do, with God's help.

All who are able may stand.

ASSOCIATION REPRESENTATIVE
addressing the members of the association
Do you, the ministers and delegates of this association,
confirm the covenant made this day with _____ **?**
name(s)

Do you agree to offer encouragement
and to sustain *him/her/them*
in the continued preparation
for ordained ministry
in the church of Jesus Christ,
to pray for *him/her/them* ,
and to recognize *him/her/them*
in this special relationship with the association?

ASSOCIATION MEMBERS
We do, with praise and thanksgiving to God.

PRAYER OF RECOGNITION

All who are able may stand.

LEADER
Let us pray.

God of the prophets and martyrs
in every age and land,
we thank you for those in our generation
who hear and answer your call
to prepare for the ordained ministry of your church.
Grant your Holy Spirit to _____
name(s)

that *he/she/they* **may grow in faith,
be filled with courage,
and increase in love.
Confirm in** *her/him/them*
**the call to ministry you intend,
that** *she/he/they* **may find in service to you
the liberty that comes to those
who give themselves for others;
through Jesus Christ,
who came not to be served, but to serve,
and who served you even to death
for our redemption.**

ALL
Amen.

DECLARATION

ASSOCIATION REPRESENTATIVE
**In the name of Jesus Christ,
and on behalf of the** _____ **Association**
                          association
of the _____ **Conference**
            conference
**of the United Church of Christ,
I declare that you are** *a student/students* **in care
of this association.**

ALL
Thanks be to God.

*The association representative(s) may give a greeting of
Christian love, such as a handshake with appropriate
words, to the student(s) in care. The proper certificate and
a symbolic gift may be given to each student.*

*A Service of Word and Sacrament or a Service of the
Word may continue, or a hymn and a benediction may
close the order.*

Order for Ordination to Ministry

INTRODUCTION

In this order the people of God celebrate Christ's gift of ministry to the church. In planning the service, set the time so that people from other local churches within the association, representatives of other Christian communions, and guests from synagogues or other communities of faith may participate. Services of ordination held on Sunday mornings prohibit the enrichment afforded by this participation.

Representatives of the association committee on the ministry, in full consultation with the ordinand and the local church where the service will be held, plan the service of ordination. The conference may be represented in the planning. Lay and ordained people may share in the leadership of the service.

This order may be incorporated within a Service of Word and Sacrament or within a Service of the Word. The installation of the pastor may immediately follow the order for ordination. It is fitting that a sermon be preached concerning the ministry of all people of God and the particular ministry of those ordained in and on behalf of the church. The service may be enriched by the generous use of music. Plans should be made in consultation with the music leaders of the local church.

The ordinand may sit with the congregation until requested to come forward.

OUTLINE

This order may be incorporated into a Service of Word and Sacrament or a Service of the Word following the sermon. An affirmation of faith and a hymn may precede the Order for Ordination to Ministry.

    Greeting
    Presentation
    Exhortation
    Examination
    Acclamation
    Laying on of Hands
    Declaration

The Order for Installation of a Pastor may begin, following the instructions in that order. If installation does not follow immediately, a hymn may be sung and a Service of Word and Sacrament or a Service of the Word continues, omitting the affirmation of faith.

Following the sermon, all who are able may stand and unite in an affirmation of faith and a hymn. After the hymn, all may be seated except the representative(s) of the association, the representative(s) of the local church, and the ordinand. The ordinand may remain in the congregation.

The greeting may be used at the opening of the service rather than at the opening of this order.

GREETING

The moderator or another representative of the association may greet the people, and they may respond in these or similar words.

ASSOCIATION REPRESENTATIVE
Grace to you and peace from God,
who is and who was and who is to come,
and from Jesus Christ the faithful witness
and the sovereign of the rulers on earth.[3]

The _____ Association
       association
of the _____ Conference
       conference
of the United Church of Christ
greets you in the name of Jesus Christ,
the head of the church.

PEOPLE
To God, who by the power at work within us
is able to do far more abundantly
than all that we ask or think,
be glory in the church
and in Christ Jesus to all generations,
for ever and ever.
Amen.[4]

PRESENTATION

A representative of the local church that is requesting the ordination may address a representative of the association

*in these or similar words. The ordinand's full name may be
used in the first reference. Thereafter, the first name only
may be used.*

LOCAL CHURCH REPRESENTATIVE
addressing the association representative
_____ United Church of Christ,

local church
after carefully considering the call to ordained ministry
of _____,

full name of ordinand
respectfully requests that the _____ Association

association
ordain _____ to the ministry

name
of the church of Jesus Christ,
consistent with scripture
and with the traditions of the church universal,
and according to the faith and order
of the United Church of Christ.

ASSOCIATION REPRESENTATIVE
addressing the congregation
The _____ Association has reviewed the request

association
of _____ United Church of Christ.

local church
We have prayerfully examined _____

name
concerning *her/his* **fitness for ministry in Christ's church.**
We are pleased,
on behalf of the United Church of Christ,
to authorize the ordination of _____

name
into the Christian ministry.

addressing the ordinand

_____,

name
servant of God,
we invite you to come forward
as a sign of your consent
to receive ordination into Christian ministry.

The ordinand may leave his or her place in the congregation and may stand, if able, at the chancel before the representative(s) of the association, who review(s) the United Church of Christ's Constitution and Bylaws regarding ordination.

ASSOCIATION REPRESENTATIVE
**The United Church of Christ acknowledges
as its sole head, Jesus Christ,
Son of God and Savior.
It acknowledges as kindred in Christ
all who share in this confession.**

**It looks to the word of God
in the scriptures,
and to the presence and power
of the Holy Spirit,
to prosper its creative and redemptive work
in the world.
It claims as its own the faith
of the historic church
expressed in the ancient creeds
and reclaimed in the basic insights
of the Protestant reformers.**

**It affirms the responsibility
of the church in each generation
to make this faith its own
in reality of worship,
in honesty of thought and expression,
and in purity of heart before God.**

**In accordance with the teaching of our Lord
and the practice prevailing
among evangelical Christians,
it recognizes two sacraments:
Baptism and . . . Holy Communion.**

**The United Church of Christ recognizes
that God calls the whole church
and every member
to participate in and extend the ministry of Jesus Christ**

by witnessing to the gospel
in church and society.
The United Church of Christ seeks to undergird
the ministry of its members
by nurturing faith,
calling forth gifts,
and equipping members for Christian service.

ASSOCIATION REPRESENTATIVE
Ordination is the rite
whereby the United Church of Christ
through an association,
in cooperation with the person
and a local church
of the United Church of Christ,
recognizes and authorizes that member
whom God has called to ordained ministry,
and sets that person apart by prayer
and the laying on of hands.
By this rite
ordained ministerial standing is conferred
and authorization given
to perform the duties
and exercise the prerogatives
of ordained ministry
in the United Church of Christ.[5]

EXHORTATION

A representative of the association may then say these or similar words.

A
ASSOCIATION REPRESENTATIVE
Hear these words
from the prophet
Isaiah:
I heard the voice
of the Holy One
saying,

B
ASSOCIATION REPRESENTATIVE
Hear these words
from the
apostle Paul:
How are people
to call upon one
in whom

C
ASSOCIATION REPRESENTATIVE
Hear these words
from Jesus Christ
to the first
disciples:
Follow me, and I
will make you

"Whom shall I send, and who will go for us?" Then I said, "Here I am! Send me!"[6]

How wonderful it is to see a messenger coming across the mountains, bringing good news, the news of peace! The messenger announces victory and says to Zion, "Your God reigns."[7]

The Spirit of God is upon me, because the Holy One has anointed me to bring good news to the poor, heal the brokenhearted, proclaim liberty to the captives, and freedom to those who are bound.[8]

they have not believed? And how are they to believe in one of whom they have never heard? So faith comes from what is heard, and what is heard comes by the preaching of Christ.[9]

fishers of humanity.[10]

Hear also these words of Jesus: You know that the rulers of the Gentiles dominate them, and their great leaders exercise authority over them. It shall not be so among you; but whoever would be great among you must be your servant, and whoever would be first among you must be your slave.[11]

EXAMINATION

A representative of the association may then ask the ordinand the following questions.

ASSOCIATION REPRESENTATIVE

——————————,
      name

**before God and this congregation,
we ask you:
Are you persuaded that God has called you
to be an ordained minister
of the church of Jesus Christ,
and are you ready with the help of God
to enter this ministry
and to serve faithfully in it?**

ORDINAND
I am.

ASSOCIATION REPRESENTATIVE
**Do you,
with the church throughout the world,
hear the word of God
in the scriptures of the Old and New Testaments,
and do you accept the word of God
as the rule of Christian faith and practice?**

ORDINAND
I do.

ASSOCIATION REPRESENTATIVE
**Do you promise to be diligent in your private prayers
and in reading the scriptures,
as well as in the public duties of your office?**

ORDINAND
I do, relying on God's grace.

ASSOCIATION REPRESENTATIVE
**Will you be zealous in maintaining
both the truth of the gospel
and the peace of the church,
speaking the truth in love?**

ORDINAND
I will, relying on God's grace.

ASSOCIATION REPRESENTATIVE
**Will you be faithful
in preaching and teaching the gospel,**

**in administering the sacraments and rites of the church,
and in exercising pastoral care and leadership?**

ORDINAND
I will, relying on God's grace.

ASSOCIATION REPRESENTATIVE
Will you keep silent all confidences shared with you?

ORDINAND
I will, relying on God's grace.

ASSOCIATION REPRESENTATIVE
**Will you seek to regard all people
with equal love and concern
and undertake to minister impartially
to the needs of all?**

ORDINAND
I will, relying on God's grace.

ASSOCIATION REPRESENTATIVE
**Do you accept the faith and order
of the United Church of Christ;
and will you,
as an ordained minister in this communion,
ecumenically reach out toward all who are in Christ
and show Christian love
to people of other faiths
and people of no faith?**

ORDINAND
I do and I will, relying on God's grace.

ACCLAMATION

*Those official delegates of the association (clergy and others
so designated) who are able may stand.*

ASSOCIATION REPRESENTATIVE
addressing the members of the association
**People of God,
you have heard the promises _____ has made.**
<small>name</small>
What is your will?

ASSOCIATION MEMBERS
By the grace of God,
he/she is worthy!
Let us ordain *her/him*.
Come, Holy Spirit.

ASSOCIATION REPRESENTATIVE
Will you support _____ **in the ministry of Christ?**

name

ASSOCIATION MEMBERS
We will.

*The people may show their approval and support by
applause, a hymn, or some other means.*

LAYING ON OF HANDS

*The ordinand may kneel, if able. A leader may invite those
who are to share in the laying on of hands to come forward. The congregation may be given an opportunity to
participate in the ordination in a symbolic way. "Veni
Creator, Spiritus" or another hymn may be sung by the
choir alone or with the congregation.*

ASSOCIATION REPRESENTATIVE
**The laying on of hands is the symbolic act
whereby the church in every age
recognizes God's call to ministry
in the lives
of faithful women and men
and asks the Holy Spirit
to confer on them
gifts for ordained ministry.**

*Those who have come forward to lay on hands may now
do so. Silence may be observed. Then an association representative may lead in prayer.*

ASSOCIATION REPRESENTATIVE
Let us pray.

Eternal God,
in wisdom you govern all things,
and from the beginning
you have chosen faithful people
to serve you in ministry,
calling some apostles, some prophets, some evangelists,
some pastors and teachers,
to equip all your people
for the work of the ministry
and for building up the body of Christ.[12]
Now bless and sanctify by your Holy Spirit
your servant _____,
name

whom we, in your name and in obedience to your will,
by prayer and with the laying on of hands,
ordain to the ministry of the church,
committing to *him/her* **the authority**
to preach your word,
administer the sacraments,
and exercise the responsibilities
of pastor and teacher.

Bestow on _____
name

the power of your Holy Spirit,
confirming what we do.
Let the same mind be in *her/him*
that was also in Christ Jesus.
Enable *him/her* **to nourish your people**
in the faith of the gospel.
Fill *her/his* **speech with truth**
and *her/his* **life with purity.**
Increase the faith of _____ **in you,**
name

strengthen *him/her* **in the day of trouble,**
prosper *his/her* **words and works**
that your name may be glorified and your truth exalted;
through Jesus Christ our Sovereign and Savior.

PEOPLE
Amen.
Thanks be to God!

DECLARATION

The newly ordained minister may rise.

ASSOCIATION REPRESENTATIVE
**In the name of Jesus Christ,
the head of the church,
and by the authority of the _____ Association**
association

of the _____ Conference
conference

**of the United Church of Christ,
I declare you to be ordained
into the ministry of Jesus Christ.**

*A Bible may be presented to the newly ordained minister
with these or other words.*

ASSOCIATION REPRESENTATIVE
**Receive at our hands this Bible
of which you are appointed as an interpreter.
Be diligent in the study of its message
that you may speak with the authority of truth,
and be a faithful minister of the word and sacraments.**

*A certificate of ordination may be presented, and a gesture
of Christian love may be made with these or other words.*

ASSOCIATION REPRESENTATIVE
**You are granted ordained ministerial standing
in the United Church of Christ;
and in behalf of its people,
we offer you the hand of Christian love.**

The leaders may greet the newly ordained minister.

*If the newly ordained minister is to be installed within this
service, the Order for Installation of a Pastor follows the
Order for Ordination to Ministry. See the introduction to
that order, beginning on page 412, for instructions.*

*If installation does not immediately follow, a hymn may be
sung. A Service of Word and Sacrament or a Service of the
Word continues. It is appropriate that the newly ordained
minister serve communion and give the benediction.*

Order for Installation of a Pastor

INTRODUCTION

In this order the association, at the request of a local church, confirms and celebrates the covenant between a local church and a newly called pastor and teacher and reaffirms the covenantal relationship of all the churches in the association. In planning the service, set the time so that people from other churches within the association, representatives of other Christian communions, and guests from synagogues or other communities of faith may participate. Services of installation held on Sunday mornings prohibit the enrichment afforded by this participation.

Representatives of the association committee on the ministry, in full consultation with the pastor to be installed and the local church requesting the service, plan the service of installation. Conference representatives may participate in the planning. Lay and ordained people may share in the leadership of the service.

This order may be incorporated within a Service of Word and Sacrament or a Service of the Word. It is fitting that a sermon be preached concerning the ministry of all the people of God and the particular ministry of a pastor and teacher within the life of the church. The service may be enriched by the generous use of music. Plans should be made in consultation with the music leaders of the local church.

When the order for installation is part of a service of ordination, only the covenant, prayer, and declaration need to be used.

The person to be installed may sit with the congregation until requested to come forward at the presentation.

OUTLINE

This order may be incorporated into a Service of Word and Sacrament or a Service of the Word following the sermon. An affirmation of faith and a hymn may precede this order. When it is used immediately following the Order for Ordination to Ministry, begin with the covenant.

> **Greeting**
> **Presentation**
> **Exhortation**
> **Covenant**
> **Prayer of Installation**
> **Declaration**

A hymn may be sung. A Service of Word and Sacrament or a Service of the Word continues, omitting the affirmation of faith.

Following the sermon, all who are able may stand and unite in an affirmation of faith and a hymn. After the hymn, all may be seated except the representative(s) of the local church, the representative(s) of the association, and the pastor who is to be installed. The pastor to be installed may remain among the congregation.

The greeting may be used at the opening of the service rather than at the opening of this order.

When the Order for Installation of a Pastor is part of a service of ordination, begin with the covenant on page 417.

GREETING

The moderator or another representative of the association may greet the people, and they may respond in these or similar words.

ASSOCIATION REPRESENTATIVE

The _____ Association
            association
of the _____ Conference
            conference
of the United Church of Christ
greets you in the name of Jesus Christ,
the head of the church in heaven and on earth.

Therefore, since we are surrounded
by so great a cloud of witnesses,
let us also lay aside every weight and sin
which clings so closely,
and let us run with perseverance the race
that is set before us.

PEOPLE

Let us look to Jesus
the pioneer and perfecter of our faith,
who for the joy that was waiting
endured the cross,
despising the shame,
and is seated at the right hand
of the throne of God.[13]

PRESENTATION

A representative of the local church that is requesting the installation may address a representative of the association in these or similar words. The pastor's full name may be used in the first reference. Thereafter, the first name only may be used.

LOCAL CHURCH REPRESENTATIVE
addressing the association representative

_____ United Church of Christ,
_{local church}
under the guidance of the Holy Spirit,
has called _____ as its pastor and teacher
_{full name of pastor}
and respectfully requests that the
_____ Association install *her/him*
_{association}
in this ministry among us,
according to the faith and order
of the United Church of Christ.

ASSOCIATION REPRESENTATIVE
addressing the congregation

The _____ Association has reviewed
_{association}
the request of _____ United Church of Christ.
_{local church}
We have prayerfully examined _____,
_{name}
and we are pleased to install *him/her*
as your pastor and teacher.

addressing the pastor

_____,
_{name}
servant of God,
we invite you to come forward
as a sign of your acceptance
of the call to this office.

The pastor may leave his or her place in the congregation and may stand, if able, before the representative(s) of the association.

ASSOCIATION REPRESENTATIVE
**Installation is the action
of an association
of the United Church of Christ
in cooperation with a local church.
Installation confirms and celebrates
the covenantal relationship
among a local church,
its pastor and teacher,
and the United Church of Christ.
Installation is a sign
that these covenantal partners are committed
to share mutually in the mission
of the United Church of Christ
and of the ecumenical church.**

EXHORTATION

Representative(s) of the association may read these or other words from scripture.

ASSOCIATION REPRESENTATIVE
addressing the congregation
**Hear these words from the apostle Paul:
We beg you, our brothers and sisters,
to pay proper respect
to those who work among you,
who guide and instruct you
in the Christian life.
Treat them with the greatest respect and love
because of the work they do.
Be at peace among yourselves.**

ASSOCIATION REPRESENTATIVE
addressing the pastor
We urge you, our _sister/brother_**,
warn the idle,
encourage the timid,
help the weak,
be patient with all.**

ASSOCIATION REPRESENTATIVE
addressing all

See that no one pays back wrong for wrong,
but at all times
make it your aim to do good
to one another and to all people.
Be joyful always,
pray at all times,
be thankful in all circumstances.
This is what God wants of you,
in your life in Christ Jesus.[14]
Amen.

When this order immediately follows the Order for Ordination to Ministry, begin this order with the covenant.

COVENANT

The pastor may remain before the representative(s) of the association.

ASSOCIATION REPRESENTATIVE
addressing the congregation

Dear friends,
_____ United Church of Christ has declared that,
    local church
having gathered
under the guidance of the Holy Spirit,

it has called _____
               name
to minister in this place
as pastor and teacher
and that it now receives *him/her*
as appointed by God
for this ministry.
The _____ Association
       association
of the United Church of Christ has declared
that *she/he* **has met all the necessary conditions**
for installation to this office.

ASSOCIATION REPRESENTATIVE
addressing the pastor

———————,
name

**seeing that you are called to ordained ministry
by the grace of God
and that ——————— United Church of Christ**
local church
**has been led to call you as pastor and teacher,
are you willing to enter this covenant
with its members who are one in Christ
with us in the ——————— Association?**
association

PASTOR
I am willing, and I promise to serve this church faithfully,
preaching and teaching the word of God,
administering the sacraments,
and fulfilling the pastoral office,
according to the faith and order
of the United Church of Christ.

ASSOCIATION REPRESENTATIVE
addressing the congregation

Members of ——————— United Church of Christ,
local church
**will those who are able rise and affirm your covenant
with your pastor and teacher?**

*Members of the church who are able stand for the
remainder of the covenant.*

LOCAL CHURCH MEMBERS
We, the members
of ——————— United Church of Christ,
local church

receive ——————— as our pastor and teacher,
name
promising to labor with *him/her* in the ministry of the gospel
and to give *him/her* due honor and support.

We gather with *her/him*
and with the United Church of Christ
as a sign of our mutual ministry in Christ's name.

ASSOCIATION REPRESENTATIVE
addressing the association members

Members of _____ Association,
association

will those who are able rise and affirm your covenant
with _____ United Church of Christ
local church
and its pastor and teacher?

Members of the association who are able stand for the
remainder of the covenant.

ASSOCIATION MEMBERS
We, the members of the _____ Association
association
of the United Church of Christ,
gather with you,
the people and the pastor and teacher
of _____ United Church of Christ,
local church
as a sign of our covenant
and in celebration of our mutual ministry in Christ's name.

PRAYER OF INSTALLATION

All who are able may stand as a representative of the asso-
ciation prays in these or similar words.

ASSOCIATION REPRESENTATIVE
Let us pray.

Almighty God,
you have called your servants
to make promises before you;
now enable us to keep our vows
that we may remain steadfast in faith
and fruitful in every good work.
Bless, we pray, your servant _____
name
to whom the care of your people
in this church is now committed.
Pour out your Holy Spirit on *him/her*,
on the people of _____ United Church of Christ,
local church

and on all the churches of the _____ **Association**
association

that our mutual ministry may be served
with all faithfulness, diligence, and courage.
Grant us the spirit of power and of love
and of a sound mind.
Make our ministry a means of awakening the careless,
strengthening the faithful,
comforting the afflicted,
building up your church,
and converting sinners to you.
Guard us against the snares of temptation
that we may be kept pure in heart,
fervent in spirit,
and valiant against evil.
And at the last, by your grace,
receive us in your eternal home,
where, with you and the Holy Spirit,
Christ reigns in glory,
one God, for ever and ever.

ALL
Amen.

DECLARATION

ASSOCIATION REPRESENTATIVE
**In the name of Jesus Christ,
and on behalf of the** _____ **Association**
association

of the _____ **Conference**
conference

**of the United Church of Christ,
I declare you duly installed as pastor and teacher
of** _____ **United Church of Christ.**
local church

ALL
Thanks be to God.

_The people may show their approval and support by
applause, a hymn, or some other means. The association_

representative(s) may make a gesture of Christian love to the newly installed person, such as a handshake with appropriate words. The congregation and newly installed person may be seated.

Separate charges or one common charge may be given the pastor and congregation. The charge to the pastor and teacher may be presented dramatically by symbolically illustrating diverse pastoral functions. At the font and table, the sacramental ministries may be reviewed; at the pulpit, the preaching of the word. A key to the church building, a copy of the church constitution, a stole, a Bible, or other symbols may be used in a similar way.

If representatives from other Christian communions or from synagogues or other communities of faith have been invited and are present, a representative from among them may be given an opportunity to bring greetings to the local church and the newly installed pastor and teacher following the charge. The same courtesy may be extended to a representative of the civic community.

At the conclusion of this order, a hymn may be sung. A Service of Word and Sacrament or a Service of the Word continues, omitting the affirmation of faith. It is appropriate that the newly installed pastor serve communion and give the benediction.

Order for Commissioning

INTRODUCTION

In this order the people of God celebrate Christ's gift of diverse ministries to the church. In planning the service, set the time so that people from other local churches within the association and other guests may participate. Commissionings held on Sunday mornings prohibit the enrichment afforded by this participation.

Representatives of the association committee on the ministry, in full consultation with the candidate and the local church or agency requesting the service, plan the service of commissioning. Lay and ordained people may share in the leadership of the service.

Commissioning may be incorporated within a Service of Word and Sacrament or within a Service of the Word. It is fitting that a sermon be preached concerning the ministry of all the people of God and the special ministry of commissioned ministers within the life of the church.

The candidate may sit with the congregation until requested to come to the chancel at the presentation.

OUTLINE

This order may be incorporated into a Service of Word and Sacrament or a Service of the Word following the sermon. An affirmation of faith and a hymn may precede the Order for Commissioning.

> **Greeting**
> **Presentation**
> **Exhortation**
> **Examination**
> **Covenant**
> **Prayer of Commissioning**
> **Declaration**

A hymn may be sung. A Service of Word and Sacrament or a Service of the Word continues, omitting the affirmation of faith.

Following the sermon, all who are able may stand and unite in an affirmation of faith and a hymn. After the hymn, all may be seated except the representative(s) of the local church or agency presenting the candidate, the representative(s) of the association, and the candidate for commissioning. The candidate may remain among the congregation.

The greeting may be used at the opening of the service rather than at the opening of this order.

GREETING

The moderator or another representative of the association may greet the people, and they may respond in these or similar words.

ASSOCIATION REPRESENTATIVE

The _____ Association
          association
of the _____ Conference
       conference
of the United Church of Christ
greets you in the name of Jesus Christ,
the head of the church,
who calls us to the ministry of reconciliation.

Hear these words from the apostle Paul:
My sisters and brothers,
I want you to know the truth about gifts
from the Holy Spirit.
There are different kinds of spiritual gifts,
but the same Spirit gives them.

PEOPLE

There are different ways of serving,
but the same God is served.

ASSOCIATION REPRESENTATIVE

There are different abilities to perform service,
but the same God gives ability to each of us
for our particular service.

PEOPLE

The Spirit's presence is shown in some way
in each person for the good of all.[15]

PRESENTATION

A representative of the local church or agency that is requesting the commissioning may address a representative of the asssociation in these or similar words. The candidate's full name may be used in the first reference. Thereafter, the first name only may be used.

LOCAL CHURCH/AGENCY REPRESENTATIVE
addressing the association representative
Friend in Christ,

——————————,
  local church/agency
under the guidance of the Holy Spirit,
has called ———————————
             full name of candidate
to serve as ———————————
          position
and respectfully requests that the
——————————— Association commission *her/him*
    association
for this ministry,
according to the faith and order
of the United Church of Christ.

ASSOCIATION REPRESENTATIVE
addressing the congregation
The ——————————— **Association has reviewed**
    association
the request of ———————————.
         local church/agency
We have prayerfully examined ———————————
                      name
concerning *his/her* **fitness for this ministry,**
and we are pleased to commission *him/her*
to serve as ———————————.
         position

addressing the candidate

——————————,
    name
servant of God,
we invite you to come forward as a sign of your acceptance
of the call to this commissioned ministry.

The candidate may leave her or his place in the congregation and may stand, if able, at the chancel before the representative(s) of the association who review(s) the United Church of Christ's Constitution and Bylaws regarding commissioning.

ASSOCIATION REPRESENTATIVE
**The United Church of Christ acknowledges
as its sole head, Jesus Christ,
Son of God and Savior.
It acknowledges as kindred in Christ
all who share in this confession.**

**It looks to the word of God in the scriptures,
and to the presence and power of the Holy Spirit,
to prosper its creative and redemptive work in the world.
It claims as its own the faith of the historic church
expressed in the ancient creeds
and reclaimed in the basic insights
of the Protestant reformers.**

**It affirms the responsibility of the church
in each generation to make this faith its own
in reality of worship,
in honesty of thought and expression,
and in purity of heart before God.**

**In accordance with the teaching of our Lord
and the practice prevailing
among evangelical Christians,
it recognizes two sacraments:
Baptism and . . . Holy Communion.**

**The United Church of Christ recognizes
that God calls the whole church and every member
to participate in and extend the ministry of Jesus Christ
by witnessing to the gospel in church and society.
The United Church of Christ seeks to undergird
the ministry of its members
by nurturing faith,
calling forth gifts,
and equipping members for Christian service.**

ASSOCIATION REPRESENTATIVE
Commissioning is an act whereby
the United Church of Christ through an association,
in cooperation with a person
and a local church of the United Church of Christ,
recognizes and authorizes that member
whom God has called to a specific church-related ministry
which is recognized by that association,
but not requiring ordination or licensing.
By this act the status of commissioned minister is conferred
and authorization granted to perform duties
necessary to and for the specific ministry.[16]

EXHORTATION

ASSOCIATION REPRESENTATIVE
Hear these words from the apostle Paul:
At all times make it your aim
to do good to one another and to all people.
Be joyful always,
pray at all times,
be thankful in all circumstances.
This is what God wants of you,
in your life in Christ Jesus.[17]

EXAMINATION

A representative of the association may then ask the candidate the following questions.

ASSOCIATION REPRESENTATIVE

———————————,
    name

before God and this congregation, we ask you:
Are you persuaded that God has called you
to the ministry of ——————————,
              position
and are you ready with the help of God
to enter this ministry on behalf of the whole church
and to serve faithfully according to the faith and order
of the United Church of Christ?

CANDIDATE
I am.

ASSOCIATION REPRESENTATIVE
**With the church throughout the world,
do you hear the word of God
in the scriptures of the Old and New Testaments,
and do you accept the word of God
as the rule of Christian faith and practice?**

CANDIDATE
I do.

ASSOCIATION REPRESENTATIVE
**Will you perform the duties
of your commissioned ministry
at** _____
place of service
**as one summoned by God to labor,
giving God the glory
and looking to God for your strength?**

CANDIDATE
I will, trusting in God's grace.

COVENANT

ASSOCIATION REPRESENTATIVE
addressing the congregation
Members of _____,
local church/agency
**will those who are able rise and affirm your covenant
with** _____
name
as a commissioned minister in your midst?

*Members of the local church and/or agency who are able
stand for the remainder of the covenant.*

LOCAL CHURCH/AGENCY MEMBERS
We receive you as a commissioned minister among us.
We promise to labor with you
as your brothers and sisters in Christ.
We gather with you and the United Church of Christ
as a sign of our mutual ministry in Christ's name.

ASSOCIATION REPRESENTATIVE
addressing the association members

Members of the _____ **Association ,**
association

will those who are able rise and affirm your covenant

with _____
local church/agency

and its newly commissioned member?

Members of the association who are able stand.

ASSOCIATION MEMBERS
We, the members of the _____ Association
association

of the United Church of Christ,
gather with you,
the people and the one commissioned,
as a sign of our covenant
and in celebration of our mutual ministry in Christ's name.

PRAYER OF COMMISSIONING

All who are able may stand as a representative of the association prays in these or similar words.

ASSOCIATION REPRESENTATIVE
Let us pray.

Almighty God,
who out of your great love gathered one church
by the power of the Holy Spirit
to be the light of the world,
we thank you for those in all ages
who have given their lives to tend it,
to care for it, to lead it,
and to serve in every way to forward its ministry.
Now we thank you especially for _____ **,**
name
whom we commission in your name
for the ministry to which you have called *him/her*.
Guide, inspire, empower _____ **,**
name
and keep *her/him* **faithful to your call**
that by *her/his* **life,**

your church may continue to be blessed
and its mission brought closer
to the fulfillment you intend;
through Jesus Christ,
the pioneer and perfecter of our faith.

ALL
Amen.

DECLARATION

ASSOCIATION REPRESENTATIVE
**In the name of Jesus Christ,
and on behalf of the** _____ **Association**
<small>association</small>

of the _____ **Conference**
<small>conference</small>

**of the United Church of Christ,
I declare that you are commissioned
in the United Church of Christ.**

ALL
Thanks be to God.

The people may show their approval and support by applause, a hymn, or other means. The representatives of the association and local church or agency may extend the hand of Christian love to the newly commissioned minister.

The congregation and newly commissioned minister may be seated.

Separate charges or one common charge may be given to the congregation and to the newly commissioned minister. The charge to the commissioned minister may be dramatically presented with symbols of the position.

At the conclusion of this order, a hymn may be sung. A Service of Word and Sacrament or a Service of the Word continues, omitting the affirmation of faith.

Order for
Affirmation of Ministry
(Installation of Lay Leaders)

INTRODUCTION

In this order the people of God in a local church celebrate the diverse ministries to which God calls all baptized people. It is a service of recognition and installation for those who consent to serve in an elected or appointed office in the church. Equally, it is a service of recognition and affirmation for those actively engaged in a variety of ministries in the world (community service, ministries in the work setting, caring for others, and the like). It is used when people want to be recognized and supported and to be called to accountability by the local church of which they are members.

The service is a reminder that to be a Christian is to be a servant. All ministry in the church is Christ's ministry. In union with Christ and in partnership with each other, Christians are called to serve according to the gifts given to them.

The pastor and other representatives of the local church, including the people to be affirmed, plan the service. Local customs and traditions may require significant adaptation of the printed order.

It is appropriate that the Order for Affirmation of Ministry be held within a Sunday service of the church or at a gathering of the church specifically called for this purpose. This order may be incorporated within a Service of Word and Sacrament or a Service of the Word. It is especially fitting that parts of this service consist of original material prepared particularly for the occasion.

OUTLINE

This order may be incorporated into a Service of Word and Sacrament or a Service of the Word following the sermon. An affirmation of faith and a hymn may precede the Order for Affirmation of Ministry.

>Greeting
>Introduction
>Presentation
>Covenant

>Laying on of Hands

>Prayer
>Declaration
>Greeting of Christian Love

A hymn may be sung. A Service of Word and Sacrament or a Service of the Word may continue, omitting the affirmation of faith.

Following the sermon, all who are able may stand and unite in an affirmation of faith and a hymn. After the hymn, all may be seated except the leaders and those whose particular ministry is being affirmed. These people may take their places before the congregation during the singing of the hymn.

The greeting may be used at the opening of the service rather than at the opening of this order.

GREETING

A leader may greet the people, and they may respond in these or similar words.

LEADER
Grace, mercy, and peace to you from Jesus Christ, the head of the church in heaven and on earth.

PEOPLE
To God be glory in the church
and in Christ Jesus to all generations,
for ever and ever.
Amen.[18]

INTRODUCTION

A leader may explain the purpose of the service in these or similar words and may lead the people in the responsive reading of scripture.

LEADER
**Affirmation of ministry is the act
whereby a local church
of the United Church of Christ
recognizes the diverse gifts of its members
and celebrates the particular ministry
of each person in the life of the church
or in various settings in the life of the world.**

**There are different kinds of spiritual gifts,
but the same Spirit gives them.**

PEOPLE
There are different ways of serving,
but the same God is served.

LEADER
**There are different abilities to perform service,
but the same God gives ability to each of us
for our particular service.**

PEOPLE
The Spirit's presence is shown in some way
in each person for the good of all.

LEADER
**Christ is like a single body,
which has many parts.**

PEOPLE
It is still one body
even though it is made up of different parts.

LEADER
**If one part of the body suffers,
all the other parts suffer with it;
if one part is praised,
all the other parts share its happiness.**

PEOPLE
All of us are Christ's body,
and each one is a part of it.[19]

PRESENTATION

*The pastor or another representative of the local church
may name the offices or the settings of ministry and the
people to be recognized in the following or a similar
manner. Use one or both, depending upon the ministries.*

🅰   *for ministries within the church*

LEADER
**These people have been called by God,
in accordance with the faith and order of this church,
to serve among us.
They have accepted their call
and are before us in witness to their willingness to serve.**

Ⓑ   *for ministries outside the church*

LEADER
**These people have been called by God
to serve in various ministries in God's world.
They have accepted their call
and desire to witness to that call
in the presence of this congregation.**

*The names of the people and their respective offices or
ministries may be read.*

COVENANT

*The pastor or another representative of the local church
may lead the people whose ministries are being affirmed
and the congregation in promises of mutual support.*

LEADER
addressing the people being affirmed

**Sisters and brothers in Christ,
it is an honor to be entrusted
with responsibility for particular service
in the ministry of the church,
whether gathered or scattered.**

The duties of each person may be outlined briefly.

LEADER
**Having prayerfully considered
the duties and responsibilities of your ministry,
are you prepared to serve with the help of God
in Christ's name
and for the glory of God?**

INDIVIDUALS
I am.

LEADER
**Do you promise
to exercise your ministry diligently and faithfully,
showing forth the love of Christ?**

INDIVIDUALS
I do, relying on God's grace.

LEADER
addressing the congregation

**Members of this household of faith,
you have heard the promises
of our brothers and sisters in Christ
who have answered God's call to service.
Let us affirm our intention
to live in covenant with them.
Will those who are able
rise and witness to the commitment
we now make?**

All who are able stand.

PEOPLE
We gather in celebration of the joy
that is ours to be partners with you
in the service of Jesus Christ.
We promise to love you,
honor your leadership,
and assist you
that together we may be a faithful church
of Jesus Christ.

The congregation may be seated.

_If it is not the tradition of the local church to ordain elders
or deacons or if there is no one present to be so ordained,
the service continues with the prayer on the next page._

LAYING ON OF HANDS

PASTOR
**The laying on of hands is the symbolic act
whereby the church in every age
recognizes God's call to ministry
in the lives of faithful women and men
and asks the Holy Spirit
to confer upon them the gifts of ministry.
We lay hands upon you, _____,
for the position of** _deacon/elder_ . name(s)

*The candidates who are able may kneel. The pastor
and other representatives of the local church may place
hands upon the head of each candidate in silence.
After hands have been laid upon all, the pastor may
say these or similar words.*

PASTOR
**May the Holy Spirit strengthen you
for the ministry of** *deacon/elder* **in Christ's church
and equip you with everything good to do God's will.
Receive authority to execute the office of** *deacon/elder*
in the name of Christ.

PEOPLE
Amen.

The newly ordained may stand.

PRAYER

*This prayer, or one prepared specifically for the occasion,
may be offered by the pastor or another representative.*

LEADER
Let us pray.

**Eternal God,
you have called these people
to serve you in this household of faith and in the world,
which you have entrusted to our care and keeping.
Send your Holy Spirit on them
that they may serve among us
with honor and faithfulness.
Help them to be diligent in their duties
that your church may prosper
in the mission you place before it.
May their example prove worthy
for all of us to follow,
as we are united in Christ's ministry,
to the glory of your name.**

PEOPLE
Amen.

DECLARATION

The pastor or another representative of the local church may declare that the act of installation or recognition has occurred. Individual positions may be named.

LEADER
**In the name of Jesus Christ,
and on behalf of the people of** _____
of the United Church of Christ,
 local church
I rejoice to announce:

Ⓐ *for all together*	Ⓑ *for individual positions*	Ⓒ *for individual ministries*
You are installed in your respective positions.	**You are installed as** _____ . position	**You are recognized and affirmed in your ministry in** _____ . setting

GREETING OF CHRISTIAN LOVE

The congregation may show approval and support by applause, a hymn, or other means. Representatives of the local church may greet those installed or recognized, using these or other words. At the conclusion the participants may return to their places in the congregation.

LEADER
**In accordance with the faith and order of this church,
I extend to you the hand of Christian love.**

PEOPLE
Thanks be to God.

At the conclusion of this order, a hymn may be sung. A service of Word and Sacrament or a Service of the Word may continue, omitting the affirmation of faith.

Order for Reception of a Local Church into the United Church of Christ

INTRODUCTION

In this order the United Church of Christ celebrates the covenant made between the churches of an association and a local church seeking admission to an association. In planning the service, set the time so that people from the member churches of the association and other guests may participate. A service of reception held on a Sunday morning will prohibit the enrichment afforded by this participation.

Representatives appointed from the local church and the association plan the service of reception. Lay and ordained people may share in the leadership of the service.

The order for reception may be incorporated within a Service of Word and Sacrament or a Service of the Word. It is recommended that it be held in the place of worship of the local church requesting the service.

It is especially fitting that original material be prepared particularly for the occasion. Provision is made in this order for the local church and the association to describe their history, ministry, and mission.

OUTLINE

This order may be incorporated into a Service of Word and Sacrament or a Service of the Word following the sermon. A hymn may precede the Order for Reception of a Local Church into the United Church of Christ.

> **Greeting**
> **Introduction**
> **Covenant**
> **Prayer**
> **Declaration**

A hymn may be sung. A Service of Word and Sacrament or a Service of the Word continues, omitting the affirmation of faith.

Following the sermon, all who are able may stand and sing a hymn.

The greeting may be used at the opening of the service rather than at the opening of this order.

GREETING

The moderator or another representative of the association may greet the people, and they may respond in these or similar words.

ASSOCIATION REPRESENTATIVE
**Grace, mercy, and peace to you from Jesus Christ,
the head of the church in heaven and on earth,
and from the _____ Association**
association
of the _____ Conference
conference
of the United Church of Christ.

LOCAL CHURCH MEMBERS
In the name of Jesus Christ we greet you,
our sisters and brothers in faith.

ASSOCIATION REPRESENTATIVE
**Hear these words from the apostle Paul:
Our brothers and sisters,
we must thank God at all times for you.
It is right for us to do so,
because your faith is growing so much
and the love each of you has for the others
is becoming greater.**

ASSOCIATION MEMBERS
That is why we ourselves boast about you
in the churches of God.[20]

INTRODUCTION

All may be seated except the representative(s) of the association and the representative(s) of the local church, who may continue the dialogue in this or a similar manner.

ASSOCIATION REPRESENTATIVE
addressing the congregation
We are here to enter a covenant.
The people of God known as _____
local church

and the churches of God gathered
in the _____ **Association**
      association
rejoice to affirm that by the grace of God
we intend to be the church together.

LOCAL CHURCH REPRESENTATIVE
We, the people of God in _____ ,
                        local church

Here may follow a summary of the faith of the local
church based on its covenant or other documents or using
words similar to the following.

believe in God, the Eternal One,
accept Jesus as the Christ,
and look to the Holy Spirit
to create and renew the church.
We are organized for Christian worship,
for the nurture of the Christian community of faith,
and for the mission of Christian witness,
in accordance with the word of God
as we receive it in the scriptures.

This is the story of our pilgrimage of faith.

Several members may recount significant parts of the his-
tory, ministry, and mission of the local church.

ASSOCIATION REPRESENTATIVE
We, the _____ **Association share your faith.**
      association
This is the story of our pilgrimage.

Representative(s) of the association may recount significant
parts of the history, ministry, and mission of the association,
including the relationship of the association to the confer-
ence and the General Synod of the United Church of Christ.

COVENANT

The act of covenanting may take diverse forms. The following may be adapted for use in particular situations.

LOCAL CHURCH REPRESENTATIVE
addressing the local church members
Sisters and brothers in ⎯⎯⎯⎯⎯⎯,
                                                  local church
let us affirm our intention to live in covenant
with the churches of the ⎯⎯⎯⎯⎯⎯ Association.
                                                association
Will those who are able
rise and witness to the commitment we now make?

The members who are able stand for the remainder of the covenant.

LOCAL CHURCH MEMBERS
We gather in celebration of the joy that is ours
to share the love of Christ with you.

ASSOCIATION REPRESENTATIVE
addressing the association members
Members of the ⎯⎯⎯⎯⎯⎯ Association,
                                    association
let us affirm our intention to live in covenant
with ⎯⎯⎯⎯⎯⎯.
              local church
Will those who are able
rise and witness to the commitment we now make?

Association members who are able stand.

ASSOCIATION MEMBERS
We gather in celebration of the joy that is ours
to share the love of Christ with you.

We promise you:
We will be concerned for your welfare;
we will be co-workers with you in your mission;
we will turn to you for assistance
in the work Christ calls us to do together.

An association covenant, a special covenant written for this occasion, the Statement of Faith of the United Church of Christ, one of the ancient creeds, or another

*unison declaration of common faith may be said by all.
Affirmations of faith are in the Resource Section, beginning on page 509.*

PRAYER

*All who are able may stand and join hands. This or a sim-
ilar prayer may be offered.*

ASSOCIATION REPRESENTATIVE
Let us pray.

ALL
**Holy God,
who in Jesus Christ has made a new and eternal covenant
with all who turn to you in faith,
witness the covenant we make today.
Confirm this relationship.
Bless our intentions, hopes, and commitments
with the fruit of holiness.
Light our way
with the lamp of your word
and the fire of your Holy Spirit.
Move us on the journey of faith
and enable us to walk with all your people
toward the day of justice and peace in all the earth;
through Jesus Christ,
who lives and reigns with you and the Holy Spirit,
one God, for ever and ever.
Amen.**

DECLARATION

All who are able may stand.

ASSOCIATION REPRESENTATIVE
**In the name of Jesus Christ,
and on behalf of the _____ Association**
                              association
of the _____ Conference
                conference
of the United Church of Christ,

I declare that _____ is a member in good standing
                      local church

of the _____ **Association.**
              association

ALL
Thanks be to God.

*All present may show their approval and support by
applause, a hymn, or some other means. The association
representative(s) may make a gesture of Christian love,
such as a handshake with appropriate words, to the repre-
sentative(s) of the local church.*

*At the conclusion of this order, a hymn may be sung. A
Service of Word and Sacrament or a Service of the
Word continues, omitting the affirmation of faith.*

Resources

Music

The music in this book was composed for the United Church of Christ by Alice Jordan and by Ronald A. Nelson.

Complete musical arrangements, beginning on this page, are followed by melody lines, beginning on page 467. When page references to music are given in the services, they refer to the complete musical arrangements.

The words of the texts are adapted by the Office for Church Life and Leadership. The words of the "Invitation" are adapted by permission from *Services of the Church*, #2. Copyright © 1969 United Church Press. The words of the "Song of Simeon" are the English translation prepared by the International Consultation on English Texts.

Prayer for Mercy (Trisagion)

Ronald A. Nelson

Prayer for Mercy (Kyrie)

Ronald A. Nelson

Gloria

Ronald A. Nelson

Doxology

Ronald A. Nelson

Invitation

Ronald A. Nelson

Holy, Holy, Holy (Sanctus)

Ronald A. Nelson

Ho - ly, ho - ly, ho - ly God of love and majesty, the whole u-ni-verse speaks of your glo-ry, O God Most High. Bless - ed is the one who comes in the name of our God! Ho -

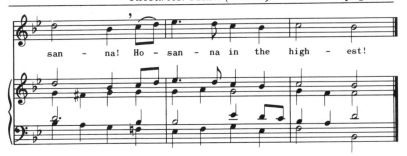

san - na! Ho - san - na in the high - est!

Memorial Acclamation I

Ronald A. Nelson

Christ's death, O God, we pro-claim. Christ's res-ur-rec-tion we de - clare. Christ's com - ing we a - wait. Glo-ry be to you, O God.

Memorial Acclamation II

Ronald A. Nelson

Christ's death, O God, we pro-claim. Christ's res-ur-rec-tion we de-clare. Christ's com-ing we a-wait. Glo-ry be to you, O God.

Lamb of God (Agnus Dei)

Ronald A. Nelson

Je - sus, Lamb of God: have mer - cy on

us. Je - sus, bear - er of our sins:

have mer - cy on us. Je - sus, re -

deem-er of the world: give us your peace.

Song of Simeon (Nunc Dimittis)

Ronald A. Nelson

na - tions and the glo - ry — of your peo - ple Is - ra-el.

Prayer for Mercy (Trisagion)

Alice Jordan

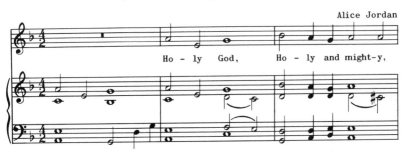

Ho - ly God, Ho - ly and might-y,

Ho - ly Im-mor-tal One, Have mer - cy up - on us.

Gloria

Alice Jordan

Glo - ry to God the Cre - a - tor, and to the Christ, and to the Ho - ly Spir - it: as it was in the be - gin - ning, is now, and will be for ev - er. A - men.

Doxology

Alice Jordan

Invitation

Alice Jordan

This is the joy-ful feast of the peo-ple of God. Men and wom-en, youth and chil-dren, come from the east and the west, from the north and the south, and gath-er a-bout Christ's ta-ble.

Holy, Holy, Holy (Sanctus)

Alice Jordan

Memorial Acclamation

Alice Jordan

Christ's death, O God, we pro-

claim. Christ's res-ur-rec-tion we de-clare. Christ's

com-ing we a-wait.___ Glo-ry be to you, O God.

Lamb of God (Agnus Dei)

Alice Jordan

Je - sus, Lamb of God: have mer - cy on us.

Je - sus, bear - er of our sins: have mer - cy on us.

Je - sus, re-deem-er of the world: give us your peace.

Song of Simeon (Nunc Dimittis)

Alice Jordan

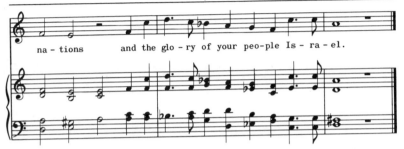

na - tions   and the glo - ry of your peo - ple Is - ra - el.

Prayer for Mercy (Trisagion)

Ronald A. Nelson

Ho - ly God,   Ho - ly and might - y One,

Ho - ly Im - mor-tal One,   Have mer-cy__ up-on   us.

Prayer for Mercy (Kyrie)

Ronald A. Nelson

Lord,   have mer - cy   up - on__   us.__

Christ,   have mer - cy   up - on__   us.__

Lord,   have mer - cy   up - on   us.__

Gloria

Ronald A. Nelson

Glo-ry to God the Cre-a - tor, and to the Christ,
and to the Ho - ly Spir - it: as it was
in the be-gin-ning, is now, and will be for ev-er.
A - men. A - men.

Doxology

Ronald A. Nelson

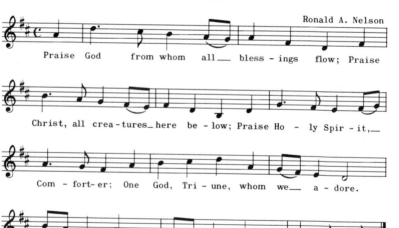

Praise God from whom all___ bless - ings flow; Praise
Christ, all crea-tures___here be - low; Praise Ho - ly Spir - it,___
Com - fort-er; One God, Tri - une, whom we___ a - dore.
A - - men. A - - men.___

Invitation

Ronald A. Nelson

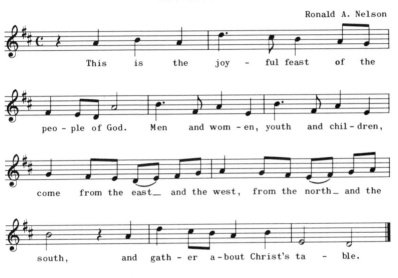

This is the joy - ful feast of the peo - ple of God. Men and wom - en, youth and chil - dren, come from the east_ and the west, from the north_ and the south, and gath - er a - bout Christ's ta - ble.

Holy, Holy, Holy (Sanctus)

Ronald A. Nelson

Ho - ly, ho - ly, ho - ly God of love and_ maj - es-ty, the whole u - ni-verse speaks of your glo - ry, O God Most High. Bless - ed_ is the_ one who comes in the name_ of our_ God! Ho - san - na! Ho - san - na in the high - est!

Memorial Acclamation I

Ronald A. Nelson

Christ's death, O God, we pro-claim. Christ's
res-ur-rec-tion we de - clare. Christ's com - ing we a -
wait.___ Glo - ry be to you, O God.

Memorial Acclamation II

Ronald A. Nelson

Christ's death, O God, we pro-claim. Christ's
res-ur-rec-tion we de - clare. Christ's com - ing we a -
wait.___ Glo - ry be to you, O God.

Lamb of God (Agnus Dei)

Ronald A. Nelson

Je - sus, Lamb of God: have mer-cy on us.

Je - sus, bear-er of our sins: have mer-cy on us.

Je-sus, re-deem-er of the world: give us your peace.

Song of Simeon (Nunc Dimittis)

Ronald A. Nelson

Ho - ly One, now let your ser - vant go in —

peace; your word has been ful - filled: my own

eyes have seen the sal -va -tion which_ you have pre-pared in the

sight of ev - 'ry peo - ple: a — light to re-veal you to the

na-tions and the glo -ry— of your peo-ple Is - ra - el.

Prayer for Mercy (Trisagion)

Alice Jordan

Ho - ly God, Ho - ly and might - y,

Ho - ly Im-mor-tal One, Have mer - cy up - on us.

Gloria

Alice Jordan

Glo - ry to God the Cre - a - tor, and to the Christ, and to the Ho - ly Spir - it: as it was in the be - gin - ning, is now, and will be for ev - er. A - men.

Doxology

Alice Jordan

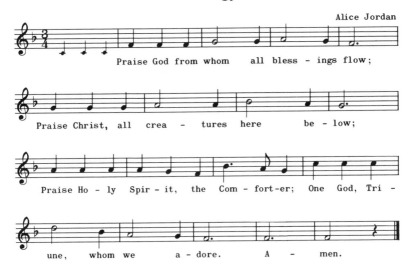

Praise God from whom all bless - ings flow;
Praise Christ, all crea - tures here be - low;
Praise Ho - ly Spir - it, the Com - fort-er; One God, Tri -
une, whom we a - dore. A - men.

Invitation

Alice Jordan

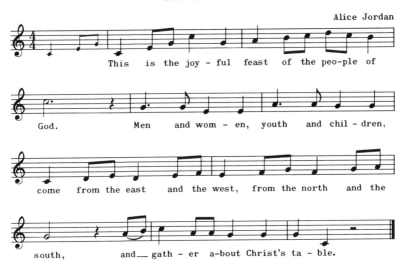

This is the joy - ful feast of the peo-ple of
God. Men and wom - en, youth and chil - dren,
come from the east and the west, from the north and the
south, and— gath - er a-bout Christ's ta - ble.

Holy, Holy, Holy (Sanctus)

Alice Jordan

Ho - ly, ho - ly, ho - ly God of love_ and maj - es-ty, the whole u - ni-verse speaks of your glo-ry, O God Most High. Bless-ed is the one who comes in the name of our God! Ho-san - na in_ the high - est!

Memorial Acclamation

Alice Jordan

Christ's death, O God, we pro-claim. Christ's res-ur-rec-tion we de - clare. Christ's com-ing we a-wait._ Glo - ry be to you, O God.

Lamb of God (Agnus Dei)

Alice Jordan

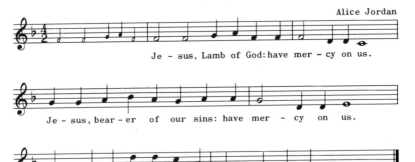

Je - sus, Lamb of God: have mer - cy on us.

Je - sus, bear - er of our sins: have mer - cy on us.

Je - sus, re-deem-er of the world: give us your peace.

Song of Simeon (Nunc Dimittis)

Alice Jordan

Ho - ly One, now

let your ser-vant go in peace; your word has been ful-filled: my own

eyes have seen the sal-va - tion which you have pre-pared in the

sight of ev - 'ry peo - ple: a light to re-veal you to the

na - tions and the glo - ry of your peo-ple Is - ra-el.

Resources for the Church Year

ADVENT

GREETING

In the desert of life,
prepare a pathway for God.
In the wilderness,
make a highway for our God.
Every valley shall be raised up,
every mountain and hill made low;
and the glory of God shall be revealed among us.[1]

CALL TO WORSHIP

LEADER
**How beautiful upon the mountains are the feet of those
who bring good news,
who proclaim peace,
who bring good tidings,
who proclaim salvation,
who say to Zion:**

PEOPLE
Your God reigns![2]

LEADER
**God comes in the power of love and justice;
therefore let us wait with eagerness
and worship with joy.**

PEOPLE
God comes to judge the world with righteousness,
the people with truth.

ALL
**Let the heavens be glad;
let the earth rejoice;
let the sea roar and all that fills it.[3]
Shout for joy,
all the earth!**

SENTENCES

Behold, I send my messenger before your face,
who shall prepare your way before you.[4]

INVOCATION

Creating and sustaining God,
in your presence there is life.
Living water springs up,
and deserts blossom where you pass.
Seeking the life that comes from you,
we have gathered before you.
Our hearts are ready, O God,
our hearts are ready.
Delight us with your presence,
and prepare us for your service in the world;
through the grace of Jesus Christ.
Amen.

CONFESSION

CALL TO CONFESSION
John the Baptist called people to repentance,
to prepare them
for the coming of God's reign.
Let us, too, repent,
that we may be ready
for God who comes to us.

PRAYER OF CONFESSION
God,
we confess that it is not easy
to wait for you.
Our world worships the power
that acts quickly through force;
how difficult it is for us
to wait for the power of your rule
which comes slowly through love.
We admit,

that while claiming to desire
your reign of peace and justice,
we take part in the ways of war, hatred, and injustice.
We leave little room for you to act in our lives.
We turn now to you
in repentance and openness to your Spirit.
Forgive us,
and show us how to clear a path for you.
Come to us in your Christ,
and reveal your reign on earth.
Amen.

ASSURANCE OF PARDON
God says:
Remember these things, O Israel,
for you are my servant;
you will not be forgotten by me.
I have swept away your transgressions like a cloud,
and your sins like mist;
return to me,
for I have redeemed you.[5]
I say to you
in the name of Jesus the Christ,
our sins are forgiven.

PREFACE

Because, O God,
you faithfully come to redeem your people,
we give you thanks and praise.

GENERAL PRAYER

In all our restless activity and all our attempts
to predict, control, and secure our lives,
we thirst for water;
our spirits yearn for you.

Without your aid,
our best efforts fall short
of bringing the life for which we long.

We do not know how to create
just and loving relationships and societies;
we need your help.
Come to us in Christ,
and show us the way to true life.
Empower us by your Spirit
that we may take part in your labor
to bring new life on earth.
Come quickly, Christ Jesus,
bright Morning Star of the world,
and shine on us with your light.
Amen.

BENEDICTION

You shall go out in joy
and be led forth in peace;
and all the mountains and hills shall break into singing
and all the trees of the field shall clap their hands.[6]
God reigns!
Go in peace.

CHRISTMAS

GREETING

Have no fear.
Behold, I bring you good news of a great joy
which shall be for all people.
God has visited us;
day has dawned upon us.
For unto us a child is born this day,
who is Christ the Lord.[7]

SENTENCES

Let us go to Bethlehem
and see this thing that has happened,
which God has made known to us.[8]

CALL TO WORSHIP

LEADER
**Glory to God in the highest,
and on earth
peace and goodwill toward all.**[9]

PEOPLE
For out of God's own being,
Jesus has come to bring love and light to all people.

LEADER
**Jesus is our Emmanuel—God With Us—
come to gather our tears and laughter,
our work and play into God's love.**

ALL
**Glory to God in the highest,
and on earth
peace and goodwill toward all.**[10]

INVOCATION

We come before you in awe, O God,
freshly aware of your glory and your love
embodied in the midst of this world.
Here amid dirt and straw,
amid noise of cattle and labor of birth,
we perceive your work.
We dare to believe that it is you, God,
coming to be among us in Jesus,
and so we praise you with songs of joy.
Glory be to you, O God,
now and for ever.
Amen.

CONFESSION

CALL TO CONFESSION
God loves this world
of flesh and blood, stone and tree,
sheep and oxen, star and field.

God loves the world so much
that God comes to us in Jesus.
Yet we are careless with God's creation.
Let us confess our sin.

PRAYER OF CONFESSION

How amazing is your love, great God!
You are not distant from us
in some faraway heaven;
you have come close to us in a child born of simple parents
and cradled in a borrowed bed of straw.

We confess we abuse this created world.
When we stand by while the earth is despoiled
and its destruction threatened,
God, forgive.
When we inflict physical or emotional pain
on those with whom we share our lives,
God, forgive.
When we abuse or neglect our own bodies,
God, forgive.
By your great love, God,
draw us into new ways of living.
Teach us to cherish and nurture life in this fragile world,
in the manner of Jesus the Christ,
whose birth we celebrate today.
Amen.

ASSURANCE OF PARDON

Hear the good news:
In compassion,
God forgives us,
enabling us to turn from the ways of violence and death;
God shows us how to choose and cherish life.
I say to you in the name of Jesus:
Our sins are forgiven.
Rejoice and sing!

PREFACE

We rejoice in the good news
of the birth of Jesus;

with the angels, the shepherds,
and the faithful of every nation,
we glorify your holy name.

GENERAL PRAYER

Loving God,
we thank you
that you have come into our lives
and that you act with saving power
to make all things new.
We thank you for pouring out your life
into the human form of Jesus
and for the continual rebirth of Christ
in the human heart.
Touched by your Word made flesh,
we would embody, incarnate, and signify your love
on this earth.
May the joy of Christmas never end,
but continue through the ages
until at last your reign of justice and peace
is fully established on this earth.
We pray in the name of Jesus, the Word.
Amen.

BENEDICTION

LEADER
Glory to God in the highest!

PEOPLE
Jesus is born!
God has come to us and shared our common lot,
and so we rejoice!

LEADER
**Go forth rejoicing in the love of God,
the peace of Christ,
and the power of the Holy Spirit.**
PEOPLE
Amen.

CHRISTMASTIDE

GREETING

In many ways the Holy One has spoken of old,
but now God has been made known in Christ,
the image of the invisible God,
the firstborn of all creation.
Let us sing a new song to the God who loves us
and who receives us as children and heirs with Christ.

CALL TO WORSHIP

LEADER
**People of God,
sing and rejoice!
God has come to us in Jesus the Christ,
to reconcile and make new.**

PEOPLE
God has entered our existence of joy and sorrow,
taking on human likeness in Jesus, born of Mary.

LEADER
**Therefore, we rejoice,
praising God and singing:**

ALL
**Glory be to God in the highest,
on earth peace to those who will the good.**[11]
Christ is born. Alleluia!

SENTENCES

The heavens are telling the glory of God;
and the firmament proclaims God's handiwork.[12]

INVOCATION

Our faces are sometimes lined with worry, O God;
our days are full of stress and struggle.
Yet we come today

grateful that in the midst
of this crowded and troubled world,
your child was born, lived, and died,
full of grace and truth.
Surprise us with your presence;
renew our sense of wonder;
and give us peace and courage
to live as your people in the world.
May you be glorified in us,
as in Jesus Christ,
in whose name we pray.
Amen.

CONFESSION

CALL TO CONFESSION
We live as if Christ had never been born.
We abuse the privileges
that are ours as children of God.
Let us confess our sin before God.

PRAYER OF CONFESSION
God, you have come to us in Jesus,
your true child,
in whom you give us power to be your children.
Yet, O God,
we confess that we turn from your love,
fearing the comfort and challenge of being your children.
We are your own,
yet we refuse you,
clinging to the security of familiar ways
rather than accepting the new life you offer.
We tolerate hatred, violence, and injustice
in the world you loved so well
that you sent the child Jesus,
begotten from your own being.

We trust not in ourselves,
but in your great compassion.
Forgive us,

and renew a right spirit within us
that we may live as your children
and once again praise you;
through the grace of Jesus Christ.
Amen.

ASSURANCE OF PARDON
Hear the good news, children of God:
In Jesus Christ,
God forgives and frees you.
Live by the Spirit.

PREFACE

Because you came to us in a baby,
a sign we can understand,
O God, we glorify you.
For your great love by which you call us children,
we praise you.
With people of every time who have testified to your love,
we sing.

GENERAL PRAYER

Blessed are you, O God,
for you have visited and redeemed your people,
coming to us in Jesus,
delivering us from all enemies,
remembering your holy covenant,
the oath you swore to our ancestors in the faith.
You have come to set us free
that we may serve you without fear
all the days of our lives.
In Christ you have given us knowledge of salvation
and forgiveness of sin.
You have come to us to give light
to those who sit in darkness and in the shadow of death,
to guide our feet in the way of peace.
Therefore we praise you
with psalms and hymns and carols

and with thankfulness in our hearts
for your gift of yourself in Jesus.
Through your Spirit, may we put on compassion,
kindness, humility, and patience
to understand and forgive one another.
Bind us together in the perfect harmony of love.

May the peace of Christ rule in our hearts
that we may be instruments of your peace on earth.
We offer all words and deeds and prayers in Jesus' name.
Amen.[13]

BENEDICTION

Depart in peace,
for you have seen God's salvation,
a light for the nations.
May the love of God guide you,
the word of Christ dwell in you richly,
and the gift of the Spirit give you power,
now and for ever.
Amen.

EPIPHANY

GREETING

The Word became flesh and dwelt among us,
full of grace and truth,[14]
the life and light of humanity.
Great is God's love for us.
Alleluia!

CALL TO WORSHIP

LEADER
Jesus said:
I am the light of the world.
Whoever follows me will never walk in darkness,
but have the light of life.[15]

PEOPLE
We have seen the light of Christ
like a star shining in the sky;
and like the Magi,
we have come to worship.

ALL
Glory be to God,
and to Jesus Christ,
the Word of Light,
in whom God is made known
in the power of the Holy Spirit.
Amen.

SENTENCES

Alleluia.
We have seen the star in the East
and have come to worship the Ruler of the Jews.[16]

INVOCATION

We thank you, God,
that you have spoken to people of faith
at many times and in various ways,
and that in Jesus, your living Word,
you have revealed yourself among us.
We come longing once more to know your presence
and to hear your word.
We come eager to follow Jesus.
We rejoice that you are with us always
when we gather in Christ's name.
Amen.

CONFESSION

CALL TO CONFESSION
God has come to us in Christ,
but we often live as if it made no difference.
Let us confess our sin.

PRAYER OF CONFESSION
Loving God,
you have come to us in Jesus;
yet we confess that we often refuse to receive you.
We live in the world
as if we did not know you.
Showing your love for all peoples,
you guided sages from distant lands
to worship Jesus, your child.
Although we know of this love,
we limit our love with safe boundaries,
building walls rather than bridges,
denying our connection with all those you love.

Forgive us, God,
and give us new hearts to love and serve you.
Write your Word within us.
Make yourself known to us as we live today.
For we pray in the name of Jesus the Christ,
in whom you most fully have revealed yourself.
Amen.

ASSURANCE OF PARDON
Be of good courage,
for God sent the Word into the world not to judge
but to save.
I say to you in the name of Jesus Christ:
Your sin is forgiven.
Through the power of the Spirit,
let us live as children of God.
Amen.

PREFACE

Because, O God,
you have manifested yourself in Jesus the Christ,
begotten from the heart of your love,
Word of Truth,
Light of Light,
we give you thanks and praise.

GENERAL PRAYER

A

We give you thanks, O God,
for those who believed Jesus
to be your Promised One.
We thank you for Mary,
who praised your name
because you chose her
as mother of the Christ.
We thank you for sages
who were led from the East
by signs in the sky to greet
the holy birth.
We give you thanks for John,
who bore witness to Jesus.
Most of all,
we give thanks that
when Jesus was baptized,
you showed your
affirmation of Jesus as your
beloved child and servant.

Through the word
of many witnesses,
we too name Jesus
as our Christ and Savior,
our Light and Life.
Shine in our hearts through
the light of Christ
that we may be signs
of your presence on earth,
making peace
and doing justice.
May your people be a light
to the nations,
through Jesus,
your faithful servant.
Amen.

B

LEADER
**As sages from the East
offered you their best,**

PEOPLE
So may we honor you,
O Christ,
with our highest visions
and finest energies.

LEADER
**As you turned the water
to wine at Cana,**

PEOPLE
So come to your church now,
and teach us to change
human tears to joyful song.

LEADER
**As you were baptized
to fulfill all righteousness,**

PEOPLE
So may your church
humbly do your will.

LEADER
**As you gave light to those
who followed you on earth,**

PEOPLE
So be our light
as we follow you on city
streets or country roads.

ALL
**Be revealed among us
in power, in word, in
sacrament, and in places
where we live and work.
Glory be to you, O Christ,
now and for ever.
Amen.**

BENEDICTION

You are the light of the world.
Let your light so shine
that others may see the good things you do
and glorify God.[17]
God is with us now and always.
Go in peace.

LENT

GREETING

Let us keep our eyes on Jesus,
the pioneer and perfecter of our faith,
who for the joy that was waiting
endured the cross,
despising the shame,
and is seated at the right hand of the throne of God.[18]

CALL TO WORSHIP

LEADER
**We have gathered in the presence of God our creator,
who sets before us the ways of life and death.**

PEOPLE
We have gathered in the presence of Jesus the Christ,
who calls us to accept the cost of discipleship
that we may know its joy.

LEADER
**We have gathered in the presence of the Spirit,
who sustains us in trial and rejoicing.**

ALL
**In our living and in our dying,
we belong to God.
In the shadow of God's wings,
we sing for joy.
Let us worship God.**

SENTENCES

Jesus says:
If you would come after me,
deny yourself and take up your cross and follow me.[19]

INVOCATION

We gather to worship, O God,
under the shadow of the cross,
sign of human shame and divine wisdom.
Like Jesus, we would follow faithfully in your way;
like Jesus, we would live to you and die to you.
We are your people;
we belong to you.
We offer you our worship and our lives.
May your name be glorified in your church
as we are open to your presence today;
through Jesus the Christ.
Amen.

CONFESSION

CALL TO CONFESSION
In every time, prophets and apostles have come
to call the people of God
to repentance and newness of life.
We too are called to admit our sin
and to commit ourselves anew to follow in God's way.
Let us pray.

PRAYER OF CONFESSION
We confess, gracious God,
that we are not worthy of your love for us.
You lead us out of the land of slavery;
yet when the journey is hard,
we long to return to the comfort of our chains.
You speak to us through your prophets,
telling us how our rebellion hurts and angers you;
yet we harden our hearts and close our ears.

You come to us in Jesus,
revealing your love for all people
and suffering pain for us;
still we do not turn
in love and obedience to you.

We do that which we ought not to do,
and we leave undone those things we ought to do.
There is no health in us.
Sinful and rebellious as we are,
we cannot trust in ourselves
and the things that we do;
we can trust only in your grace.

Speak the word, O God,
and we shall be made free.
Forgive us,
receive us,
and give us courage to serve you
with renewed hearts and wills;
through the grace of Jesus Christ.
Amen.

ASSURANCE OF PARDON
Do not fear.
I say to you
in the name of Jesus Christ:
Your sins are forgiven.
Your faith has made you free.
Anyone who is in Christ Jesus is a new creation;
the old has passed away.
Behold, the new has come.[20]
Thanks be to God!

PREFACE

Because you have come to us in Jesus Christ,
enduring the cross
so that we might know eternal life,
it is right
that we should give you thanks and praise.

GENERAL PRAYER

Faithful God,
we praise you that you love us
and that you have come to us in Jesus
to reconcile the world to yourself.
We thank you that Jesus walked the path of obedience
all the way to the cross
and that you raised Jesus up
to draw us to yourself.
Jesus handed himself over to death,
knowing that unless a grain of wheat falls to the ground
and dies,
it will not bear fruit.

Teach us,
like Jesus,
to hand ourselves over in love for you,
for one another,
and for all people.
As we who have been baptized into Jesus Christ enter
into the life of the world,
may we die with Christ
that we may also rise with Christ.
May we take part in your work
of suffering and redeeming love,
lifting up the oppressed,
binding the brokenhearted,
challenging the powerful,
drawing all into a community of love.

We lift up our prayers for the world
still so full of suffering,
still so shadowed by crosses,
knowing you have loved your creation from the beginning.
We join our hearts with yours
in love for the world,
and we offer ourselves to you;
through Jesus Christ,
in whose name we pray.
Amen.

BENEDICTION

Seeing that we are surrounded
by so great a cloud of witnesses,
the faithful of all times
who have given themselves to God's loving will,
let us run with patience the path God sets before us,
encouraged by the love of God,
renewed by the grace of Christ,
and empowered by the presence of the Spirit,
now and for ever.
Amen.

EASTER

GREETING

Christ has been raised from the dead.
"O death, where is your victory?
O grave, where is your sting?"
Thanks be to God,
who gives us the victory through our Lord Jesus Christ.[21]

CALL TO WORSHIP

LEADER
**Praise God, who brings life out of death
and hope out of despair.**

PEOPLE
Praise God, who has raised Jesus Christ from the dead.

LEADER
**Praise God,
who gathers up the fragments left by human destruction
and creates new possibilities.**

PEOPLE
Christ has risen!

LEADER
Christ has risen indeed!

SENTENCES

LEADER
Sing to God!

PEOPLE
For God has done excellent things!

LEADER
**Sing, O heaven;
and be joyful, O earth!**

PEOPLE
For God has comforted the people!

LEADER
Thanks be to God!

PEOPLE
For God has given us the victory![22]

INVOCATION

We rejoice, mighty God,
that you have raised Jesus Christ from the dead.
We praise you and glorify your name.
New life blossoms where dead hopes were buried.
Today the world is made new.
Be known among us in resurrection power;
through Jesus, our crucified and risen Savior.
Amen.

CONFESSION

CALL TO CONFESSION
Easter morning takes us by surprise,
awakening us to the doubt and despair
that have been rooted in our lives.
Let us now confess to God.

PRAYER OF CONFESSION
If, at times, we deny you:
God forgive.
If, at times, when the risks of discipleship are high,
we are nowhere to be found:

God forgive.
If, at times,
we wash our hands of responsibility:
God forgive.
If, at times,
we cast our lot with powerful oppressors
and seek to buy freedom with silver:
God forgive.
If, at times,
fear keeps us from witnessing to your truth,
or prejudice keeps us from believing it:
God forgive.

In the bright light of Easter morning,
our sin is exposed,
but your grace is revealed.
Tender God,
we are bold to come before you
and ask you to forgive us.
Help us to leave behind our foolish doubt
so that with joy we may witness to your awesome deeds
in Jesus the Risen One.
Amen.

ASSURANCE OF PARDON
Hear the good news:
In raising Jesus from the dead,
God has brought life and immortality to light.
And hear the good news:
By God's great mercy,
we have been born anew to a living hope
through the resurrection of Jesus Christ
from the dead.[23]
In the name of Jesus,
I say to you:
Our sins are forgiven.
All things are made new.
Doubt no more;
Christ is with us always.
Alleluia!
Amen.

PREFACE

Because you have done the completely unexpected deed,
because you have raised Jesus to eternal life,
because you grant us the presence
of the risen Christ among us,
because you offer eternal life to those who trust in you,
we praise and magnify your name.

GENERAL PRAYER

God of ceaseless new beginnings,
we rejoice that through your powerful love
Jesus Christ has risen from the dead.
In the resurrection you have shown that neither trouble
nor persecution, hardship nor poverty,
danger nor death can separate us from your love.
Free us to trust in you
that we may live in the confidence of your children.

In the resurrection you were victorious
over sin, violence, and oppression.
Free us to risk ourselves in the struggle for justice and peace
that we may be your partners
in restoring all creation to your will.

In the resurrection you have opened the gates of eternal life.
Free us from the fear of death
that we may serve you with courage.

In the resurrection you bring new possibilities
out of hopeless situations.
Free us from all despair
that we may bring your hope to those who have lost heart.

Through the presence of Jesus Christ among us,
draw us into a community of freedom, hope, and love.
Work your new creation among us
that we may serve you without fear.
God Most Holy, God Most Loving, God Most Knowing,
we praise your name for ever;
through Jesus our risen Christ and Savior.
Amen.

BENEDICTION

Rejoice, people of God!
Christ is risen from the dead!
Go in peace to love and serve God.
Christ is with you always,
even to the end of the age!
Amen.

EASTERTIDE

GREETING

Jesus said:
I am the vine, you are the branches.
Whoever abides in me, and I in that person,
will bear much fruit;
for apart from me you can do nothing.
This is my commandment,
that you love one another, as I have loved you.[24]

CALL TO WORSHIP

LEADER
**We are gathered in the presence of the risen Christ,
who remains with us for ever.**

PEOPLE
When we abide in the love of Christ,
love, joy, and peace grow.

LEADER
**We are rooted in Christ's love
that we may bear these fruits
together with all God's people.**

ALL
**With the faithful of every race, tribe, people, and nation
we sing:
Blessing, glory, wisdom, thanks, honor, and might
be to God for ever and ever.
Amen.**[25]

SENTENCES

LEADER
Jesus commanded: Love one another.

PEOPLE
We come to worship the God who is love
that we may learn to love one another.

LEADER
**Jesus said: No longer do I call you servants;
now I call you my friends.**

PEOPLE
We come to worship the God
whose friends we are through Christ.

LEADER
**Let us sing praise to God
and live in love and friendship toward the human family;
through Jesus Christ.
Amen.**[26]

INVOCATION

Holy God, the earth is full of your glory,
and so we worship you.
Our hearts are on fire with the awareness
that Christ is with us,
and so we thank you.
Our fears have been calmed
in the bright light of the Resurrection Day,
and so we praise you.
Do not leave us, we pray.
Let us abide for ever in the assurance of your love;
through the grace of Jesus Christ.
Amen.

CONFESSION

CALL TO CONFESSION
With all the signs of new life in Christ around us,
we still cling to our old ways.
Let us confess our sin to God and to one another.

PRAYER OF CONFESSION

When we do not accept as our sisters and brothers in Christ
those who are different from us,
forgive us, O God.
When we oppose you by opposing those
who disrupt our routines and challenge our assumptions,
forgive us, O God.
When we willfully disobey you and lose faith in your future,
forgive us, O God.

God, in your mercy,
restore us to newness of life.
Bind together your church universal
through the coming of your Holy Spirit.
Empower us to witness with courage
to the presence of Jesus Christ among us.
Amen.

ASSURANCE OF PARDON

Take heart:
God's Spirit empowers us to move from the ways of death
to the ways of new life.
Our sins are forgiven.
Let us forgive one another
and give ourselves to one another
in the joyful community of the risen Christ.
Amen.

PREFACE

Because you have raised Jesus from the dead
and because you have raised us up
to be a community of faith through Christ,
we praise you with joy.

GENERAL PRAYER

We praise you, O God,
that by the life, death, and resurrection of Jesus Christ,
you have delivered us from the power of death,
making us alive to serve you.

Free us from pride of self
that we may live in community with one another
and with all your people.
Free us from fear of the principalities and powers
of this world
that we may live and speak with courage,
guided by your Spirit.

Keep us rooted and grounded in your love,
and fill us with the power of your Spirit.
Be glorified in our life together;
through Jesus our risen Savior.
Amen.

BENEDICTION

You are a chosen people,
a royal priesthood,
a holy nation,
God's own people.
Go into the world in peace,
declaring the praises of God
who has called you out of darkness
into wonderful light.[27]

May the God of hope
fill you with all joy and peace in believing
so that by the power of the Holy Spirit
you may abound in hope;[28]
through the grace of Jesus Christ.
Amen.

PENTECOST

GREETING

In the last days, says God,
I will pour out my Spirit upon all people.
Your sons and daughters shall prophesy.
Your young people shall see visions,

and your old people shall dream dreams.[29]
People of God,
we have been baptized into one Spirit
and one body through Jesus Christ.
Let us worship God with joy.

CALL TO WORSHIP

LEADER
The Spirit descends like a dove,
bringing peace to unite the world
in a just and caring community.

PEOPLE
The Spirit comes like a breath,
bringing life to renew the people of God.

LEADER
The Spirit spreads like fire,
bringing energy for witnessing to the love of God.

ALL
Spirit of the living God,
come to us and transform our lives by your power.

SENTENCES

You shall receive power
when the Holy Spirit comes upon you;
and you shall be my witnesses in Jerusalem
and in all Judea and Samaria,
and to the end of the earth.[30]

INVOCATION

We thank you, compassionate God,
that you sent your Spirit
to encourage those whom Jesus left behind
that they might not be alone.
Through the comfort of your presence,
you empowered them to witness to your love.

Today we also seek the encouragement of your presence.
Do not leave us alone, O God,
but send your Spirit to us
that we may worship and serve you with joy;
through Jesus our crucified and risen Savior.
Amen.

CONFESSION

CALL TO CONFESSION
Jesus said:
You shall receive power
when the Holy Spirit has come upon you,[31]
but we fear the Spirit's power.
Let us confess our slowness
to embrace the new life of the Spirit.

PRAYER OF CONFESSION
We admit to you, God of our life,
that our celebration of the coming of your Spirit
is often an empty ritual.
Through the Spirit you offer us life,
but we cling to the ways of death.
Through the Spirit you offer us freedom,
but we cling to our chains.
Through the Spirit you offer us unity,
but we continue building walls
between ourselves and others.
Through the Spirit you offer us power,
but we shrink away in fear and doubt.

Forgive us, O God,
that we refuse the gifts you offer.
Allow us to touch the risen Christ
that our doubt may be overcome.
Let us sing and dance with joy,
truly celebrating your presence.
Let us move with courage into the world
with the word of your love.
We pray in the powerful name of Jesus.
Amen.

ASSURANCE OF PARDON

People of God, leap up, dance!
The Spirit is here in healing power.
Your sins are forgiven.
Rise up in the new life of the Spirit.

PREFACE

Baptized by your Spirit into one body,
we testify to your faithfulness toward those
of every time, nation, people, and language,
and we give you thanks.

GENERAL PRAYER

Eternal Spirit of the universe,
we thank you that you do not leave us alone
but place your word within us and in the midst
of our life together.
You are no statue made of silver or gold,
but a living reality on the face of the earth.
Give us courage and commitment
to let your winds blow through us
and to let your life be revealed among us.
Empowered by your Spirit,
may we care for the needs of all people,
break bread together with joy,
and praise you day by day.
Grant us your peace;
through Jesus who lives among us.
Amen.

BENEDICTION

And now to the one who by the power at work within us
is able to do far more than we ask or imagine:
be glory in the church
and in Jesus Christ to all generations.[32]
Go in the Spirit of the living God!
Amen.

SUNDAYS AFTER PENTECOST

GREETING

The body is a unit,
though it is made up of many parts;
and though all its parts are many,
they form one body.
So it is with Christ.
For we were all baptized by one Spirit into one body—
whether Jews or Greeks, slaves or free—
and given one Spirit to drink.[33]
Let us worship God in Spirit and in truth.

CALL TO WORSHIP

LEADER
**How lovely is your dwelling place,
O God of hosts!**

PEOPLE
My soul longs, yea, faints for your courts;
my heart and flesh sing for joy to the living God.

LEADER
**Even the sparrow finds a home,
and the swallow a nest for herself,
where she may lay her young, at your altars,
O God of hosts, my ruler and God.**

ALL
**Blessed are those who dwell in your house,
ever singing your praise.
Blessed are those whose strength is in you.[34]**

SENTENCES

Thanks be to God,
who in Christ always leads us in triumph,
and through us spreads the fragrance
of the knowledge of God everywhere.[35]

INVOCATION

We thank you, living God,
that in Jesus Christ
you have built a house not made with hands,
a people among whom you live.
We thank you that you have called us
and that we belong to you.
We come now,
longing to know the touch of your Spirit
that we may be encouraged to serve you in the world.
Come to us that we may recognize you
and sing your praise;
through the grace of Jesus Christ.
Amen.

CONFESSION

CALL TO CONFESSION

Let us confess our sin,
trusting in God's grace.

PRAYER OF CONFESSION

We have promised to live as your people, God.
Yet, we confess that we fail you and one another.
We do not honor one another as we should.
As the body of Christ,
we are often disjointed and clumsy.
We do not work together as one to your glory.
We refuse your cry for help
in the voices of the poor and hungry.
We have not been faithful
to the trust you have placed in us.
Merciful God,
receive us as we are, and forgive us.
Encourage us with your love
that we may commit ourselves anew to live
as those who belong to you;
through the grace of Jesus Christ.
Amen.

ASSURANCE OF PARDON

Hear the good news:
In the life, death, and resurrection of Jesus,
we learn that God's love has no bounds.
In Christ we are forgiven
and are empowered to begin anew.
Thanks be to God!

PREFACE

You have called us into your church, O God,
to accept the cost and joy of discipleship,
to serve you in serving the entire human family,
to proclaim the gospel to all the world
and resist the powers of evil,
to share in Christ's baptism and eat at Christ's table,
to join in Christ's passion and victory.[36]
In gratitude we accept your call,
praise your holy name,
and testify to your loving deeds.

GENERAL PRAYER

We give you thanks, eternal God,
for those who have run the race of faith before us
and now surround us like a cloud of witnesses.
We thank you for those
who pass the word of your love to each new generation.
We thank you for martyrs and saints
who give themselves in love for you
and in the pursuit of peace and justice on earth.
We give you thanks, infinite God,
for the church around the world.
We thank you that we count
as our brothers and sisters in Christ,
people of all races, tongues, and nations.
From the villages of India to the mountains of Peru,
from the cities of Russia to the plains of Canada,
your name is praised.

We thank you for those who witness faithfully to you
in the midst of political or economic oppression.
May all your people, wherever they are, be one.

We give you thanks, living God,
that here and now you give us parts to play
in the great drama of your love.
Speak through us and move through us
that the story of your mighty deeds will be known
in our time and place.
With faithful people of all ages,
may we be Christ's body on earth,
for it is in the name of Christ Jesus that we pray.
Amen.

BENEDICTION

May God's face shine upon us;
may Christ's peace rule among us;
may the Spirit's fire burn within us,
as we scatter into the world
until we meet again.
Amen.

Affirmations of Faith

I believe in God,
　　the Father almighty,
　　Creator of heaven and earth.

I believe in Jesus Christ, his only Son, our Lord.
　　He was conceived by the power of the Holy Spirit
　　and born of the Virgin Mary.
　　He suffered under Pontius Pilate,
　　was crucified, died, and was buried.
　　He descended to the dead.
　　On the third day he rose again.
　　He ascended into heaven,
　　and is seated at the right hand of the Father.
　　He will come again to judge the living and the dead.

I believe in the Holy Spirit,
　　the holy catholic church,
　　the communion of saints,
　　the forgiveness of sins,
　　the resurrection of the body,
　　and the life everlasting.
Amen.[37]

COLOSSIANS 1:15-20 (ADAPTED)

Christ is the image of the invisible God,
the firstborn of all creation;
for in Christ all things were created, in heaven and on earth,
visible and invisible,
whether thrones or dominions
or principalities or authorities—
all things were created through Christ and for Christ.
Christ is before all things,
and in Christ all things hold together.
Christ is the head of the body, the church;

Christ is the beginning, the firstborn from the dead,
that in everything Christ might be preeminent.
For in Christ all the fullness of God was pleased to dwell,
and through Christ all things are reconciled to God,
whether on earth or in heaven,
making peace by the blood of Christ's cross.

NICENE CREED

We believe in one God,
    the Father, the Almighty,
    maker of heaven and earth,
    of all that is, seen and unseen.

We believe in one Lord, Jesus Christ,
    the only Son of God,
    eternally begotten of the Father,
    God from God, Light from Light,
    true God from true God,
    begotten, not made,
    of one Being with the Father.
    Through him all things were made.
    For us and for our salvation
    he came down from heaven:
    by the power of the Holy Spirit
    he became incarnate from the Virgin Mary,
    and was made man.
    For our sake he was crucified under Pontius Pilate;
    he suffered death and was buried.
    On the third day he rose again
    in accordance with the scriptures;
    he ascended into heaven
    and is seated at the right hand of the Father.
    He will come again in glory
    to judge the living and the dead,
    and his kingdom will have no end.

We believe in the Holy Spirit, the Lord, the giver of life,
    who proceeds from the Father [and the Son].
    With the Father and the Son
    he is worshiped and glorified.

He has spoken through the prophets.
We believe in one holy catholic and apostolic church.
We acknowledge one baptism for the forgiveness of sins.
We look for the resurrection of the dead,
and the life of the world to come. Amen.[38]

SALEM CHURCH COVENANT

We covenant with the Lord and one with an other
and doe bynd our selves in the presence of God,
to walke together in all his waies, according as he is pleased
to reveale himself unto us in his blessed word of truth.[39]

"FAITH" FROM THE KANSAS CITY STATEMENT

We believe in God the Father,
infinite in wisdom, goodness, and love,
and in Jesus Christ, his Son, our Lord and Savior,
who for us and our salvation lived and died and rose again
and liveth evermore,
and in the Holy Spirit, who taketh of the things of Christ
and revealeth them to us,
renewing, comforting, and inspiring the souls of men.

We are united in striving to know the will of God
as taught in the holy scriptures,
and in our purpose to walk in the ways of the Lord,
made known or to be made known to us.

We hold it to be the mission of the church of Christ
to proclaim the gospel to all mankind,
exalting the worship of the one true God,
and laboring for the progress of knowledge,
the promotion of justice, the reign of peace,
and the realization of human brotherhood.

Depending, as did our fathers, upon the continued guidance
of the Holy Spirit to lead us into all truth,
we work and pray for the transformation of the world
into the kingdom of God,
and we look with faith for the triumph of righteousness,
and the life everlasting.[40]

UNITED CHURCH OF CHRIST STATEMENT OF FAITH

We believe in God, the Eternal Spirit, Father of our Lord Jesus Christ and our Father, and to his deeds we testify:

He calls the worlds into being,
   creates man in his own image
   and sets before him the ways of life and death.

He seeks in holy love to save all people from aimlessness and sin.

He judges men and nations by his righteous will declared through prophets and apostles.

In Jesus Christ, the man of Nazareth, our crucified and risen Lord,
   he has come to us
   and shared our common lot,
   conquering sin and death
   and reconciling the world to himself.

He bestows upon us his Holy Spirit,
   creating and renewing the church of Jesus Christ,
   binding in covenant faithful people of all ages,
   tongues, and races.

He calls us into his church
   to accept the cost and joy of discipleship,
   to be his servants in the service of men,
   to proclaim the gospel to all the world
   and resist the powers of evil,
   to share in Christ's baptism and eat at his table,
   to join him in his passion and victory.

He promises to all who trust him
   forgiveness of sins and fullness of grace,
   courage in the struggle for justice and peace,
   his presence in trial and rejoicing,
   and eternal life in his kingdom which has no end.

Blessing and honor, glory and power be unto him.
Amen.[41]

UNITED CHURCH OF CHRIST STATEMENT OF FAITH
ADAPTED BY ROBERT V. MOSS

We believe in God, the Eternal Spirit, who is made known
to us in Jesus our brother, and to whose deeds we testify:

God calls the worlds into being,
>   creates humankind in the divine image,
>   and sets before us the ways of life and death.

God seeks in holy love to save all people from aimlessness
and sin.

God judges all humanity and all nations by that will of
righteousness declared through prophets and apostles.

In Jesus Christ, the man of Nazareth, our crucified and
risen Lord,
>   God has come to us
>   and shared our common lot,
>   conquering sin and death
>   and reconciling the whole creation to its Creator.

God bestows upon us the Holy Spirit,
>   creating and renewing the church of Jesus Christ,
>   binding in covenant faithful people of all ages,
>   tongues, and races.

God calls us into the church
>   to accept the cost and joy of discipleship,
>   to be servants in the service of the whole
>   human family,
>   to proclaim the gospel to all the world
>   and resist the powers of evil,
>   to share in Christ's baptism and eat at his table,
>   to join him in his passion and victory.

God promises to all who trust in the gospel
>   forgiveness of sins and fullness of grace,
>   courage in the struggle for justice and peace,
>   the presence of the Holy Spirit in trial and rejoicing,
>   and eternal life in that kingdom which has no end.

Blessing and honor, glory and power be unto God.
Amen.[42]

UNITED CHURCH OF CHRIST STATEMENT OF FAITH
IN THE FORM OF A DOXOLOGY

We believe in you, O God, Eternal Spirit,
God of our Savior Jesus Christ and our God,
and to your deeds we testify:

> You call the worlds into being,
>> create persons in your own image,
>> and set before each one the ways of life and death.

> You seek in holy love to save all people from aimlessness and sin.

> You judge people and nations by your righteous will declared through prophets and apostles.

> In Jesus Christ, the man of Nazareth, our crucified and risen Savior,
>> you have come to us
>> and shared our common lot,
>> conquering sin and death
>> and reconciling the world to yourself.

> You bestow upon us your Holy Spirit,
>> creating and renewing the church of Jesus Christ,
>> binding in covenant faithful people of all ages, tongues, and races.

> You call us into your church
>> to accept the cost and joy of discipleship,
>> to be your servants in the service of others,
>> to proclaim the gospel to all the world
>> and resist the powers of evil,
>> to share in Christ's baptism and eat at his table,
>> to join him in his passion and victory.

> You promise to all who trust you
>> forgiveness of sins and fullness of grace,
>> courage in the struggle for justice and peace,
>> your presence in trial and rejoicing,
>> and eternal life in your realm which has no end.

Blessing and honor, glory and power be unto you.
Amen.[43]

PRINCIPLES OF THE CHRISTIAN CHURCH

Christ is the only head of the church.
Christian is a sufficient name for the church.
The Holy Bible is a sufficient rule of faith and practice.
Christian character is the only requirement for membership.
The right of private judgment and the liberty of conscience
are rights and privileges for all.
Union of all Christ's followers is sought.[44]

FROM THE PREAMBLE TO THE DESIGN FOR THE CHRISTIAN CHURCH (DISCIPLES OF CHRIST)

We confess that Jesus is the Christ,
   the Son of the living God,
   and proclaim him Lord and Savior of the world.
In Christ's name and by his grace
   we accept our mission of witness
   and service to all people.
We rejoice in God,
   maker of heaven and earth,
   and in the covenant of love
   which binds us to God and one another.
Through baptism into Christ
   we enter into newness of life
   and are made one with the whole people of God.
In the communion of the Holy Spirit
   we are joined together in discipleship
   and in obedience to Christ.
At the table of the Lord
   we celebrate with thanksgiving
   the saving acts and presence of Christ.
Within the universal church
   we receive the gift of ministry
   and the light of scripture.
In the bonds of Christian faith
   we yield ourselves to God
   that we may serve the one whose kingdom has no end.
Blessing, glory, and honor be to God for ever.
Amen.[45]

General Resources

PRAYER OF OUR SAVIOR

A

Our Father in heaven,
hallowed be your name,
your kingdom come,
your will be done,
on earth as in heaven.
Give us today our daily bread.
Forgive us our sins
as we forgive those who sin against us.
Save us from the time of trial
and deliver us from evil.
For the kingdom,
the power,
and the glory are yours
now and for ever.
Amen.[46]

B

Our Father,
who art in heaven,
hallowed be thy name.
Thy kingdom come.
Thy will be done
on earth as it is in heaven.
Give us this day our daily bread.
And forgive us our trespasses,
as we forgive those who trespass against us.
And lead us not into temptation,
but deliver us from evil.
For thine is the kingdom,
and the power,
and the glory,
for ever and ever.
Amen.

C

Our Father, who art in heaven,
hallowed be thy name.
Thy kingdom come.
Thy will be done on earth as it is in heaven.
Give us this day our daily bread.
And forgive us our debts,
as we forgive our debtors.
And lead us not into temptation,
but deliver us from evil.
For thine is the kingdom,
and the power,
and the glory,
for ever.
Amen.

COMMANDMENTS

A

THE TEN COMMANDMENTS
God spoke these words, saying,
I am the Holy One your God.
You shall have no other gods before me.
You shall not make for yourself a graven image.
You shall not take the name of God in vain.
Remember the Sabbath day; keep it holy.
Honor your father and your mother.
You shall not kill.
You shall not commit adultery.
You shall not steal.
You shall not bear false witness against your neighbor.
You shall not covet anything that is your neighbor's.[47]

B

THE GREAT COMMANDMENT
You shall love God with all your heart,
and with all your soul, and with all your mind.
This is the great and first commandment.
And the second is like it:
You shall love your neighbor as yourself.[48]

WORDS OF COMFORT FROM SCRIPTURE

A

I know that my Redeemer lives,
and at last will stand upon the earth;
and after my body has wasted away,
then without my flesh I shall see God,
whom I shall see for myself,
and my eyes shall behold, and not as a stranger.

Job 19:25-27, adapted

B

Holy One,
you are my shepherd,
I shall not want;
you make me lie down
in green pastures.
You lead me
beside still waters;
you restore my soul.
You lead me
in paths of righteousness
for your name's sake.
Even though I walk through
the valley of the shadow
of death, I fear no evil;
for you are with me;
your rod and your staff,
they comfort me.
You prepare a table
before me in the presence
of my enemies;
you anoint my head
with oil, my cup overflows.
Surely goodness and mercy
shall follow me all the days
of my life;
and I shall dwell
in your house for ever.

Psalm 23, adapted

C

The Lord is my shepherd,
I shall not want;
he makes me lie down
in green pastures.
He leads me
beside still waters;
he restores my soul.
He leads me
in paths of righteousness
for his name's sake.
Even though I walk through
the valley of the shadow
of death, I fear no evil;
for you are with me;
your rod and your staff,
they comfort me.
You prepare a table
before me in the presence
of my enemies;
you anoint my head
with oil, my cup overflows.
Surely goodness and mercy
shall follow me all the days
of my life;
and I shall dwell in the
house of the Lord for ever.

Psalm 23, adapted

D

LEADER
A reading from the Psalms:
Hear, O Holy One, when I cry aloud,
be gracious to me and answer me!

PEOPLE
You have said:
"Seek my face."
My heart says to you,
"Your face, dear God, do I seek."

LEADER
Hide not your face from me.
Turn not your servant away in anger,
you who have been my help.

PEOPLE
Cast me not off,
forsake me not,
O God of my salvation!

LEADER
Even if my father and my mother forsake me,
you will take me up.

PEOPLE
Teach me your way, O God;
and lead me on a level path because of my enemies.

LEADER
Give me not up to the will of my adversaries;
for false witnesses have risen against me,
and they breathe out violence.

PEOPLE
I believe that I shall see the goodness of God
in the land of the living!

LEADER
I wait for you.
Strengthen me,
and give courage to my heart.

PEOPLE
Yes, God, I wait for you.
Psalm 27:7-14, adapted

God is our refuge and strength,
a very present help in trouble.
Therefore we will not fear
though the earth should change,
though the mountains shake
in the heart of the sea;
though its waters roar and foam,
and though the mountains tremble with its tumult.

"Be still, and know that I am God.
I am exalted among the nations,
I am exalted in the earth!"
The God of hosts is with us;
the God of Jacob is our refuge.
Psalm 46:1-3, 10-11

☒

LEADER
**If I lift up my eyes to the hills,
where shall I find help?**

PEOPLE
My help will come from the Holy One,
who made heaven and earth.

LEADER
**Would God let your foot stumble?
Would God, your guardian, sleep?**

PEOPLE
The Holy One, the guardian of Israel,
will neither slumber nor sleep.

LEADER
**The Holy One will keep you from all evil,
will guard your life.**

PEOPLE
The Holy One will guard your going
and your coming,
from this time forth and for evermore.
Psalm 121:1-4, 7-8, adapted

🄶

LEADER
Out of the depths I call to you.
O God, hear my voice!

PEOPLE
Let your ears be attentive to my voice!

LEADER
If you should mark our sins,
O God,
who could stand?

PEOPLE
But there is forgiveness with you,
so that you may be revered.

LEADER
I wait for the Holy One.
My soul waits, and in God's word I hope.

PEOPLE
My soul waits for the Holy One,
more than the watcher waits for the morning.

LEADER
O Israel,
depend on the Holy One,
for with God there is steadfast love,
with God there is plenteous redemption.

PEOPLE
God will redeem Israel from all sins.
Psalm 130, adapted

🄷
The Spirit of the Holy One is upon me,
because the Holy One has anointed me
to bring good news to the afflicted;
God has sent me
to heal the brokenhearted,
to proclaim liberty to the captives,
and the opening of the prison to those who are bound;
to proclaim the year of God's favor,
and the day of our God's vengeance;
to comfort all who mourn;

to grant to those who mourn in Zion
a garland instead of ashes,
the oil of gladness instead of mourning,
the mantle of praise instead of a faint spirit;
that they may be called oaks of righteousness,
the planting of the Holy One,
that God may be glorified.
Isaiah 61:1-3, adapted

Ⓘ
And when they came to the place which is called The Skull,
there they crucified Jesus, and the criminals,
one on the right and one on the left.
One of the criminals who were hanged railed at Jesus,
saying, "Are you not the Christ?
Save yourself and us!"
But the other rebuked him, saying,
"Do you not fear God,
since you are under the same sentence of condemnation?
And we indeed justly,
for we are receiving the due reward of our deeds;
but this man has done nothing wrong."
And he said, "Jesus, remember me
when you come in your reigning power."
And Jesus said to him,
"Truly, I say to you,
today you will be with me in Paradise."
Luke 23:33, 39-43, adapted

Ⓙ
Let not your hearts be troubled;
believe in God,
believe also in me.
In my Father's house are many rooms;
if it were not so,
would I have told you that I go to prepare a place for you?
And when I go and prepare a place for you,
I will come again and take you to myself,
that where I am you may be also.
I will not leave you desolate;

I will come to you.
Yet a little while, and the world will see me no more,
but you will see me;
because I live, you will live also.
These things I have spoken to you,
while I am still with you.
But the Counselor, the Holy Spirit,
whom the Father will send in my name,
will teach you all things,
and bring to your remembrance all that I have said to you.
Peace I leave with you;
not as the world gives do I give to you.
Let not your hearts be troubled,
neither let them be afraid.
adapted selections from John 14

Ⓚ
Now, since our message is that Christ
has been raised from death,
how can some of you say
that the dead will not be raised to life?
If that is true,
it means that Christ was not raised;
and if Christ has not been raised from death,
then we have nothing to preach
and you have nothing to believe.
More than that,
we are found to be lying about God
because we said God raised Christ from death—
but if it is true that the dead are not raised to life,
then God did not raise Christ.
For if the dead are not raised,
neither has Christ been raised.
And if Christ has not been raised,
then your faith is a delusion
and you are still lost in your sins.
It would also mean
that the believers in Christ who have died are lost.
If our hope in Christ is good
for this life only and no more,

then we deserve more pity than anyone else in all the world.
But the truth is that Christ has been raised from death,
as the guarantee
that those who sleep in death will also be raised.
1 Corinthians 15:12-20, Good News Bible, *adapted*

Ⓛ
But we have this treasure in earthen vessels,
to show that the transcendent power belongs to God
and not to us.
We are afflicted in every way, but not crushed;
perplexed, but not driven to despair;
persecuted, but not forsaken;
struck down, but not destroyed;
always carrying in the body the death of Jesus,
so that the life of Jesus may also be manifested
in our bodies.
For while we live
we are always being given up to death for Jesus' sake,
so that the life of Jesus may be manifested
in our mortal flesh.

So we do not lose heart.
Though our outer nature is wasting away,
our inner nature is being renewed every day.

For we know that if the earthly tent we live in is destroyed,
we have a building from God,
a house not made with hands,
eternal in the heavens.
Here indeed we groan,
and long to put on our heavenly dwelling,
so that by putting it on we may not be found naked.
For while we are still in this tent,
we sigh with anxiety;
not that we would be unclothed,
but that we would be further clothed,
so that what is mortal may be swallowed up by life.
The one who has prepared us for this very thing is God,
who has given us the Spirit as a guarantee.
2 Corinthians 4:7-11, 16; 5:1-5, adapted

OPENING WORDS

A
God is our refuge and strength,
a very present help in trouble.[49]

B
This is the day which God has made.
Let us rejoice and be glad in it.
Come, let us worship and bow down;
let us kneel before God, our Maker.[50]

C
God is spirit,
and those who worship God must worship
in spirit and in truth.[51]

D
Serve God with gladness!
Come before God's presence with singing!
Enter God's gates with thanksgiving,
and God's courts with praise!
Give thanks to God, and bless God's name!
For the Holy One is good;
God's steadfast love endures for ever,
and God's faithfulness to all generations.[52]

E
LEADER
**Blessed be the name of our God
from this time forth and for evermore!**

PEOPLE
From the rising of the sun to its setting,
the name of God is to be praised!

LEADER
**It is good to give thanks to God,
to sing praises to your name, O Most High;**

ALL
**To declare your steadfast love in the morning
and your faithfulness by night.[53]**

F

LEFT

These are the things that you shall do:
Speak the truth of one another,
render in your gates judgments
that are true and make for peace.

RIGHT

Let justice roll down like waters
and righteousness like an everflowing stream.

LEFT

Learn to do good;
seek justice, correct oppression;
defend the fatherless, plead for the widow.

ALL

Thus says the God of all,
"Keep justice, and do righteousness,
for soon my salvation will come,
and my deliverance be revealed."[54]

G

LEFT

And you shall proclaim liberty
throughout the land
to all its inhabitants;
it shall be a jubilee for you.

RIGHT

You did what was right in my eyes
by proclaiming liberty,
each to one's neighbor,
and you made a covenant before me
in the house which is called by my name.

LEFT

God is spirit,
and where the spirit of God is,
there is freedom.

ALL

For freedom Christ has set us free;
stand fast therefore,
and do not submit again to a yoke of slavery.[55]

🄷
People of God,
look about and see the faces of those
we know and love—
neighbors and friends,
sisters and brothers—
a community of kindred hearts.

People of God,
look about and see the faces
of those we hardly know—
strangers, sojourners, forgotten friends,
the ones who need an outstretched hand.

People of God,
look about and see all the images of God assembled here.
In me, in you, in each of us,
God's spirit shines for all to see.

People of God, come.
Let us worship together.[56]

🄸
LEADER
**We are summoned here
by our holy God,
who calls us each by name
and gathers us together
in the unity of Jesus Christ.**

PEOPLE
From classroom and kitchen and carpool,
we are called into God's presence.
Young and old and middle-aged,
individuals and families,
softspoken and outspoken,
we hear our names being called to join in worship.

LEADER
**This house of worship is a place
to pursue God's vision for all people:
unity and joy and faith
expressed through different gifts.
Let us worship together![57]**

Ⓙ

LEADER
Be still, and know that God is.

PEOPLE
God was, also, in the beginning.

LEADER
**And when all human striving has ceased,
God will still be.**

PEOPLE
From everlasting to everlasting,
God is God and alone is worthy to be worshiped.

LEADER
Let us sing praise to our God.[58]

PREPARATORY PRAYERS

Ⓐ

O almighty God,
from whom every good prayer comes,
and who pours out on all who desire it
the spirit of grace and supplication,
deliver us, when we draw nigh to you,
from coldness of heart and wanderings of mind,
that with steadfast thoughts and kindled affections
we may worship you in spirit and in truth;
through Jesus Christ.
Amen.[59]

Ⓑ

Almighty God,
who has given us grace at this time with one accord
to make our common supplications unto you,
and does promise that where two or three are gathered
together in your name,
you will grant their requests,
fulfill now the desires and petitions of your servants,
as may be most expedient for them,
granting us in this world knowledge of your truth,
and in the world to come, life everlasting.
Amen.[60]

C
Almighty God, unto whom all hearts are open,
all desires known, and from whom no secrets are hid,
cleanse the thoughts of our hearts
by the inspiration of your Holy Spirit,
that we may perfectly love you
and worthily magnify your holy name;
through Christ our Lord.
Amen.[61]

D
Many of us are bored or apathetic, O God.
We have no expectation other than getting through the day.
Surprise us with the good news
that our lives can be renewed.
Open us to your amazing love
that keeps knocking at the door of our hearts
through Christ our Savior.
Amen.[62]

E
Eternal God, we come to you with hungry hearts,
waiting to be filled:
waiting to be filled with a sense of your presence;
waiting to be filled with the touch of your spirit;
waiting to be filled with new energy for service.
Come to us, we pray.
Be with us.
Touch us.
Empower us as your people that we might worship you here
and act in the world for Jesus' sake.
Amen.[63]

F
O Holy Spirit, Breath of God, blow in our lives this day.
Clear out the cobwebs of closed minds and outworn ideas.
Fill us with the freshness of your living love.
Cleanse and renew us that we might go from this place
ready to be your people in the world.
We ask this in the name of the one who came
to reconcile the world to you, even Jesus Christ.
Amen.[64]

CONFESSIONS AND ASSURANCES

CONFESSIONS

A

Almighty and most merciful God,
we have erred and strayed from your ways like lost sheep.
We have followed too much
the devices and desires of our own hearts.
We have offended against your holy laws.
We have left undone those things
which we ought to have done,
and we have done those things
which we ought not to have done.
Have mercy upon us.
Spare those, O God, who confess their faults.
Restore those who are penitent,
according to the promises declared
to all persons in Christ Jesus.
And grant, O most merciful God, for Jesus' sake,
that we may hereafter live a godly, righteous, and sober life,
to the glory of your holy name.
Amen.[65]

B

Gracious God,
you have promised to receive us when we come to you.
We confess that we have sinned against you
in thought, word, and deed.
We have disobeyed your law.
We have not loved you or our neighbors as we should.
Forgive us, O God,
and grant that we may live and serve you in newness of life;
through Jesus Christ our Savior.
Amen.[66]

C

Almighty God,
maker of all things, judge of all people,
we acknowledge and confess our manifold sins,
which we from time to time have committed,
by thought, word, and deed,

against your Divine Majesty.
We do earnestly repent
and are heartily sorry for these our misdoings.
The remembrance of them is grievous to us.
Have mercy upon us,
have mercy upon us, most merciful God;
for the sake of our Lord Jesus Christ,
forgive us all our sins;
and grant that we may ever hereafter serve and please you
in newness of life,
to the honor and glory of your name;
through Jesus Christ.
Amen.[67]

D
Almighty God, Spirit of purity and grace,
whose salvation is never far from the contrite heart,
hear our confession of sin and have mercy upon us.
For our many refusals of your call;
for all our forgotten vows;
for the excuses we have fashioned
to hide from ourselves our unfaithful lives;
for our readiness to blame others;
for our selfish luxuries
amid the oppression and sorrows of life;
for the pleadings of your spirit
to which we have not harkened,
have mercy upon us.
Amen.[68]

E
Almighty God,
too often we forget your promise.
We live in ways that bring glory only to ourselves.
We bask in the false assumption
that we are in control of our lives.
Sometimes we want to tamper with the lives
of those around us for our own ends.
Help us to love our neighbors as ourselves
and to serve you more faithfully each day.
Amen.[69]

F

Almighty and most merciful God,
God our Creator, Redeemer, and Keeper,
we have been created in your image,
but we have spoiled the perfectness of your model.
Being invisible in the eyes of the oppressor,
we have forgotten that we are highly visible in your eyes.
In failing to help our loved ones,
we have sinned against you.
Acknowledging our shortcomings and brokenness,
we confess our wretched nature,
come to you for forgiveness,
and give your name the praise.
Amen.[70]

G

Gracious God,
we confess what seems always with us:
broken things within us that seem never to mend,
empty places within us that seem always to ache,
things like buds within us that seem never to flower.
O God of love and grace,
help us accept ourselves;
lead us to do those good and true things
that are not compromised by anything within us.
As much as can be,
mend us, fill us, make us bloom.
For all these things, we will give you the glory;
through Jesus Christ our Savior.
Amen.[71]

H

Because we have seen pain without being moved,
because we forget your love with solemn pride,
because we pass by happy before poverty and sadness,
Lord have mercy,
Lord have mercy,
have mercy on us.

For speaking of love without loving our sister or brother,
for speaking of faith without living your word,

because we live without seeing our personal evil, our sin,
Christ have mercy,
Christ have mercy,
have mercy on us.

For our tranquility in our affluent life,
for our great falseness in preaching about poverty,
for wanting to make excuses for injustice and misery,
Lord have mercy,
Lord have mercy,
have mercy on us.
Amen.[72]

ASSURANCES
Ⓐ
LEADER
We confess our sins
so that we can be set free from the bondage of the past.

Therefore, I announce to you
in the name of Christ Jesus
that you are henceforth set free:
   set free from all the enslaving bonds of your past;
   set free to live powerfully in every present moment;
   set free to love God,
            to love your neighbor, and
            to work with brothers and sisters
                  in building a peaceful world.
Jesus said:
I have come that you might have life,
and have it more abundantly.
Praise God!

PEOPLE
God's name be praised![73]

Ⓑ
In spite of our tendency to pull apart,
in spite of our tenacity to our old ways,
our loving God continues to call us back together again,
showing us the true nature of forgiveness.
God does not keep score of our wrongs,

or measure how far we have wandered.
God welcomes us,
like a mother scooping up her lost children,
like a father embracing his prodigal offspring.
As we are welcomed home,
we are encouraged to learn from that forgiveness,
to offer it to ourselves and to others again and again
as God offers it to us in Jesus Christ,
our hope and our home.[74]

🄲
How we love to hang on to the past!
We get all tied up
remembering, keeping count, bearing grudges.
God doesn't.
Your past is accepted.
Let it go.
Live in the freedom God hands to you afresh each day.
Thanks be to God.[75]

PRAYERS OF THANKSGIVING

🄰
O God, giver of all good,
who continually pours your benefits upon us,
age after age the living wait upon you
and find that of your faithfulness there is no end
and that your care is unfailing.
We praise you that the mystery of our life
is a mystery of infinite goodness.
We praise you for the order and constancy of nature;
for the beauty and bounty of the earth;
for day and night, summer and winter,
seedtime and harvest;
for the varied gifts of loveliness and use
which every season brings.
We give you thanks for all the comfort and joy of life,
for our homes, for our friends, and
for all the love and sympathy and goodwill of all people.
Amen.[76]

B

O God,
we are made glad by the good news of your love
for us and for all.
We thank you for creating us
and giving us all that is necessary for life.
We thank you for your action in Christ
by which our lives are measured,
found wanting, and renewed.
Help us to remember your gifts
that we may praise you with lives of joy and service;
through Jesus Christ.
Amen.[77]

C

God, we offer you thanks and praise
for all the surprising graces which come to us,
for those that sustain our lives and those that change them:

for food, familiar diets, and startling new aromas and tastes;
for homes, places of steady surroundings,
and settings for redemptive love;
for friendships, old friends who are willingly open
in their affection and their correction,
and new friends who remind us
that your spirited presence still dwells within us and others;
for tasks to perform,
routine actions which we do well
and which give order to our days
and tasks at which we have failed
which restore a needed humility to us;
for Jesus Christ,
and for all Christ has done and will do for us
in our life as a congregation of Christ's people.

In Christ's name we pray.
Amen.[78]

D *post-communion*

Grant, O God,
that the ears which have heard the voice of your song
may be closed to the voice of clamor and dispute;

that the eyes which have seen your great love
may also behold your blessed hope;
that the tongues which have sung your praise
may speak the truth;
that the feet which have walked your courts
may walk in the region of light;
and that the bodies which have tasted your living body
may be restored in newness of life.
Glory be to you, O God![79]

Ⓔ *post-communion*
Almighty God, heavenly Father,
we praise you and extol you,
for you have again amply given us
of the blessed benefits of your sacraments.
You have satisfied us
with the food and drink of eternal life,
and you have again assigned us
the signs and seals of your mercy.
Having been fulfilled with the benefits of your altar,
behold,
we offer ourselves, our bodies and souls,
as a holy, as a precious offering,
that all of us who have just united with Jesus Christ
and through Christ with one another
may grow daily in faith,
may rejoice in hope,
and may enrich ourselves in familial love.
May praise, glory, honor, and thanksgiving
descend upon your holy name now and for ever.
Amen.[80]

PRAYERS OF INTERCESSION

Ⓐ
O God, the refuge of the poor,
and the hope of the humble,
the salvation of the needy;
hear us as we pray for those who are worn by illness,
for all who are wronged or oppressed,

and for the weary and heavy-laden,
that they may be strengthened by your grace
and healed by your consolations.
Let the dayspring from on high
visit those who sit in darkness
and in the shadow of death,
to guide their feet into the way of peace;
through Jesus Christ.
Amen.[81]

B
O God, Eternal Spirit,
you have called us into relationship
to fulfill a mission
whose meaning we yet dimly see.
Grant to the United Church of Christ
a secure sense of our identity
as people of rich human lineage,
as children of the promise,
as nobodies unless you claim us as your own.
And make us impatient with any identity
that does not propel us into the struggle
for justice, liberation, and peace.
Distribute among us gifts of faith and prayer,
of prophecy and discernment,
of love and hope
that we may never cease doing your will;
in Jesus' name.
Amen.[82]

C
Almighty God,
the fountain of all wisdom,
enlighten by your Holy Spirit
those who teach and those who learn,
that, rejoicing in the knowledge of your truth,
they may worship you and serve you
from generation to generation;
through Jesus Christ.
Amen.[83]

D

LEADER
Let us pray.
Let us pray for those who weep
and for those who cause their weeping;
PEOPLE
Hear our prayer, O God.

LEADER
For those who are without food, clothes,
and a place of shelter;

PEOPLE
Hear our prayer, O God.

LEADER
For those who live without hope and meaning;

PEOPLE
Hear our prayer, O God.

LEADER
For those who live as the objects of the whims of others;

PEOPLE
Hear our prayer, O God.

LEADER
For those who are fooling themselves;

PEOPLE
Hear our prayer, O God.

LEADER
For those who live with wars and rumors of wars;

PEOPLE
Hear our prayer, O God.

LEADER
For those who distort the good news of the gospel;

PEOPLE
Hear our prayer, O God.

LEADER
For those who make gods of things and of themselves;

PEOPLE
Hear our prayer, O God.
Amen.[84]

🅴 *one who is sick*
Loving and merciful God,
grant the assurance that you are here now.
Give the gift of quiet and rest;
pour forth the renewal of strength;
give the refreshment of sleep and relief from suffering.
Comfort those who wait,
that when this is all past,
we may praise your glorious name;
through Jesus Christ.
Amen.[85]

GENERAL PRAYERS

🅰
O God of love,
we are wayfarers in the world,
prone to erratic changes of course,
to losing sight of our goals,
to becoming so discouraged by the journey
that we will hitch a ride on anything that comes along.
Help us on our way, O God.
If we change our course,
let it be not in self-interest,
but in order to share the love of Christ
with another sojourner.
If we lose sight of our goals,
let our quest bring us as your curious people
to honest searching of our faith.
If we become weary and discouraged
and forget you are with us,
let it lead to recognition of our need for you.
As we travel in a world
that sometimes seems a trackless, hostile wilderness,
we ask that your Spirit sustain, encourage,
and enable us to go on.
In the name of Jesus Christ,
who walked before us.
Amen.[86]

B

O great and kind Spirit,
you have always been, and before you nothing has been.
There is no one to pray to but you.
The star nations all over the heavens are yours,
and yours are the grasses of the earth.
You are older than all need,
older than all pain and prayer.

O great and kind Spirit,
all over the world the faces of living ones are alike.
With tenderness have they come out of the earth
from which you give us food.
Look on your children.
With children in their arms, they face the wind
and walk the red road to the day of quiet.

O great and kind Spirit, fill us with light.
Give us strength to understand and eyes to see deeply.
Teach us to walk on soft earth as relatives to all that live.
Help us! Without you, we are nothing.
Amen.[87]

C *the hungry*

O Lord Jesus Christ,
help us always to remember that it is you whom we behold
in the weakened bodies and haunting faces
of the hungry of the world.
Grant that we may not turn away
but rather that we may receive your blessing
as a minister to the least of your brothers and sisters.
Amen.[88]

D *words*

God, Gracious Word beyond words,
let the Word we hear be in the words we choose,
   the words we use,
and join in chorus the words
of those whose song and speech
   tumble walls of sterile silence and meaningless noise;
in the name of Christ.
Amen.[89]

Ⓔ *healing*
God of All,
you have so fashioned the world
that it possesses the potential to repair its imperfections.
    And, O Eternal One,
    you have fashioned humankind by endowing us,
    as your partners,
    with the creative ability to help the repairing.
You gave us the insight to transform the simple herb
into a healing balm for the body.
    May we, as your servants,
    realize our responsibility to transform
    the herb of human caring
    into a healing balm for the aching soul.
Like ourselves, many are in need.
    We know the inner yearning for fulfillment, for purpose,
    for meaning in our lives.
May we ever come to know
that as we help others to feel fulfilled,
so shall we.
And then,
may we recognize the strength, the will, the dedication,
and the commitment to do that for which we were created:
to serve you by realizing your reign in our midst.
Amen.[90]

Ⓕ *the poor*
They sleep in doorways;
they sleep at home.
They wear ragged clothes and carry shopping bags;
they look like us.
They use poor grammar and smell;
they have good educations and are well-groomed.

All-knowing God, show us the poor—
not just the ones who have been pushed aside
in the wake of competition,
but the ones who are losing self-confidence,
the ones who are victims of the system they helped to build,
the ones whose jobs no longer exist.

Show us that there also is a poverty of the heart
when saving is more important than sharing.
Help us to find security
in sharing all our resources
so that through our total effort
we will have answered your call to be a friend in need.
Amen.[91]

ⓖ *mystery and hope*

Be with us through all the unknown days lying before us:
days when the black of night settles early in the west,
days when the strong white of winter comes from the north,
days when we look for the red of sunrise in the east,
days when the yellow noonday lingers in the south.

Touch us that we may trust you and be strong,
so that we grow in union with all our sisters and brothers,
so that we may see more deeply into ourselves.

We seek a vision from you,
a vision of your mystery,
a vision of ourselves and the love you have for us.
May we answer you honest and true, generous and brave.

Help us understand that for those who are faithful to you
life is not ended but only changed.
Help us join together with all you have created to say:
Great and powerful is our God.
God fills all heaven and earth with beauty.
We have deep hope because God has promised
everlasting life to God's faithful people.
In Christ's name we pray.
Amen.[92]

ⓗ *times of conflict*

O God, you have bound us together in a common life.
Help us,
in the midst of our struggles for justice and truth,
to confront one another without hatred or bitterness,
and to work together with mutual patience and respect.
Amen.[93]

Ⓘ *providers*
In the midst of our plenty, O God,
recall our debt to those who garner our food for us . . .
> those who pluck pineapples in the blaze of noon,
> those who buck the seas in search of fish,
> those who tend sheep and cattle through all the tantrums
> of weather,
> those who plow, and sow, and cultivate,
> and then wait in hope.
Teach us that we live
because others must fish and farm and shepherd.
Amen.[94]

Ⓙ *national holiday*
God of the nations,
guide our people by your Spirit
to go forward in justice and freedom.
Give us what outward prosperity may be your will,
but above all things give us faith in you
that our nation may give glory to your name
and blessings to all peoples;
through Jesus Christ.
Amen.[95]

Ⓚ *tragedy*
God of compassion,
you watch the ways of all of us
and weave out of terrible happenings
wonders of goodness and grace.
Surround those who have been shaken by tragedy
with a sense of your present love,
and hold them in faith.
Though they are lost in grief,
may they find you and be comforted;
through Jesus Christ,
who was dead,
but lives,
and rules this world with you.
Amen.[96]

Ⓛ *success or disaster*
Great God, help us to have such faith that neither success
nor disaster shall turn us aside from the love of you.
> In our success, help us to know that what we achieve
> > we can lose.
> In our disaster, help us to know
> > that tomorrow is a new day.

In success or disaster, assure us that your requirements are
a clean conscience,
a loving spirit,
and a forgiving heart.
Amen.[97]

Ⓜ *facing death*
God, in the struggle of my life,
be merciful to me and take me unto yourself.
When I am unable to speak in my pain,
and my face expresses my torment,
please come to my help.
When I am unable to hear anymore,
and the beating of my heart ceases,
let the Holy Spirit prepare me to receive your Word.
When death closes my eyelids,
let the beams of eternal light shine before me.

I believe in you, the only hope of my soul
and the leading torch on the way to salvation.
Do not permit my faith to fail
when all my strength is exhausted and comes to nothing.

You are the gate to salvation; in you do I hope;
your life was proof of it.
Call me when it pleases you.
In my life and in my death I belong to you.
Come, my Christ, as soon as possible.
Amen.[98]

Ⓝ *natural disaster*
God of earthquake, wind, and fire:
tame natural forces that defy control
or shock us by their fury.

Keep us from calling a disaster your justice;
and help us,
in good times or in calamity,
to trust your mercy, which never ends,
and your power,
which in Jesus Christ stilled storms,
raised the dead,
and put down demonic powers.
Amen.[99]

◙
Almighty and most gracious God,
whose very nature is to be present in good times and in bad;
in warm days and in cold;
in wind, rain, and sunny life;
in laughter and in pain;
in joy and in despair;
in work and in play;
and in all those things that are a joy of life,
open our hearts and our minds to the realities of the present
here and now.

Turn back, O God, the outer layers of our selves,
and look beneath the surface to our hidden inner depths.
Many of us hide behind polite dreams and wooden responses—
not daring to admit to others or even to ourselves
that we are vulnerable.
Yet we turn to you, trusting,
knowing that you will handle us carefully and tenderly.

Turn back the outer layers of apparent courage,
and find our fears.
Address them in us.
Acknowledge them,
even as you cause us to acknowledge them before you.
Do it not so much to rid us of them,
though we would like to be rid of them
and free from fears for ever.
How wonderful it would be
to stand in the presence of your perfect love
that casts out fear.

Turn back the outer layers of apparent confidence,
and find our worries and our anxieties.
Address them in us.
Acknowledge our uncertainties,
even as we acknowledge them before you.
Do it not so much to rid us of these fears and anxieties,
though we would like to walk along some waterway
and watch our worries and anxieties drown
in the backwash behind us.
How wonderful it would be
to stand in the presence of your perfect love
that calms fears, storms, and worries.
Still our plea would be more modest:
to know that you are present with us
and that we are not alone
in our struggle with worry.

Turn back the outer layers of apparent certainty,
and find our doubts.
Address them in us.
Help us to acknowledge doubts without shame.
Do it not to rid us of our doubts,
for we would not want to forfeit the growth
that comes from ourselves and our doubts,
even while we seek your purest presence.
So, O God, our plea is more modest:
to make our doubts building blocks
to a finer and firmer faith,
and to know that you accompany us in our journey.

We ask not that you make the hard moments of life easier,
except that our burdens are
eased by the assurance of your companionship,
heightened by the knowledge of your loving care,
strengthened by hope,
and shaped by love,
even as was the one in whose name we pray,
Jesus Christ,
our Lord and Savior.
Amen.[100]

▣ *litany of memory and potential*

LEADER
**Behold: the ripples of fire
buried deep in the dark, rich ground.**

PEOPLE
We are here.
We bring our memories and legacy.
We bring our bamboo and rice.
We bring our taro and palm.
We bring our earth and ocean.

LEADER
**Behold: the first shoots that burst out
from the ground and reach toward the sun.**

PEOPLE
We are here.
We bring our struggles and hopes.
We bring our shovels and picks
to this land of opportunity.
We bring our irons and ditches
to this land of promise.
We bring our broken hands and weeping hearts
to this land of milk and honey.

LEADER
**Behold: the golden flower that blooms with all the beauty
and the power and fragrance of almighty God!**

PEOPLE
We are not yet here,
but we are coming.
Help us, O God,
to open our minds,
to open our hearts,
to open our spirits
to the bright, new potential you have given us
in each moment of life.

LEADER
We thank you, O God.

PEOPLE
We thank you, O God.[101]

ⓠ *peace*

LEADER
Eternal God, who brought forth all worlds
from the womb of your being
and nurtured creation to splendor
in the cradle of your care:

PEOPLE
We praise you for your loving-kindness
toward all you have made
and for a universe still expanding beyond the stars.

LEADER
We rejoice that you have raised us from dust
and breathed living breath into our frames,
that we may love and serve you in perfect freedom.

PEOPLE
We lift before you a world burdened
with the power to incinerate itself
and to return to you the breathless dust
of a silenced earth.

LEADER
God, in your mercy,
show us the way of justice and peace,
lest in the defense of what cannot be defended,
we offer death a winnerless victory.

PEOPLE
Speak to all peoples,
but speak especially to us,
that our nation may not lift up sword against any nation,
neither provoke war
by a readiness that invites war.

LEADER
God, in your gentleness,
wean us from the enemy within ourselves,
that we may have grace and courage to prepare for peace
with more diligence
than any who labor to prepare for war.

PEOPLE
Forgive us for not doing anything,
because we cannot do everything,

and for not taking first steps,
because we cannot see the last step
on the journey that peace requires.

LEADER
**God, in your faithfulness,
do not turn away from us
when we place our trust in megatons of destruction
rather than in you.**

PEOPLE
From the lips of Jesus Christ,
let us hear again the call,
"Blessed are those who work for peace;
they shall be called the children of God."

LEADER
**Come, Holy Spirit,
let your tongues of fire stir us
to a Pentecost of peace,
lest the tongues of the technicians of war vaporize us
in a holocaust of hate.**

PEOPLE
Hear our prayer, O God,
for the sake of the world you pronounced good
at the dawn of creation,
and for the world you loved enough
to send us Jesus Christ,
who with you and the Holy Spirit lives and reigns,
one God, for ever and ever.
Amen.[102]

OFFERTORY SENTENCES AND PRAYERS

A
The psalmist said:
Behold, God is my helper;
God is the upholder of my life.
With a freewill offering I will sacrifice to you;
I will give thanks to your name, O God,
for it is good.
For you have delivered me from every trouble.[103]

B

Let your light so shine before people,
that they may see your good works
and give glory to God who is in heaven. [104]

C

All people shall give as they are able,
according to the blessings
which God has given them.

D

Remember the words of Jesus:
It is more blessed to give than to receive. [105]

E

What an abundance of gifts we have to offer:
  musical talent, the melody of laughter,
  the use of our hands in cooking and repairs,
  the use of our minds in problem solving,
  curiosity, compassion,
  patience, urgency,
  spiritual reservoirs, financial resources,
  obedience and courage to act.
All these gifts,
and others which bear our personal marks,
are symbolized in our offering
for the work of the church.
Let us commit ourselves in service
as we worship God with our offerings. [106]

F

Accept these offerings now placed on your altar,
O God, the giver of every good and perfect gift.
Grant that they may be symbols of our love
and of ourselves now offered more fully to you.
Use these gifts and us, we pray,
to the end that your realm may come
and your will be done on earth,
even as it is done in heaven;
through Jesus Christ our Savior.
Amen. [107]

G

All good gifts around us come from you,
O God.
You have given us life and new life in Christ.
As you have given us gifts,
so we offer our gifts
that we may be gifts to one another,
even as Jesus so taught and lived.
Amen.[108]

H

O God, most merciful and gracious,
of whose bounty we have all received,
accept, we pray, this offering of your people.
Remember in your love those who have brought it
and those for whom it is given;
and so follow it with your blessing
that it may promote peace and goodwill among all people
and advance the realm of our Savior Jesus Christ.
Amen.[109]

I

God,
we present these offerings
that they may be used
to extend your liberating reign.
With them,
we offer our varied ministries in the days ahead
that each of us may be part of your answer
to the cries of the world.
Amen.[110]

J

LEADER
What we have we bring:

PEOPLE
Our good intentions, our unknown motives,

LEADER
**Our uncertainties about life,
our grasp of truth,**

PEOPLE
Our time,
our uneasiness with what is.

LEADER
We offer this in the midst of what remains unspoken

PEOPLE
And affirm that it is received.

LEADER
Amen.

PEOPLE
Amen.[111]

COMMISSIONINGS AND BENEDICTIONS

🄰
The peace of God, which passes all understanding,
keep your hearts and minds
in the knowledge and love of God
and of Jesus Christ
and the blessing of God Almighty remain with you always.
Amen.[112]

🄱
Now to the one who is able to keep you from falling,
and to present you faultless
before the presence of God's glory with exceeding joy;
to the only wise God our Savior,
be glory and majesty, dominion and power,
both now and for ever.
Amen.[113]

🄲
The grace of God,
deeper than our imagination;
the strength of Christ,
stronger than our need;
and the communion of the Holy Spirit,
richer than our togetherness;
guide and sustain us today
and in all our tomorrows.
Amen.[114]

D
O Christ, our only Savior,
so dwell within us
that we may go forth
with the light of hope in our eyes
and the fire of inspiration on our lips,
your word on our tongues,
and your love in our hearts.
Amen.[115]

E
And now unto the one who is able to keep us from falling
and lift us from the dark valley of despair
to the bright mountain of hope,
from the midnight of desperation
to the daybreak of joy:
to God be power and authority,
for ever and ever.[116]
Amen.

F
LEADER
We have worshiped God together;

PEOPLE
Now we go our separate ways.

LEADER
May the spirit which has blessed us here

PEOPLE
Be your spirit in each day that comes!
Amen.[117]

G
May the great Ruler of all high places,
God of many names,
touch you with a wind that keeps you strong,
for all the days to come.
Amen.[118]

Notes

INTRODUCTION

1. Luke 10:27; see also Deuteronomy 6:4-5.

2. H. Strathmann, "Leitourgeo and Leitourgia in the New Testament," in *Theological Dictionary of the New Testament*, ed. Gerhard Kittel, trans. G.W. Bromily (Grand Rapids: Wm. B. Eerdmans Publishing Co., 1967), 4:226-228.

3. Amos 5:21-24, Matthew 25:31-46, Romans 12.

4. Luke 10:27-37; see also Leviticus 19:18.

5. J.D. Crichton, "A Theology of Worship," in *The Study of Liturgy*, ed. Cheslyn Jones et al. (New York: Oxford University Press, 1978), 7ff. For worship as the recapitulation of salvation history, see J.J. von Allmen, *Worship: Its Theology and Practice* (New York: Oxford University Press, 1965), 32.

6. R.T. Beckwith, "The Jewish Background to Christian Worship," in *Study of Liturgy*, Jones et al., 41ff. See also John C. Shetler et al., *Handbook on Worship* (Committee on Worship, Division of Church and Ministry, Pennsylvania Southeast Conference, United Church of Christ, 1981), 3-5.

7. Lucien Deiss, *Springtime of the Liturgy*, trans. M.J. O'Connell (Collegeville, Minn.: Liturgical Press, 1967), 3-19. See also Ilion T. Jones, *A Historical Approach to Evangelical Worship* (New York: Abingdon Press, 1954), 37-52.

8. Deiss, *Springtime of the Liturgy*, 26, and Beckwith, "Jewish Background," 43.

9. Dom Gregory Dix, *The Shape of the Liturgy* (Westminster: Dacre Press, 1954), 336-337.

10. Acts 15.

11. Deiss, *Springtime of the Liturgy*, 73ff., 123ff. See also Charles Yrigoyen, Jr., and George E. Bricker, eds., *Catholic and Reformed: Selected Writings of John Williamson Nevin* (Pittsburgh: Pickwick Press, 1978), 327.

12. Dix, *Shape of the Liturgy*, 5, 103ff.

13. Deiss, *Springtime of the Liturgy*, 123-127.

14. Marion J. Hatchett, *Commentary on the American Prayer Book* (Minneapolis: Seabury Press, 1980), 3.

15. Hatchett, *Commentary*, 5, and D.H. Tripp, "Protestantism and the Eucharist," in *Study of Liturgy*, Jones, 257-259.

16. Massey Hamilton Shepherd, Jr., "The History of the Liturgical Renewal," in *The Liturgical Renewal of the Church*, ed. Theodore Otto Wedel et al. (New York: Oxford University Press, 1960), 21ff.

17. Karl Barth, *The Knowledge of God and the Service of God According to the Teaching of the Reformation*, 211ff., cited in A. Allan McArthur, *The Christian Year and the Lectionary* (London: S.C.M. Press, 1958), 21-22.

18. *Baptism, Eucharist and Ministry*, Faith and Order Paper No. 111 (Geneva: World Council of Churches, 1982), paragraph 12, p. 12.

19. Quoted and discussed in Paul Whitman Hoon, *The Integrity of Worship* (Nashville: Abingdon Press, 1971), 47ff.

20. Massey H. Shepherd, Jr., "Liturgy and Ecumenism," in *Ecumenical Trends* 10 (May 1981): 68.

21. *The Lord's Day Service* (Philadelphia: United Church Press, 1964), 5.

22. *A Book of Worship for Free Churches* (New York: Oxford University Press, 1948), v.

23. *Book of Worship* (Evangelical and Reformed Church) (St. Louis: Eden Publishing

House, 1947), 3-4. Copyright renewed by United Church Press.

24. Hebrews 13:8, adapted.

25. For example, see the discussion of the womb of God in Jurgen Moltmann, "The Motherly Father: Is Trinitarian Patripassianism Replacing Theological Patriarchalism?" *Concilium* (New York: Seabury Press, 1981), 143: 51-56. See also Phyllis Trible, "The Nature of God," in *The Interpreter's Dictionary of the Bible*, Supplementary Volume, ed. Keith Grim et al. (Nashville: Abingdon Press, 1976), 368-369.

26. *Inclusive Language Guidelines for Use and Study in the United Church of Christ* (New York: United Church of Christ, 1980), 1-2.

27. It is especially important that words like *blind, black, poor*, and others not be used judgmentally. Likewise, optional directions concerning standing, sitting, kneeling, or movement should take into account the physical limitations of leaders and members of the congregation. Where fermented wine is used for Holy Communion, grape juice should be available for alcoholic individuals and others who wish to abstain from the use of alcoholic beverages.

28. Geoffrey Wainwright, "Recent Eucharistic Revision," in *Study of Liturgy*, Jones, 287.

29. "Eucharist with Children: Report of the Bad Segeberg Consultation," in *And Do Not Hinder Them*, ed. Geiko Muller-Fahrenholz, Faith and Order Paper No. 109 (Geneva: World Council of Churches, 1982), 14-15.

30. Karl Heinrich Bierritz, "The Lord's Supper as Sacrament of Fellowship," in Muller-Fahrenholz, *And Do Not Hinder Them*, 41.

31. Bierritz, "Supper as Sacrament," 45.

32. *Baptism, Eucharist and Ministry,* commentary on paragraph 19, p. 15.

33. William H. Willimon, *The Service of God* (Nashville: Abingdon Press, 1983), 185.

34. John 12:32, *King James Version*, adapted.

35. Hatchett, *Commentary*, 4.

36. J. Edgar Park, *The Miracle of Preaching* (New York: Macmillan Co., 1936), 113, quoted in Kenneth G. Phifer, *A Protestant Case for Liturgical Renewal* (Philadelphia: Westminster Press, 1965), 107.

37. Hugh T. Kerr, ed., *A Compend of the Institutes of the Christian Religion by John Calvin* (Philadelphia: Westminster Press, 1964), 177-178, quoted in Phifer, *Protestant Case*, 74.

38. Henry Martyn Dexter, *A Handbook of Congregationalism* (Boston: Congregational Publishing House, 1880), 88.

39. Stanley Samuel Harakas, *Living the Liturgy* (Minneapolis: Light and Life Publishing Co., 1974), 7.

40. Walter M. Abbot, ed., *Documents of Vatican II* (New York: Guild Press, 1966), 144.

41. Abbot, *Documents of Vatican II*, 144.

42. Bard Thompson, *Liturgies of the Western Church* (New York: Meridian, 1961), 194.

43. The Episcopal Church, *The Book of Common Prayer* (New York: Church Hymnal Corp. and Seabury Press, 1977), 9.

44. I Peter 2:9.

45. Joseph Gelineau, "Music and Singing in the Liturgy," in *Study of Liturgy*, Jones, 440.

46. Philip H. Pfatteicher and Carlos R. Messerli, *Manual on the Liturgy—Lutheran Book of Worship* (Minneapolis: Augsburg Publishing House, 1979), 79.

47. Abbot, *Documents of Vatican II*, 171.

48. Pfatteicher and Messerli, *Manual on Liturgy*, 81.

49. Exodus 15:19-21 and 2 Samuel 6:12-15.

50. See Constance Fisher and Doug Adams, *Dancing with Early Christians* (Austin, Texas: Sharing Co., 1983); Doug Adams, *Congregational Dancing in Christian Worship*, rev. ed. (Austin, Texas: Sharing Co., 1984); and Margaret Taylor and Doug Adams, *Hymns in Action for Everyone 9 to 90 Dancing Today* (Austin, Texas: Sharing Co., 1985).

51. United Church of Christ laywoman Margaret Taylor pioneered in this area with her early works now reprinted, *Look Up and Live: Dance as Prayer and Meditation*, ed. Doug Adams (Austin, Texas: Sharing Co., 1980), and *A Time to Dance: Symbolic Movement in Worship*, ed. Doug Adams (Austin, Texas: Sharing Co., 1980).

52. See Marian B. MacLeod, *Dancing Through Pentecost: Dance Language from Pentecost to Thanksgiving*, ed. Doug Adams (Austin, Texas: Sharing Co., 1981), and Dane Packard, *The Church Becoming Christ's Body: The Small Church's Manual of Dances for Holy Seasons*, ed. Doug Adams (Austin, Texas: Sharing Co., 1981). Movement can be used creatively to celebrate the gifts of groups of different ages, cultural backgrounds, and degrees of physical mobility.

53. Joseph Gelineau, *The Liturgy Today and Tomorrow*, trans. Diana Livingstone (London: Darton, Longman and Todd, 1979), 121.

54. Dix, *Shape of the Liturgy*, 305-335.

55. Philip Carrington, *The Primitive Church Calendar, a Study in the Making of the Marcan Gospel* (Cambridge: Cambridge University Press, 1952), 1:16.

56. A. Allan McArthur, *The Christian Year and Lectionary Reform* (London: S.C.M. Press, 1958), 38.

57. See Horace T. Allen, Jr., "Introduction," in *Common Lectionary: The Lectionary Proposed by the Consultation on Common Texts* (New York: Church Hymnal Corp., 1983), 10.

58. McArthur, *Christian Year and Lectionary*, 11.

59. McArthur, *Christian Year and Lectionary*, 11. See also Dix, *Shape of the Liturgy*, 329.

60. Peter Cobb, " Calendar," in *Study of Liturgy*, Jones, 415.

61. McArthur, *Christian Year and Lectionary*, 76.

62. Cobb, "Calendar," 418.

63. A. Allan McArthur, *The Evolution of the Christian Year* (Greenwich, Conn.: Seabury Press, 1953), 42.

64. McArthur, *Evolution of the Christian Year*, 53.

65. John Wilkinson, trans., *Egeria's Travels to the Holy Land* (Jerusalem: Ariel Publishing House, 1981), 25:12.

66. McArthur, *Evolution of Christian Year*, 66-67.

67. Cobb, "Calendar," 413.

68. Wilkinson, *Egeria*, 29.

69. Edward T. Horn, III, *The Christian Year* (Philadelphia: Muhlenberg Press, 1957), 112.

70. Cobb, "Calendar," 407.

71. Wilkinson, *Egeria*, 37:6.

72. Dix, *Shape of the Liturgy*, 349.

73. McArthur, *Evolution of Christian Year*, 79.

74. Wilkinson, *Egeria*, 41.

75. Cobb, "Calendar," 411.

76. See the discussion concerning ordinary time in Allen, "Introduction," 11, 22, and in the same volume, "Comparative List of Titles for Sundays and Special Days," 51-53.

77. Wilkinson, *Egeria*, 22:2.

78. McArthur, *Christian Year and Lectionary*, 51.

79. G.G. Willis, *St. Augustine's Lectionary* (London: S.P.C.K., 1962), 9.

80. Dix, *Shape of the Liturgy*, 364.

81. McArthur, *Christian Year and Lectionary*, 27.

82. See *Common Lectionary: The Lectionary Proposed by the Consultation on Common Texts* (New York: Church Hymnal Corp., 1983). This lectionary is provisional until testing has been completed in 1989.

83. Abbot, *Documents of Vatican II*, paragraph 51, p. 155.

SERVICES OF WORD AND SACRAMENT

1. Ephesians 2:19.

2. Matthew 18:20.

3. 2 Corinthians 13:14, adapted.

4. Psalm 124:8, adapted.

5. 1 Corinthians 5:7-8, adapted.

6. John 1:1.

7. Romans 5:5.

8. Based on Luke 4:18-19.

9. 1 John 1:8-9, adapted.

10. Adapted and reprinted from *Lutheran Book of Worship*, copyright © 1978, *Lutheran Book of Worship*. Used by permission of Augsburg Publishing House.

11. *The Sacrament of the Lord's Supper: A New Text*. Copyright © 1984 Consultation on Church Union. Used by permission.

12. Adapted by permission from *Services of the Church*, #1. Copyright © 1966 and 1969 United Church Press.

13. Based on 1 Corinthians 11:23-25.

14. Beginning with "For in the night of betrayal" adapted from *An Order of Worship for the Proclamation of the Word of God and the Celebration of the Lord's Supper*. Copyright © 1968 Executive Committee, Consultation on Church Union (COCU). Used by permission. COCU has prepared a new text, rather than adapting this text. See *The Sacrament of the Lord's Supper: A New Text*.

15. International Consultation on English Texts.

16. Both texts are from the International Consultation on English Texts.

17. *Sacrament of the Lord's Supper: A New Text*. Copyright © 1984 Consultation on Church Union. Used by permission.

18. International Consultation on English Texts, adapted.

19. Adapted by permission from *Services of the Church* #1. Copyright © 1966 and 1969 United Church Press.

20. Hebrews 13:20-21, adapted.

21. *Baptism, Eucharist and Ministry*, Faith and Order Paper no. 111 (Geneva: World Council of Churches, 1982).

22. 2 Corinthians 13:14, adapted.

23. 1 John 4:7-8, *Good News Bible*.

24. Micah 6:6, 8, adapted.

25. Matthew 18:20.

26. 1 John 1:8-9, adapted.

27. Psalm 51:1-2, 10-12, adapted.

28. Romans 5:1-2, adapted.

29. Matthew 5:23-24, *Good News Bible*, adapted.

30. Romans 12:1, *Good News Bible*, adapted.

31. International Consultation on English Texts.

32. John 6:35, adapted.

33. 1 Corinthians 11:23-26, adapted.

34. Matthew 26:26-28, adapted.

35. Revelation 1:17-18.

36. The words said in giving the bread and wine in option B are used by permission from *Services of Word and Sacrament*, II. Copyright © 1966 United Church Press.

37. Adapted by permission from *Services of Word and Sacrament*, II. Copyright © 1966 United Church Press.

38. Based on Numbers 6:24-26.

39. International Consultation on English Texts, adapted.

40. Isaiah 55:2-3, *Good News Bible*.

41. John 6:35, adapted.

42. Luke 19:5-6, 9, *Good News Bible*, adapted.

43. Matthew 18:20, adapted.

44. This is an adaptation of a traditional invitation. One version can be found in *The Minister's Service Book for Pulpit and Parish Use*, ed. and comp. James Dalton Morrison (New York: Harper and Bros., 1937), 113-114.

45. Matthew 8:8, adapted.

46. John 8:10,11, adapted.

47. 1 Corinthians 11:23-25, adapted.

48. International Consultation on English Texts.

49. The words said in giving the bread and wine are used by permission from *Services of Word and Sacrament* II. Copyright © 1966 United Church Press.

50. Matthew 5:14-16, adapted.

51. Adapted by permission from *Services of the Church* #1. Copyright © 1966 and 1969 United Church Press.

52. Numbers 6:24-26, adapted.

53. John 14:27.

54. John 6:35, adapted.

55. Matthew 18:20, *Good News Bible*, adapted.

56. 1 Corinthians 11:23-26, adapted.

57. International Consultation on English Texts.

58. The words said in giving the bread and wine are used by permission from *Services of Word and Sacrament*, II. Copyright © 1966 United Church Press.

59. Numbers 6:24-26, adapted.

60. Adapted and reprinted from *Lutheran Book of Worship*, copyright © 1978 *Lutheran Book of Worship*. Used by permission of Augsburg Publishing House.

61. International Consultation on English Texts.

62. Source unknown, quoted in *Jesus Christ— The Life of the World* (Geneva: World Council of Churches, 1983).

63. Adapted by permission from *Services of the Church* #1. Copyright © 1966 and 1969 United Church Press.

64. 2 Corinthians 13:14, adapted.

65. 2 Corinthians 13:14, adapted.

66. Matthew 18:20.

67. International Consultation on English Texts.

68. Mary Ann Neeval in *Bread for the Journey: Resources for Worship*, ed. Ruth C. Duck. Copyright © 1981 The Pilgrim Press. Used by permission.

69. John 1:1.

70. International Consultation on English Texts.

SERVICES OF BAPTISM AND AFFIRMATION OF BAPTISM

1. *Baptism, Eucharist and Ministry*, Faith and Order Paper No. 111 (Geneva: World Council of Churches, 1982).

2. Ephesians 4:4-6, adapted.

3. 1 Corinthians 12:12-13, 27.

4. Mark 10:13-16, adapted.

5. Matthew 3:13-17, *Good News Bible*, adapted.

6. Matthew 28:19, adapted.

7. John 3:3, 5, adapted.

8. Romans 6:3-4, adapted.

9. Adapted by permission from *Services of the Church* #3. Copyright 1969 United Church Press.

10. Adapted by permission from *Services of the Church* #3. Copyright 1969 United Church Press.

11. John 15:5, 7, 10, 11, adapted.

12. Romans 10:8-10, *Good News Bible*, adapted.

13. Ephesians 2:19-22, adapted.

14. Adapted from *Book of Common Worship*, Church of South India. Copyright 1963 Oxford University Press. Used by permission.

15. Adapted by permission from *Services of the Church* #3. Copyright 1969 United Church Press.

16. Adapted from The Episcopal Church, *The Book of Common Prayer* (Boston: Seabury Press, 1979).

17. Adapted by permission from *Uniting Church Worship Services: Baptism and Related Services*. Copyright 1981 The Uniting Church in Australia Assembly Commission on Liturgy.

18. John 15:5, 7, 10, 11, adapted.

19. Romans 10:8-10, *Good News Bible*, adapted.

20. Ephesians 2:19-22, adapted.

21. Adapted by permission from *Services of the Church* #3. Copyright 1969 United Church Press.

22. Adapted from *Book of Common Prayer*.

23. Adapted by permission from *Uniting Church Worship Services: Baptism and Related Services*. Copyright 1981 The Uniting Church in Australia Assembly Commission on Liturgy.

SERVICES OF A CHURCH'S LIFE

1. Luke 2:10, adapted.

2. Dom Gregory Dix, *The Shape of the Liturgy*, (Westminster: Dacre Press, 1954), 356.

3. Hebrews 12:2, adapted.

4. Based on Luke 4:18-19.

5. This is an adaptation of a traditional invitation. One version can be found in *The Minister's Service Book for Pulpit and Parish Use*, ed. and comp. James Dalton Morrison (New York: Harpers & Bros., 1937), 113-114.

6. Psalm 100: 1, 2, 5, adapted.

7. Psalm 51: 10, 11, 7, adapted.

8. 1 John 1:8-9, adapted.

9. Psalm 51:1-3, adapted from The Episcopal Church, *The Book of Common Prayer* (Boston: Seabury Press, 1979).

10. Romans 5: 6, 8, adapted.

11. Hebrews 10: 19, 21-22, *Good News Bible*, adapted.

12. John 13:1, 2, 4-17, *Good News Bible*, adapted.

13. John 8:12, adapted.

14. Based on Psalm 139:11-12.

15. 1 John 1:5, 7; adapted.

16. Based on John 1:1-4, 14, 10, 12; 3:19.

17. This service is adapted and reprinted from *Lutheran Book of Worship*, copyright © 1978 *Lutheran Book of Worship*. Used by permission of Augsburg Publishing House.

18. John 1:1, 4-5, adapted.

19. 1 Corinthians 12: 12-13, 27, adapted.

20. Matthew 5:23-24, *Good News Bible*, adapted.

21. Order from Consultation on Church Union, Research Park, 151 Wall Street, Princeton, N.J. 08540.

22. Genesis 22:'17.

23. Isaiah 11: 6.

24. Matthew 12: 48-50, adapted.

25. Psalm 51:1-3, adapted from *Book of Common Prayer*.

26. Psalm 51:1-3, adapted from *Book of Common Prayer*.

27. Adapted from *Book of Common Prayer*.

28. 1 Timothy 1:15, adapted from *Book of Common Prayer*.

29. 1 John 1:9, adapted.

30. Psalm 32:5, adapted.

31. Adapted from *Book of Common Prayer*.

32. 2 Corinthians 13:14, adapted.

33. Psalm 103:1-5, adapted.

34. Luke 11:9-10, adapted.

35. Adapted and reprinted from *Lutheran Book of Worship*, copyright © 1978 *Lutheran Book of Worship*. Used by permission of Augsburg Publishing House.

36. Exodus 20:1-17, adapted.

37. Mark 12:29-31, adapted.

38. Matthew 5:3-12, adapted.

39. Adapted by permission from *Services of the Church* #2. Copyright © 1969 United Church Press.

40. Psalm 32:3-5, adapted.

41. 1 John 1:8-9, adapted.

42. Hebrews 4:14, 16, adapted.

43. Adapted from *Book of Common Prayer*.

44. Psalm 51:1-2. 10-12, adapted.

45. Romans 5:6, 8, adapted.

46. Matthew 11:28-30, *Good News Bible*.

47. John 8:10, 11, adapted.

48. Adapted and reprinted from *Lutheran Book of Worship*, copyright © 1978 *Lutheran Book of Worship*. Used by permission of Augsburg Publishing House.

49. Adapted by permission from *Services of the Church* #1. Copyright © 1966 and 1969 United Church Press.

50. John 14:27.

51. Matthew 18:20.

52. Psalm 46:1-3, *Good News Bible*.

53. Hebrews 4:16, adapted.

54. Romans 5:8, adapted.

55. Adapted by permission from *Services of the Church* #1. Copyright © 1966 and 1969 United Church Press.

56. Galatians 6:2.

57. Psalm 51:1-2, 10-12, adapted.

58. Romans 5:8, adapted.

59. Adapted by permission from *A United Methodist Rite for Anointing* by Timothy J. Crouch, O.S.L. Copyright 1986 Order of St. Luke (P.O. Box 429, Hackettstown, N.J. 07840).

60. Adapted by permission from *Pastor's Manual*, Church of the Brethren. Copyright 1978 The Brethren Press.

61. Adapted from *Book of Common Prayer*.

62. Adapted by permission from *Pastor's Manual*, Church of the Brethren. Copyright 1978 The Brethren Press.

63. Adapted from *Book of Common Prayer*.

64. Numbers 6:24-26, adapted.

65. 2 Corinthians 13:14, adapted.

66. Luke 10:9. Scripture taken from *Holy Bible: New International Version*. Copyright © 1978 by the New York International Bible Society. Used by permission of Zondervan Bible Publishers.

67. Mark 11:24.

68. Romans 12:2, *Good News Bible*.

69. Adapted by permission from *Pastor's Manual*, Church of the Brethren. Copyright 1978 The Brethren Press.

70. Luke 11, 9-10, adapted.

71. Psalm 51:1-2, 10-12, adapted.

72. Adapted by permission from *Services of the Church* #2. Copyright © 1969 United Church Press.

73. 1 John 1:9, adapted.

74. Adapted by permission from *Pastor's Manual*, Church of the Brethren. Copyright 1978 The Brethren Press.

75. Adapted by permission from *A United Methodist Rite for Anointing* by Timothy J. Crouch, O.S.L. Copyright 1986 Order of St. Luke (P.O. Box 429, Hackettstown, N.J. 07840).

76. Adapted by permission from *Pastor's Manual*, Church of the Brethren. Copyright 1978 The Brethren Press.

77. Adapted from *Book of Common Prayer*.

78. Adapted from *Book of Common Prayer*.

79. Adapted by permission from *Pastor's Manual*, Church of the Brethren. Copyright 1978 The Brethren Press.

80. Adapted from *Book of Common Prayer*.

81. Adapted from *Book of Common Prayer*.

82. Numbers 6:24-26, adapted.

SERVICES OF MARRIAGE

1. 2 Corinthians 13:14, adapted.
2. Based on 1 John 4:7.
3. Based on an unpublished prayer by Ann Asper Wilson.
4. Based on Matthew 19:6.
5. Based on Matthew 19:6.
6. Adapted from *The Worshipbook—Services.* Copyright © MCMLXX The Westminster Press. Adapted by permission.
7. This prayer, except for the blessing of the children, is adapted from The Episcopal Church *The Book of Common Prayer* (Boston: Seabury Press, 1979).
8. International Consultation on English Texts.

9. Based on Gospel and Epistle accounts.
10. Philippians 4:7, adapted.
11. Numbers 6:24-26, adapted.
12. 2 Corinthians 13:14, adapted.
13. Adapted from *A Service of Christian Marriage.* Copyright © 1979 by Abingdon. Used by permission.
14. Adapted from *A Service of Christian Marriage.* Copyright © 1979 by Abingdon. Used by permission.
15. Based on Matthew 19:6.
16. 1 John 4:7-8, adapted.
17. Based on Matthew 19:6.

SERVICES OF MEMORIAL AND THANKSGIVING

1. Adapted from *The Worshipbook—Services.* Copyright MCMLXX The Westminster Press. Adapted by permission.
2. Matthew 25:23, adapted.
3. International Consultation on English Texts.
4. Matthew 25:40, adapted.
5. Adapted from "In Time of Death" (p. 128) in *Prayers for Daily Use* by Samuel H. Miller. Copyright © 1957 by Samuel H. Miller. Reprinted by permission of Harper and Row, Publishers, Inc.
6. Adapted from The Episcopal Church, *The Book of Common Prayer* (Boston: Seabury Press, 1979).
7. *Book of Common Prayer.*
8. Numbers 6:24-26, adapted.
9. Psalm 145:18-19, adapted.
10. John 11:25-26, adapted.
11. Revelation 1:17-18
12. Isaiah 41:10, adapted.
13. Romans, 6:3-4, *Good News Bible,* adapted.
14. Romans 6:5, adapted.
15. Revelation 14:13, adapted.
16. 2 Corinthians 13:14, adapted.
17. Romans 14:8-9, adapted.

18. Psalm 116:4, 8, 12-13, adapted and reprinted from *Lutheran Book of Worship,* copyright © 1978 *Lutheran Book of Worship.* Used by permission of Augsburg Publishing House.
19. Romans 8:1, 28, 38-39, adapted.
20. International Consultation on English Texts.
21. *Book of Common Prayer.*
22. International Consultation on English Texts, adapted.
23. Hebrews 13:20-21, adapted.
24. Numbers 6:24-26, adapted.
25. 1 Thessalonians 4:13-14, adapted.
26. 1 Corinthians 15:54, 55, 57, adapted.
27. John 16:22, adapted.
28. Revelation 22:12, 13, adapted.
29. International Consultation on English Texts.
30. Adapted by permission from *Services of the Church* #5. Copyright © 1969 United Church Press.
31. Adapted from *Book of Common Prayer.*
32. Adapted from a prayer by John Henry Cardinal Newman quoted in *Services of the Church* #5.
33. Romans 15:13.
34. Philippians 4:7, adapted.

SERVICES OF RECOGNITION AND AUTHORIZATION

1. 2 Timothy 2:1-2, 15, *Good News Bible,* adapted.
2. *Constitution and Bylaws of the United Church of Christ,* rev. ed., 1984, Preamble and Article V, paragraph 20.
3. Revelation 1:4, 5, adapted.
4. Ephesians 3:20-21, adapted.
5. *Constitution and Bylaws of the United Church of Christ,* rev. ed., 1984, Preamble and Article V, paragraphs 2, 17, and 19.

6. Isaiah 6:8, adapted.
7. Isaiah 52:7-8, *Good News Bible,* adapted.
8. Isaiah 61:1, adapted.
9. Romans 10:14, 17, adapted.
10. Matthew 4:19, adapted.
11. Matthew 20:25-27, adapted.
12. Ephesians 4:11-12, adapted.
13. Hebrews 12:1-2, adapted.
14. 1 Thessalonians 5:12-18, *Good News Bible.*
15. 1 Corinthians 12:1, 4-7, *Good News Bible,*

adapted.

16. *Constitution and Bylaws of the United Church of Christ*, rev. ed., 1984, Preamble and Article V, paragraphs 17 and 24.

17. 1 Thessalonians 5:15-18, *Good News Bible*, adapted.

18. Ephesians 3:21, adapted.

19. 1 Corinthians 12:4-7, 12, 26-27, *Good News Bible*, adapted.

20. 2 Thessalonians 1:3-4, *Good News Bible*, adapted.

RESOURCES

1. Isaiah 40:3-5, adapted.
2. Isaiah 52:7, adapted.
3. Psalm 96:11.
4. Matthew 11:10, adapted.
5. Isaiah 44:21-22, adapted.
6. Isaiah 55:12, adapted.
7. Luke 2:10-11, adapted.
8. Luke 2:15, adapted.
9. Luke 2:14, adapted.
10. Luke 2:14, adapted.
11. Luke 2:14, adapted.
12. Psalm 19:1, adapted.
13. Based on Luke 1:68-79 and Colossians 3:12-17.
14. John 1:14, adapted.
15. John 8:12, adapted.
16. Matthew 2:2, adapted.
17. Matthew 5:14, 16, adapted.
18. Hebrews 12:2, adapted.
19. Mark 8:34, adapted.
20. 2 Corinthians 5:17, adapted.
21. 1 Corinthians 15:20, 55, 57, adapted.
22. Adapted by permission from *A Book of Worship for Free Churches*. Copyright © 1948 Board of Home Missions of the Congregational and Christian Churches; copyright renewed 1976 by United Church Press.
23. 1 Peter 1:3, adapted.
24. John 15:5, 12, adapted.
25. Revelation 7:12, adapted.
26. Ruth C. Duck in *Bread for the Journey: Resources for Worship*, ed. Ruth C. Duck. Copyright © 1981 The Pilgrim Press. Used by permission.
27. 1 Peter 2:9, adapted.
28. Romans 15:13.
29. Acts 2:17, adapted.
30. Acts 1:8, adapted.
31. Acts 1:8.
32. Ephesians 3:20-21, adapted.
33. 1 Corinthians 12:12-13, adapted.
34. Psalm 84:1-5, adapted.
35. 2 Corinthians 2:14, adapted.
36. Based on the Statement of Faith of the United Church of Christ.
37. International Consultation on English Texts.
38. International Consultation on English Texts, adapted. The only change is the omission of the word *men* in line 13, a commonly accepted practice in the ecumenical church.
39. This covenant of the first Non-Separatist congregationally organized Puritan Church in America (1629) disclaimed any superior ecclesiastical power and took for granted Calvinist belief.
40. The historical reorganization of Congregationalism effected at the 1913 National Council structured a more coherent and efficient relationship between the churches and their affiliated missionary societies. The statement of faith adopted there lifted up freedom of conscience, autonomy of the local church, relationships with other communions in matters of common Christian concern, and church unity in three sections: "Faith" (included here), "Polity," and "The Wider Fellowship."
41. Approved by the Second General Synod of the United Church of Christ, 1959.
42. Revised 1976, by Robert V. Moss, Jr., President of the United Church of Christ, 1969-1976.
43. Approved by the Executive Council in 1981 for use in connection with the twenty-fifth anniversary of the United Church of Christ.
44. The first five principles were generally held early in the history of the various branches of the Christian Church that later became the United Church of Christ. Even documents of the twentieth century sometimes show only five principles. Very early, however, especially in the West and South, the sixth principle of union was affirmed but given various interpretations from cooperation to merger.
45. Adopted by the General Assembly, Kansas City, Mo., 1968. The first line of the preamble, omitted here, reads "As members of the Christian Church."
46. International Consultation on English Texts.
47. Exodus 20:1-17, paraphrase.
48. Matthew 22:37-39, adapted.
49. Psalm 46:1.
50. Psalms 118:24, 95:6, adapted.
51. John 4:24, adapted.
52. Psalm 100:2,4-5, adapted.
53. Psalms 113:2-3, 92:1-2, adapted.
54. Adapted by permission from *Christian Worship: A Service Book*, ed. G. Edwin Osborn. Copyright 1953, 1958 Bethany Press.
55. Adapted by permission from *Christian*

Worship: A Service Book, ed. G. Edwin Osborn. Copyright 1953, 1958 Bethany Press.

56. Ann Asper Wilson in *Worship: Inclusive Language Resources*. Copyright 1977 United Church of Christ Office for Church Life and Leadership.

57. Used by permission of the author, Laura A. Loving.

58. William C. Smith, Jr., in *Worship: Inclusive Language Resources*. Copyright 1977 United Church of Christ Office for Church Life and Leadership.

59. William Bright, nineteenth-century church historian and hymn writer, adapted.

60. John Chrysostom, Bishop of Constantinople, 4th century, adapted.

61. Gregorian Sacramentary, 7th century, adapted.

62. Used by permission of the author, Sally Stevens Smith.

63. Used by permission of the author, Sally Stevens Smith.

64. Used by permission of the author, Sally Stevens Smith.

65. Adapted from The Episcopal Church, *The Book of Common Prayer* (Boston: Seabury Press, 1979).

66. Adapted by permission from *Services of the Church* #1. Copyright 1966, 1969 United Church Press.

67. Adapted by permission from *The Hymnal* (Evangelical and Reformed). Copyright United Church Press.

68. Used by permission of the author, Howard A. Worth.

69. Used by permission of the author, Cynthia S. Mazur-Bullis.

70. Jeremiah A. Wright, Jr., in *Worship: Inclusive Language Resources*. Copyright 1977 United Church of Christ Office for Church Life and Leadership.

71. Used by permission of the author, Richard D. Leach.

72. Translated and adapted from the Spanish. Source unknown.

73. Used by permission of the author, James R. Lahman.

74. Used by permission of the author, Laura A. Loving.

75. Used by permission of the author, R. Kenneth Ostermiller.

76. Used by permission from *A Book of Worship for Free Churches*. Copyright © 1948 Board of Home Missions of the Congregational and Christian Churches; copyright renewed 1976 by United Church Press.

77. Adapted by permission from *Services of the Church* #1. Copyright 1966, 1969 United Church Press.

78. Used by permission of the author, Donald M. Proctor.

79. From the Liturgy of Malabar quoted in *Services of the Church* #1.

80. Laszlo Ravasz, 1929, in *"Lift Thy Head, O Zion. . .,"* Hungarian Reformed Tradition Series I, ed. Aladar Komjathy (Passaic, N.J.: Hungarian Reformed Church). Used by permission.

81. Adapted by permission from *The Hymnal* (Evangelical and Reformed). Copyright United Church Press.

82. Used by permission of the author, Robert D. Webber.

83. Adapted from *Book of Common Prayer*.

84. Used by permission of the author, William A. Hulteen, Jr.

85. Adapted by permission from *A United Methodist Rite for Anointing* by Timothy J. Crouch, O.S.L. Copyright 1986 Order of St. Luke (P.O. Box 429, Hackettstown, N.J. 07840).

86. Used by permission of the author, Glen E. Rainsley.

87. Used by permission from the 1982 Convocation of Lower Sioux, The Episcopal Church, Diocese of Minnesota and Diocese of North Dakota, Order for Celebrating Holy Eucharist.

88. From the Archives of the United Church of Christ from the papers of Robert V. Moss, President of the United Church of Christ, for Ash Wednesday 1975. Used by permission.

89. Used by permission of the author, William A. Hulteen, Jr.

90. Adapted from "A Service of Worship for Access Sabbath/Sunday 1982," The Healing Community. Used by permission.

91. Used by permission of the author, Paul B. Robinson.

92. Used by permission from the 1982 Convocation of Lower Sioux, The Episcopal Church, Diocese of Minnesota and Diocese of North Dakota, Order for Celebrating Holy Eucharist.

93. Adapted from *Book of Common Prayer*.

94. Richard Wong, *Prayers from an Island* (Richmond, Va.: John Knox Press). Copyright 1968 M.E. Bratcher. Used by permission.

95. Adapted and reprinted from *Lutheran Book of Worship*, copyright © 1978 *Lutheran Book of Worship*. Used by permission of Augsburg Publishing House.

96. Adapted by permission from *The Worshipbook—Services*. Copyright MCMLXX The Westminster Press. Adapted by permission.

97. Richard Wong, *Prayers from an Island* (Richmond, Va.: John Knox Press). Copyright 1968 M.E. Bratcher. Adapted by permission.

98. Adapted by permission from a prayer of Gyorgy Szendrei, galley slave and pastor of the Reformed Church of Balogh, Gomor County, Hungary, enslaved during the Counter-Reformation, trans. Francis Vitez.

99. Adapted by permission from *The Worshipbook—Services*. Copyright MCMLXX

The Westminster Press. Adapted by permission.

100. Arthur D. Gray, from the Twelfth General Synod, 1979, adapted.

101. Used by permission of the author, Alpha D. Goto.

102. Used by permission of the author, Thomas E. Dipko.

103. Psalm 54:4, 6-7, adapted.

104. Matthew 5:16, adapted.

105. Acts 20:35.

106. Used by permission of the author, Laura A. Loving.

107. Adapted by permission from *A Book of Worship for Free Churches*. Copyright © 1948 Board for Home Missions of the Congregational and Christian Churches; copyright renewed 1976 by United Church Press.

108. Used by permission of the author, Roger D. Knight.

109. Adapted from *Book of Worship* (Evangelical and Reformed Church). Copyright United Church Press. Used by permission.

110. Jerry W. Paul in *Worship: Inclusive Language Resources*. Copyright 1977 United Church of Christ Office for Church Life and Leadership.

111. Used by permission of the author, William A. Hulteen, Jr.

112. Adapted by permission from *Services of the Church* #1. Copyright © 1966, 1969 United Church Press.

113. Adapted from *Book of Worship* (Evangelical and Reformed Church). Copyright United Church Press. Used by permission.

114. Used by permission of the author, Roger D. Knight.

115. G.C. Binyon, *Prayers for the City of God* (London: Longmans, Green and Co., 1927).

116. Martin Luther King, Jr. Quoted from *Eerdmans Book of Famous Prayers*, comp. Veronica Zundel. Copyright 1983 Lion Publishing. Adapted and used by permission of the American publisher.

117. Elizabeth A. Hambrick-Stowe in *Worship: Inclusive Language Resources*. Copyright 1977 United Church of Christ Office for Church Life and Leadership.

118. Adapted by permission from the 1982 Convocation of Lower Sioux, The Episcopal Church, Diocese of Minnesota and Diocese of North Dakota, Order for Celebrating Holy Eucharist.